© 2019 Sheldon B. Lubar

Published by the Milwaukee County Historical Society
910 N. Old World Third St.
Milwaukee, WI 53203

ISBN 978-0-938076-01-8

Printed in Canada
Production: Market Engineers LLC
Front cover photograph by Erol Reyal

Climbing My Mountain

My Life, Words, and Values

Sheldon B. Lubar

Dedication

There is only one person I could dedicate this book to, and that is my wife and teammate, Marianne. In this book I tell how we met and grew together and came to share a belief that family was always what it was about. The excitement of being parents and the gratification and pride of seeing our children mature and give us eleven grandchildren were all gifts from heaven. Long ago Marianne told me that we make a good team, and we do. We love each other and our family.

The book is also dedicated to those who follow us: Kris, David, Susan, Joan, and their spouses; our eleven grandchildren: John, Maddie, and Joe Thomson; Joe, Hannah, and Patrick Lubar; Simen, Izzy, and Sonja Solvang; Isaac and Charlotte Siegel; our first great-grandchildren, Reid Lubar McElhenny and River Yang Thomson; and all the generations that will follow them.

Foreword

I was eighteen years old before I saw a mountain. In fact, until then I had been out of Wisconsin only on a few visits to Chicago. But I knew long before I saw one that I would love the mountains, since I was drawn to books and movies about the West, especially stories of the Mountain Men. But I truly had no idea how awesome they were. However, this book is not about mountains; it is about myself, my family background, my wife, our four children and our eleven grandchildren, and in particular my life and my values. *Climbing My Mountain* is a metaphor for this journey.

I am writing this story because I want my children, grandchildren, and our future descendants to know about what came before. This book is self-serving in a way, since it gives me the opportunity to re-think how my life and how my career developed and set it down in some sensible order. Hopefully, my words, experiences, and decisions will provide my family and other readers with an understanding of me and my times. If *Climbing My Mountain* helps them in their future as productive and honest citizens, it will all be worthwhile.

My methodology in writing this book has been straightforward. I am the author. The first section is a memoir that describes the events of my life as I remember them. The second section includes many of the speeches I have written and presented over the decades. In these speeches, the reader will find the principles and views I have spoken of, believe in, and live by. In both the memoir and the speeches, you can be assured that what I said, I meant.

Exactly who am I? I am someone who believes strongly in lifelong education, self-discipline, and enlightened self-interest. I am a capitalist who believes in saving and investing. This means postponing the consumption of wealth for the reward of building greater and more productive assets in the future. I believe in a healthy mind and body. For me that means running, swimming, hiking, walking, skiing, and moderation in what I eat, drink, and do. It also means being direct and truthful always. I believe in giving back. It was Winston Churchill who first wrote, "We make a living by what we get, but we make a life by what we give." No one makes it up the mountain of life by themselves. Since I graduated from college, I have felt an obligation to give back to my country and my community. I have been more able than most to do so, and it has been gratifying for me and helpful to others. I believe in education. There is no end to learning in a lifetime; it is the pathway to a good and successful life. I believe in civility. I believe in the fair and equal treatment of all persons, but I also recognize that those who study more, work harder, and have the capitalist mentality will achieve the greatest intellectual and material rewards. Finally, I am guided by the ancient words of Heraclitus: "Nothing endures but change."

Part One

My Life

Part One
Contents

Chapter 1

In the Beginning

Let me start by telling you about my parents. I don't know too much about the Lubar or Stern families before them, but I believe they lived in their home countries for hundreds of years before coming to America. My mother, Charlotte Stern, who was always known as Lottie, was born on April 15, 1896, in Milwaukee. Her parents, Bertha Fromstein and Jacob Stern, were both born in Kishinev, Russia—Jacob in about 1850 and Bertha in 1870. Jacob came to the U.S. alone in about 1888 and after a year or so went home to gather his wife and children.

The whole family came to America to stay in the 1890s. They lived on Tenth Street and Central Avenue (now Somers Street) in Milwaukee, sharing a small house with no indoor plumbing that held about ten people, including six or eight children, a cousin, and my mother's parents. Historically this area was known as the Haymarket. In Europe, my grandfather was a baker. In the U.S., he became a peddler who would venture into the countryside with a horse and wagon, peddling pots, pans, and other such wares. My mother attended Fourth Street School, now known as Golda Meir School, across from the Schlitz brewery. Her first job was with Gimbels Department Store. I remember her as a very beautiful lady—kind, caring, independent, and doing all she could for her children.

My father, Joseph Lubar, was born on May 7, 1893, in Rossava, a village in what is now Ukraine. His father, Solomon, was born in about 1850 and died in about 1901, when my father was just a boy. Dad was the youngest of eight children: three boys and five girls. His mother's name was Esther Koslov. The family's business was wheat-milling, which involved buying wheat from surrounding farms and grinding it into flour, which they sold at retail. It was apparently a good business until Solomon died. After that my father's two older brothers came to

1

America, where their oldest sister and her husband had already settled. The other four sisters married and remained in Europe. To the best of my knowledge, they were never in touch again. My father graduated from a military high school in 1911 and shortly thereafter traveled to Hamburg, Germany, where he boarded a ship to Philadelphia and then went on to Milwaukee, where he joined the rest of his family.

Joseph Lubar was one of the earliest Milwaukeeans to be drafted into the U.S. Army when our country entered World War I in 1917. He had a brief training period at Camp Grant, Illinois, then went off to France, assigned to Company B, 47th Infantry, 3rd Army. My father fought in the trenches in three of the four major engagements that involved American troops under the leadership of General John J. Pershing. His battles were Aisne-Marne, St. Mihiel, and Meuse-Argonne. He was wounded at Aisne-Marne and received the Purple Heart, but he returned to duty in six weeks. He also received the Soldier's Victory Medal and, following the Armistice, spent the year of 1919 with General Pershing's Composite Regiment, "Pershing's Own," showing the American flag in Europe's principal capitals.

My father was truly a two-fisted man's man. He was a very hard worker, whether at his business or maintaining our home. I was fortunate to grow up with loving parents who considered educating and caring for their children to be an important part of their life's mission. In the Depression days of the 1930s and early '40s, almost all families struggled, but my memory is that we were better off than most.

I was born on May 21, 1929, at Mount Sinai Hospital in Milwaukee. I have two older sisters: Esther, who was born in 1922 and married Bob Sametz, and Dorothy, born in 1925 and married to Don Zucker. Around the time of my birth, our family moved to a large duplex on Sherman Boulevard, directly across the street from Sherman Park. I loved school and attended Townsend Street School from kindergarten (for two years) through fourth grade. In those days, the Milwaukee Public Schools were considered among the best anywhere. My school was almost a mile away, and I walked that mile four times a day: to classes in the morning, home for lunch, back to school, and then home again. There was no day that my mother wasn't there to greet her children and cook and clean for them. Above all, my parents loved their children.

I was the "baby" of our family and the only boy, with two adoring sisters. As I look back on those days, I realize that my family instilled in me a feeling of self-confidence and self-importance. Whether it was deserved or not, I believe their unconditional support enabled me to be comfortable with risks and adventures throughout my life. I developed confidence in my judgment.

In 1939, at the urging of my sister Dorothy, my parents decided to move from the West Side across town to Whitefish Bay on the East Side. They bought a lot on Wildwood Avenue and built a home that was very close to both Cumberland Grade School and Whitefish Bay High School. I was ten years old at the time and entering fifth grade. That move to the East Side changed my life. It brought new friends, new surroundings, and a different, more progressive teaching approach in the schools. There was plenty of open space, and the teachers were caring, serious, and well-schooled. My classmates were from middle-income white families. That doesn't mean there weren't cliques and clubs, but we all got along, reading, studying, and playing together. Whitefish Bay was truly an ideal place for a young person to grow and develop.

Cumberland School had a football team with uniforms and pads that I played on for one year. As I look back, I realize I wasn't very good, but I did play as a lineman on the first team. Our other sports were soccer, track, and ice-skating. During those days, Milwaukee winters were mean, with much snow and below-zero weather. I loved my classes and always did very well, especially in mathematics and the sciences. I was at Cumberland from fifth through eighth grade and then went on to high school.

In all honesty, I can say I was a good student in high school. I took four years of mathematics, sciences, history, and English. I went out for football for three years and finally realized it was a waste of my time. In my senior year, I ran track, which I should have focused on as a freshman. During my days at Whitefish Bay High School, the school had no gymnasium, swimming pool, or other athletic facilities. But we did have gym classes. Until there was snow on the ground, we played tag football outside. When winter came, we would repeatedly run up and down four flights of stairs to the tower. Try it yourself some time! The tower consisted of one room with a boxing ring that was used for individual matches or simply group punching. Don't ask me to explain. It was not fun for most of us.

Although I was an above-average student, I can't honestly say that I worked up to my capacity. I did all my studying at school during the study hall periods. Nor did I excel on any of the sports teams, although I thought of myself as a good athlete and a very fast runner. It was only many years later that I started understanding myself. I realized that I wasn't a team player; I was more of a loner.

As I look back on those early times, there was nothing remarkable in either my childhood or my high-school days. I did very well academically in grade school and was a "B" student in high school. I never felt challenged or stimulated by any of our fine teachers. I don't know what I was thinking about in those days, and if I excelled at anything, it was at being normal and civil. If I thought about the future, the main events were going to college and seeing our country—particularly the West and the Rocky Mountains.

The crowd I traveled with lived in Whitefish Bay, Shorewood, and on the East Side of Milwaukee. It was a very social life, revolving around our confirmation class at Temple Emanuel, which was across the street from what is now the University of Wisconsin-Milwaukee. On most weekends there were girl-and-boy parties. The host would assign each boy a date to pick up and escort to the party, which was usually a dance with music provided by a pair of boys who would play popular phonograph records. Refreshments were served, but never any alcohol or substantial food. Occasionally there would be a live band. It made for busy weekends and the development of very decent social skills.

We lived close to Lake Michigan, and it was not uncommon for me to skip out of fall classes early and play on the bluffs above the lake with some of my pals. We would make mud slides, take mud baths, and jump into the water to rinse off. Of course, I ultimately got caught, but it was great fun while it lasted. How very quickly my high school days passed! Before I knew it, June, 1947, was upon me and I was graduating from high school.

I couldn't wait to get off on my own and go to college, but first I wanted to travel. My dream was to buy an old car and drive west during the summer between high school and college. I hooked up with three other guys who had somehow come up with the same idea: my cousin, Roger Pokrass; a friend of his, Howard Gould; and Mickey Morton, the son of friends of my parents.

In June, 1947, we set off in high style in Roger's new Chrysler convertible and Mickey's new Buick convertible. We drove west through Yellowstone National Park to California, then down the coast from San Francisco to Los Angeles. Roger and I went on to San Diego and continued even further to Tijuana, Mexico. I can't remember all the details, but it was an unforgettable journey of about three weeks. Except in the large cities, we slept outside in our sleeping bags wherever we stopped. We were really rookies, and I sometimes wonder how we managed to do it all and return in one piece. I guess the times were quite different then: far fewer cars on the road, friendly people everywhere, and a nonthreatening experience in all ways. It was on this trip that I first become acquainted with the Rocky Mountains. They have been a constant in my life ever since.

Chapter 2

The University of Wisconsin

If there was one thing I knew from the moment I could understand anything, it was that all the Lubar children would go to college. That was the mission of our parents, and the logical school, the affordable school, was the University of Wisconsin in Madison. Tuition at that time was forty dollars per semester.

I enrolled at UW-Madison in the fall of 1947, when the student body was dominated by veterans of World War II. The GI Bill enabled them to get a college education, and many veterans did. That bill was definitely the single best government program I've ever heard of. It not only rewarded soldiers and sailors who had given years of their lives to win World War II, but it also created a new generation of educated and productive citizens. Most of the veterans wore some pieces of their military uniforms at school, so when you looked up Bascom Hill while classes were changing, the campus looked like a combination Army and Navy base.

Veterans were given preference for housing, which meant that there was no space for incoming freshmen in the dormitories. As a result, my roommate and I rented a room at the Langdon Bend House, an old rooming house at the bend of Langdon Street. My roommate was Mayer Franklin, who had been a friend since we first met at Townsend Street School in kindergarten. Mayer was very intelligent and studied like no one I had ever known. The result was that I studied just as hard, and after our first year we both made freshman honors and were elected to Phi Eta Sigma, the freshman honors fraternity.

I enjoyed school and liked the feeling of learning new things and being independent—especially being independent. My freshman courses were advanced chemistry, algebra, English, European history, and ROTC. I joined a fraternity during the second semester and moved into the fraternity house for my second year. I did not want to join a fraternity, but my friends all belonged, so I went along. Although I enjoyed the friendship and social aspects of fraternity life, I didn't like the group living experience. At the end of my second year, I moved out of the frat house into a room on the second floor of a very large house on Lake Mendota. It was much more quiet and private, and the fraternity house was only a mile away. My studying was always done at the university library.

Perhaps eight or nine years earlier, my father had established the Wisconsin Liquor Company of Oshkosh, a warehouse for wholesaling wine and liquor that was a satellite of a Milwaukee company by the same name. Later the majority owners of the company, my uncles, Messrs. Peckarsky and Pokrass, split up. The branch warehouses around the state went to Peckarsky, and Pokrass took the Milwaukee operation. Ownership of the Oshkosh business was divided: 51 percent Peckarsky and 49 percent Joe Lubar. After several severe disagreements, my father left the business and told me he could no longer help me financially. I told him, "Don't worry, Dad. I can handle it with a summer job and working at a meal job." At that time, tuition was still forty dollars per semester, and my room cost ten dollars per month. I could handle it without much trouble, and the experience changed my life. At age twenty-one I was on my own, and it was through being on my own that I met Marianne.

To back up just a little, the job I found at the beginning of my junior year was waiting on tables at the Shoreland House, a small girl's dormitory located on Lake Mendota. I got the job through my lifelong friend, Bill Bachman, who also worked there. In exchange for my labor, I received lunch and dinner and a much-expanded social life. My academic path had shifted in the meantime. At the start of my junior year, I changed my major from general studies to the School of Commerce, seeking a degree in business administration. It's worth noting that in 1950 there was no School of Business; it was called the School of Commerce. The required courses included accounting (which I didn't care for), public utilities, money and banking, and several others I've long since forgotten.

It wasn't the study of business that I had anticipated. Not that I knew what that was, but my instincts told me I wasn't on the right track. Compounding my uncertainty was the fact that our country was involved in the Korean War. If you dropped out of school, you were subject to the draft. Putting it all together, I concluded that I wanted to have a college degree in hand at the end of four years and then, if possible, go on to law school. With all the uncertainty in the outside world, an undergraduate degree was a priority, and I reasoned that a law degree would provide me with the maximum of opportunities no matter where my career might take me.

The upshot was that I spent my third year in the School of Commerce, where things became more interesting, with courses like investments, ethics, and statistics, and then I enrolled in UW's Law School. I was able to combine my fourth year in both Law and Commerce, which gave me a Bachelor of Business Administration in June, 1951, and a Bachelor of Law in 1953. Without any doubt, my time at the Law School was the most intellectually challenging of my entire education and certainly the most enjoyable.

It was during the winter of 1950-1951 that Marianne Segal, a young woman from Kenosha, moved into Shoreland House as a freshman. As she describes it, I became "her waiter." That was sixty-nine years ago in 2019. It didn't take long for both of us to realize that this was it. Of all life's choices and all life's game-changers, this for both of us was the most important. In Marianne's words, "We are a good team." I realize this more every day.

We became engaged in 1951 and were married in Milwaukee on August 31, 1952. Marianne's parents, Marcia and Israel Segal, held the wedding at the Astor Hotel that afternoon, and by about 4 p.m. we were off on our honeymoon. Our destination was the Colorado Hotel in Glenwood Springs, Colorado, in the middle of the Rocky Mountains. On our way out the door, Marianne's father gave me $500. Thank you, Mr. Segal, I needed it more than I understood at that moment. Marianne's parents were wonderful people. Her father was born in Maine in 1896. His parents had emigrated earlier from Lithuania. Her mother was born in 1906 in what is now Belarus. They met in Kenosha, where Mr. Segal's sister lived. Together the Segals started an upscale ladies clothing store that operated very successfully until their retirement in the early 1960s.

We drove Marianne's car through the West to Denver. In 1952 Denver was smog-free, and when we awoke on that first morning, there were the foothills of the Rockies right outside our hotel window, set against a beautiful blue sky and brilliant sunshine. It was awesome. We drove into the mountains and finally reached the Colorado Hotel in Glenwood Springs. While we were there, we met two slightly older and rather colorful young men from Chicago who had made the trip west on the train. Since we had a car, they persuaded us to drive to Aspen, which was about an hour away. The entire drive was through open ranchland in 1952—no buildings, no development of any kind. Aspen itself was a relic of an old mining town. The only memorable buildings were the Jerome Hotel, which is now ten times the size it was then, and the Red Onion, a small restaurant and bar. We went to the Red Onion for lunch and encountered the best jazz quartet I had ever heard. The group consisted of students from the Juilliard School of Music in New York who were enrolled at the Aspen Music School for the summer. They were fabulous. After lunch, Marianne and I went up the ski lift. It was a single chair that went a relatively short distance up the face of Ajax Mountain. Little did I realize that we would return twenty years later as skiers and hikers, or that we would be there every year thereafter to the present. It was a wonderful honeymoon. We didn't have much money, but Marianne and I made memories that we still talk about.

Once back in Madison, we moved into what would be our home for the next year at 10 E. Wilson Street. The house was an older brick building divided into four apartments. We were on the first floor, and our unit had a large bedroom, a small kitchen, a good-sized living room, and a full bathroom. Across the street was the State Office Building, and two blocks away was the capitol on Capitol Square. It was great. Though eating was never on my mind, Marianne turned out to be a fabulous cook. This was the beginning of one of our best years, but more were ahead.

We lived in Madison until July, 1953. Instead of continuing in college, Marianne decided to get a job to support us, while I focused on finishing my last year at the Law School. Marianne went to work for the Department of Agriculture in the capitol. It couldn't have been a better or more enjoyable year. We loved each other, we helped each other, and everything we did was fun. My grades were the best ever, and I won first prize in the will-drafting contest sponsored by the Wisconsin Bankers Association and the Wisconsin Bar Association. Everything seemed to be working.

The Korean War complicated life for us. I expected to be drafted after graduation, and I reasoned that, if I was going in, I wanted to go in as an officer. I had two years of infantry ROTC training, but I had chosen not to continue. Now, two years later, I decided to try for a Navy officer program. My eyesight was below what was required, and I thought I could slip by with contact lenses. This was 1951, in the early days of contact lenses. I bought one of those early pairs and practiced wearing them. After almost going blind in one eye, I gave up on that plan. Next I was back to the Army and ROTC. I managed to squeeze past the eye exam, but the tension must have caused my blood pressure to elevate, and they rejected me. My last stop was the U.S. Air Force. During my last year in school, I applied to the Air Force for a direct commission in their Judge Advocate Division, which would follow graduation and admission to the bar. My term of enlistment would be three or four years, with a first lieutenant's rank and a salary of $5,000 per year. You can't imagine my happiness when my application was accepted. Thinking back, I believe the idea of three years as an officer at good pay and a chance for real experience as a lawyer appealed to me.

That last year passed quickly, and in June, 1953, I graduated. Because of my impending call-up, I was sworn in as a member of the bar early, and we started packing. As proof that even the best of plans can go awry, in mid-June I received a letter from the Air Force thanking me for my interest and advising me that, because the Korean War had ended and budget cuts had been imposed, the program I had enrolled in had been canceled. Good morning, Shel, and welcome to the real world! I might add here that Marianne and I were expecting our first child in the fall.

Chapter 3

Going to Work

With the Air Force possibility eliminated, Marianne and I were back to square one. As a father, I was not subject to the draft, so the military was no longer a factor. The reality was that I had to hit the street, find a job, and start supporting my wife and child. What I clearly remember is that I felt confident I would find something worthwhile. I wasn't aware that the U.S. economy was slowing at the time, or that most openings for professional job-seekers are filled before graduation. I started my search by contacting the Law School placement office, which produced two interviews but no offers. Next I made my own list of employers who I thought could use my newly developed talents in tax and estate planning. These were law firms, accounting firms, and the trust departments of banks. I was particularly interested in a job in Milwaukee with one of the three downtown banks: First Wisconsin, M&I, or the Marine.

Marianne and I had moved from Madison to Kenosha after graduation, and we were living on the second floor of her parents' home. From early July until the end of August, I would arise early and put on a shirt, tie, and suit. Marianne would drive me to the depot of the North Shore Railroad, which took me to either Chicago or Milwaukee. I had pretty much exhausted my hopes for Milwaukee. I had only one real possibility in my hometown, a small but well-regarded law firm, but I didn't see myself there, and neither did the head of the firm. I had drawn no interest from any of the Chicago law firms I called on, but three of the four principal banks I contacted were encouraging. I was seriously considering a firm offer from the First National Bank of Chicago. Their interest was a life-saver for me, and, despite my desire to come back to Milwaukee and build my career on a smaller stage, I was relieved to have a job with a first-rate institution.

We were in Milwaukee on the weekend after I received the First National offer, and by chance I encountered my Uncle Sam Pokrass. He was a powerful, successful man who had grown up with my father in Russia. He asked how I was doing, and I explained that I was about to move to Chicago for a job with the First National Bank. He then said that his business, the Wisconsin Liquor Company, banked with the Marine National Exchange Bank, and that he considered the Marine's president, Eliot Fitch, a friend. Did I want him to call Mr. Fitch and provide an introduction? Of course, I said "Yes." Early the next week I met with Mr. Fitch. We had a very good conversation, with him asking the questions and me answering. The subject was mainly my background, but toward the end of our meeting he told me about the history of the bank, which was the oldest in Milwaukee. You knew from the minute you met him that Mr. Fitch was a patrician. He was very smart, well-dressed, and self-assured. After we'd talked for about thirty minutes, he looked at me and said, "Well, I think we can find a place for you in the bank, young man. When would you like to start?" Without betraying my joy and excitement, I said, "October 1." He said, "Fine. Report to Mr. Thomas Moore, head of our Trust Department."

I am unable to adequately express the enormous joy I felt. In 1953 big banks, big law firms, and big companies didn't hire Jewish people. I believe I was the first in Milwaukee at a large bank. From the beginning, I knew what I was up against, but that only motivated me more. Joining the Marine was another life-changer; I knew I was on the way. A few weeks later, on October 1, 1953, I reported to Mr. Moore. His first words to me were, "Nice to meet someone who is working for me." I got the message but let it roll off my back. In fact, over the years I came to greatly admire Mr. Moore.

The Marine Bank smacked of the old school. It traced its roots to 1839 and was the oldest bank in Wisconsin as well as Milwaukee. The company was founded as the Wisconsin Marine and Fire Insurance Company, since President Andrew Jackson had abolished bank charters. Various alternative means were necessary to perform the functions that had previously been the responsibility of banks. After President Jackson died, banks were re-established, and the one I joined was a combination of the Marine Bank and the National Exchange Bank.

Eliot G. Fitch was a third-generation banker. His grandfather, William Grant Fitch, had come from Ohio before the Civil War and joined what became the National Exchange Bank. Eliot's father, Grant, became president of the bank in 1925. Eliot himself was a graduate of Yale University, with a master's degree from the Harvard University School of Business. He served in World War I as a lieutenant in the Army and came to the bank directly thereafter. Of the three downtown banks in 1953, First Wisconsin had about $400 million in assets, M&I about $225 million, and Marine about $140 million. Marine characterized itself exclusively as a commercial and trust bank, devoted to business lending and trust services. We did very little mortgage lending and no consumer lending at all. For that business, our officers would politely direct applicants to the M&I or First Wisconsin.

I knew very little of his background when I first met with Thomas Moore. He told me a bit about himself, including how he had come from the Guaranty Bank of New York, which a few years later was merged with J.P. Morgan & Co. to form the Morgan Guaranty Bank. After a brief conversation, Mr. Moore handed me off to Mr. Jack Geilfuss, my new boss. Mr. Geilfuss was almost the stereotype of a middle-aged Boston lawyer, which in fact he had been. Raised in Milwaukee, he had gone to Harvard Law School and then started a legal practice in Boston before returning to Milwaukee to join the Marine Bank's Trust Department. He was a man of high intelligence, high ethics, and the utmost decency in every respect. Mr. Geilfuss took me to meet Mr. Ed Young, who ran the Tax Division of the Trust Department. Ed was a graduate lawyer who knew everything possible about the federal and state tax laws. He was truly an expert and could recall every statute as well as every related case. I worked under his direction, but Jack was our ultimate boss.

I was in the Tax Division for about a year. I enjoyed my work, and our family had started to develop. Our daughter Kris was born on October 21, 1953, in Kenosha, when we were still living with Marianne's parents. Later that year, before Christmas, we moved into a rented duplex on Maryland Avenue in Milwaukee, across the street from what is now the Sheldon B. Lubar School of Business at the University of Wisconsin-Milwaukee. In 1954 we bought our first house, at 5855 N.

Shoreland Avenue in Whitefish Bay. I was back home. Marianne and I both loved that house, and we thought we would live out our lives in it—or at least I did.

Our son David was born on November 7, 1954. As I look back on our sixty-six years of marriage, I realize how young Marianne and I were, and how unaware of the real world. But I'm also struck by how confidently we took on the responsibilities of parenthood, work, and family. We did this together. I thought I worked very hard six days a week. As the mother of what would be four children, she worked harder. As I grew at the bank, I became more assertive. So did Marianne. We grew and matured together. We were a team. That was our secret.

We had a familiar routine in those years. Marianne would keep house and take care of our infants (as Ed Young would refer to them). I would carpool to the bank, come home, put on my work clothes, and paint, fix, and remove wallpaper with Marianne. On occasional weekends, my brother-in-law, Bob Sametz, would join us, and my father would come down from Sheboygan to help with electric switches, fixtures, landscaping, and lots of other tasks. Marianne's folks would arrive with bags of groceries. There was always a lot of action, but after about a year we had created a wonderful three-bedroom house in a first-rate neighborhood a short block from the Richards Grade School. Life was good. Neither of us knew anything could be better.

At the bank, in the meantime, I was promoted out of the Tax Division into Estate Administration, with an increase in my annual salary from $4,000 to $4,200. At this point I must tell the reader that I was never concerned about money. If we had enough to live our lives as they were, that was all we needed; the rest would come later. When I got that first raise, after about six months on the job, I asked if it meant I was doing well or doing poorly. I was assured it was a good raise and I was doing a good job.

That was good enough for me and, although I had thought my career would be in tax planning, I was game to learn estate administration. As it developed, I did not enjoy it. I felt I was wasting my time and not learning anything or being challenged. I had been at the bank less than two years by that time. After thinking things over, I decided to leave the Marine and join my college friend, Erv Plesko, in a securities brokerage business I had helped him start.

I told my boss I was leaving, and shortly after I received a call from Mr. Rex Reeder, the executive vice-president of the entire bank, inviting me to lunch. The first thing he asked was why I was leaving. Before I could even answer, he gave me two pieces of information. The first was that Eliot Fitch felt very badly that I was leaving, and the second was some sound advice: "Don't let go of one trapeze until you have a firm grasp on another." To this day I have not forgotten his words. I told Mr. Reeder that I was bored and restless. He then described how he spent his days, running the bank's loan portfolio, dealing with large customers, serving on the boards of some of Milwaukee's leading corporations, and other activities I could only dream of doing. When he was done, I said, "That's what I would like to do." Mr. Reeder replied, "We will start you by putting you in the Credit Department, where you will learn financial analysis and how successful businesses operate."

I didn't know it then, but I had encountered another life-changer. My days in the Credit Department were a post-graduate course in banking and finance. I would spread the numbers, do comparative-ratio analysis, and review each company's performance with the responsible loan officer. I was learning about business, including what both the good operators and the bad operators did. In addition, I enrolled at the University of Wisconsin Extension for a course in financial analysis. After a short stay in Credit—only six or nine months—I was made an officer and given a desk on the commercial lending floor. My title was assistant cashier, a title from the past that is no longer used. I was part of a team of seven or eight vice-presidents and assistant vice-presidents who had lending authority and responsibility for all the bank's commercial customers.

I was assigned to Division B, working under the direction of Senior Vice-President John P. Botch, who was better known as Jack. What a wonderful man he was! I can't describe how much I learned from his steady manner and intelligent, insightful analysis. Jack had spent his entire career at the Marine, as had most of the officers. He had not gone to college, but he was the best banker I have ever known. Jack took me under his wing and got me involved with almost every credit he was responsible for. Division B's customer base was about one-half manufacturing and the other half retailing, construction, and savings and loans, plus an assortment of small businesses. The bank's largest customer was Allen-Bradley, and they were in our division.

I spent approximately three years in commercial lending, staying until 1959. By the time I was twenty-nine, I had been promoted to vice-president and was involved in almost all our strategic decisions. Those included the formation of a bank holding company, the initial acquisition of four smaller banks, plans for a new downtown head-quarters office building (with all the necessary city approvals), and my own creation of a small-business term loan program. It was a truly engaging, broadening, and exciting experience. I could not have been happier.

At home, two more children joined Kris and David. Susan was born on October 9, 1957, and Joan on December 31, 1958. All four children started their schooling at the Whitefish Bay Nursery School at Kingo Lutheran Church. From there they enrolled at Richards School, which was only one block from our home on Shoreland Avenue. You can't begin to understand how busy Marianne was, mothering four children during the first five years of our marriage. It wasn't long before we were looking for a larger house. In 1962, after checking out several possibilities in the North Shore suburbs, we found our new home at 4447 N. Stowell Avenue in Shorewood. It was a solid brick house built in 1920. The children all enrolled at Lake Bluff School and, with this material upgrade, I was certain that this was where we would live forever. I had paid $13,000 for our Whitefish Bay home in 1954 and sold it for $20,000. My memory says that we bought the Shorewood house for $42,000. I must say this was a huge amount for me, but I felt then, as I do today, that there is no better investment for a family than a home in a neighborhood where you enjoy a happy, peaceful life.

At about this time, I had an experience that left a lasting impression on me. It was an afternoon toward the end of August, 1959, when Eliot Fitch stepped out of his second-floor office at the Marine, looked around the room, and came over to my desk. I can hear him now in his announcer-like voice: "Shel, you like football?"

"Yes," I replied.

"Albert Puelicher, president of the Marshall & Ilsley Bank and a director of the Green Bay Packers, is having a small cocktail reception at his office to introduce the new coach and general manager of the Green Bay Packers, a man by the name of Vince Lombardi. I can't make it, so would you go over and represent us?"

"Of course, Mr. Fitch. I would be delighted."

So off I went to the M&I Bank, which was a half-block away. Those in attendance were Mr. Puelicher, the presidents of perhaps three smaller local banks, and myself. I was, at twenty-nine, very much the junior attendee. Let me mention that the Packers had won only one of the twelve league games they had played the previous season.

After his introduction, Coach Lombardi reviewed his experience and his background and described how pleased he was to be in the National Football League. "Any questions?," he concluded. I realized that the other guests were there out of respect for Mr. Puelicher and for the cocktails—except me. Only one question was asked: mine. "Coach," I ventured, "the Packers had a poor year in 1958. What can we expect in the coming season?"

His reply was short and to the point. "Young man," Lombardi said, "every player in this league is a talented player. They are the best of the best college players. They are all professionals. The issue is, can I as their head coach get them to excel and give me that extra effort that makes the difference in all contests? Can I get my pass receivers to stretch an extra few inches and grab those passes they have been missing? Can I get my guards to pull a second or two quicker and make that block they have been missing? Can I get my place kicker to make those field goals he might have previously missed? In other words, can I get that extra effort out of my players that makes the difference between winning and losing in this league? If I can, we will be winners."

He did all that and more, of course. He became the best ever. I have never forgotten that afternoon and what Coach Vince Lombardi said. His words were well worth remembering, especially "extra effort."

Chapter 4

Making Progress

Things continued to move ahead for me at the Marine Bank. I was totally engaged in my commercial banking career, and to become a vice-president at age twenty-nine at the carriage-trade Marine Bank was well beyond my expectations. Mr. Reeder retired in 1957, and John Lobb succeeded him as the new executive vice-president. John was a graduate of the University of Wisconsin Law School, but he had spent the most recent part of his career in the world of institutional investments. He was in his mid-forties, extremely intelligent, and energetic. John was a builder, and I believe he saw these qualities in me.

In 1958 Congress passed the Small Business Investment Company (SBIC) Act, which authorized banks, among other institutions, to form investment companies that could acquire equity positions in small businesses. The practice had not been permitted since the Depression. John asked me to take a good look at the situation and advise him whether the Marine should organize an SBIC. Well, I dug into the legislation and regulations, considered the matter carefully, and gave John all the reasons the Marine should not get involved. He looked at me for a minute and said, "Good job, Shel, but we're going to start one. Do you want to run it?" Without hesitation, I said, "Yes." With that brief exchange, I had changed careers again. I was about to become a venture capitalist and then a private investor.

We started Marine Capital Corporation in 1959. The bank invested $150,000, and the Small Business Administration invested $150,000 in a subordinated note, so we commenced operations with $300,000 of capital. Our offices were adjacent to the bank on Water Street. I put together a small staff and went to work. Most of the investments we considered were referred to us by bank officers. The regulations allowed our company to invest up to 20 percent of its capital in any

21

enterprise defined as a small business. In short order, we made four investments: Koss Electronics, the original developer and manufacturer of headphones; Getzen Music Company, a manufacturer of trumpets and other musical instruments; and two other small companies. Marine Capital's investment was usually in the form of a convertible subordinated debenture. Since I was still a vice-president of commercial loans, I would also provide the company we were investing in with a term loan, a line of credit, or both.

We had an impressive board of directors: Eliot Fitch, Elmer Winter (CEO of Manpower), Philip Ryan (CEO of Cutler-Hammer), Bill Bunge (CEO of Mortgage Associates), John Galbreath (a mega real estate developer), Jim Davant and Jim Swoboda (partners in Paine, Webber, Jackson & Curtis), Don Mitchell (president of General Telephone & Electronics), Grady Clark (CEO of Investors Diversified), and John Kelly (my good friend and a vice-president of the Marine Bank). With myself as president and our four original investments, we went public in April, 1961. The IPO raised $10 million, in addition to the initial $150,000 Marine Bank investment. I was thirty-two years old at the time. The challenges ahead turned out to be more than I had anticipated, and they were not all enjoyable. I was about to get an advanced education in the perils of venture capital and the ups and downs of life as the CEO of a public company, even a small one.

At the outset, things looked great. We managed to get a good deal of newspaper publicity, all of which was very flattering. The market was excited about SBICs, but, as I know now, unless you show constantly increasing earnings, the stock market loses interest. I tried to explain to the analysts that we would never show steady upward earnings growth; our gains would come largely from the sale of our investments, and this would happen as opportunities presented themselves. On top of this, there was constant pressure, initially from stockholders and even from some board members, to get our capital invested. I cautioned that investing the money was easy, but picking real winners was a slow process.

After a few years, our portfolio consisted of eight new investments in addition to the original four. As things developed, we had one good-sized winner (Empire Gas), several with modest gains, and one huge investment of $750,000 that took enormous amounts of time and pain before we recovered our money. That was possible only because of our total absorption in the business, a descent into bankruptcy, and the good luck of a merger. On our other investments, we generally managed to get our capital back plus interest.

Meanwhile, the stock market had lost interest, and our stock, which went public at $15, was selling for $7.50 a share. That was not the worst of it. Let me tell you of the hard lesson I learned about borrowing money. At an early board meeting, one of our directors, who left the board during our first year, asked me how much stock I owned. I told him 100 shares at the offering price of $15 per share, for a total investment of $1,500. He asked me why I didn't own more, and I told him that was all I could afford. He then offered to guarantee a $100,000 personal loan from the First National Bank of Chicago, where he banked, which would enable me to buy 10,000 shares at the current price of $10 per share. Confident about what we could do, I accepted his offer and borrowed the $100,000, certain that my leadership of the company would result in a value of $20 or $30 per share in the near future.

This was not a wise move, but I wasn't done. In my desire to share my good fortune with my four senior managers, I offered to loan them each $10,000, or $40,000 of the $100,000 I had borrowed, to buy Marine Capital stock. They readily accepted and signed notes to me on the same terms as my bank loan from First National.

Perhaps ten months later, the same director advised me that he needed to eliminate his guarantee: Would I please repay the note? By this time the stock was selling for $7.50 a share. I was underwater to the tune of $25,000 and earning $20,000 annually. I told the director that I didn't have the money; the stock was down, and I was not able to pay. To make matters worse, two of my investment managers left the company and simply renounced their obligations.

At this point I realized how foolish I had been, and I did the only sensible thing I could: I went to Chicago and met with my banker, Jim Badger. I told Jim the whole story and promised him that, even if I didn't know how yet, he would be paid in full. Jim said, "I trust you," and he renewed the note. It took a few years, but Marine Capital was ultimately successful. I paid my loan back from the company's distribution of assets and even had a profit. The lessons I learned were not forgotten: Never borrow money unless you have an assured source of repayment, never personally guarantee business loans, and don't be a gullible nice guy—you aren't doing anyone a favor, especially yourself.

At this point, more than two years into the venture, I concluded that a stand-alone SBIC, especially one with public shareholders, was not viable. The gains, if you had any, were not predictable, and I was less than impressed with the managers of the companies we had invested in. I felt I could do better than any of them and, since I knew banking, I figured that, if we could convert Marine Capital into a financial services holding company, I could make a success out of what had been at best a struggle.

Convincing our board of this entirely new strategy was not easy. Most of the directors were rightly skeptical. Eliot Fitch had doubts, but he said, "Let's see what you can do." Our attorney, Roger Minahan, of Whyte Hirschboeck and Minahan, was not just encouraging; he was enthusiastic, so I set off looking for a base acquisition. I felt the best candidate would be a savings and loan (S&L) institution, since that was a fairly straightforward business that I understood. Wisconsin's S&Ls were all mutual companies, and so I had to look for prospects among the stock companies on the West Coast. Acquisition candidates were available there, and their outlook was very good. So I set off for California and, with the help of Kidder, Peabody & Co., a well-respected investment banking firm, I started my search. I traveled to California a good many times, investigating S&Ls in the Los Angeles, San Francisco, and Sacramento areas. There were some very interesting possibilities, but before anything jelled, a different opportunity presented itself.

Bill Bunge, one of our directors, came to me one day and said, "Why don't you buy my company, Mortgage Associates?" Bill, who owned more than 50 percent of the company, was about sixty-five years old and looking for liquidity. The other shareholders were also older men who had merged their businesses into Mortgage Associates and were just as ready to sell. I gave a good deal of thought and study to this situation. I considered the future of the enterprise, reviewed its past financial statements, checked out the key people, and concluded that Mortgage Associates could be a good base operating company. The final check I made was with my friend Dorrance Noonan. He had graduated three years ahead of me from Whitefish Bay High School, served in the Marine Corps, and gone on to college. Dorrance and I met again when I joined the Marine Bank; in fact, we carpooled downtown together for three years. He now worked at Mortgage Associates and was in charge of their home improvement loan department. I shared the situation with him and asked for his thoughts and advice. He simply said, "Buy it." Again I asked, "What do you think? What are the problems? What do you think of management?" Again came the same simple response: "Buy it." And that is what I did.

The principal business of Mortgage Associates, Inc. (MAI) was originating FHA- and VA-insured mortgage loans on single-family homes, selling the loans to various life insurance companies, and then servicing the loans for a fee of 0.5 percent. Milwaukee was the home office, and there were five branches in Minneapolis, St. Louis, Chicago, Rockford, and Gary, Indiana. The company also originated commercial real estate loans, operated a casualty insurance agency, and made FHA-guaranteed home improvement loans that were held in the company's portfolio. It was this last business that Dorrance Noonan ran. It did not take me long to decide to buy the company. The asking price was $2 million, and we settled at $1.8 million. I was convinced that we could make Mortgage Associates grow as the platform for a diversified financial holding company.

I took the proposition to the Marine Capital board, who approved it. What we needed next was approvals from the SBA to leave the SBIC program and from the SEC to remove our designation as an investment company under the 1933 act. Neither approval was forthcoming. In fact, each agency had its own set of issues that caused it to oppose the transaction.

I spoke with my contact at the First National Bank of Chicago, who ended our conversation by telling me that if Marine Capital was blocked from buying Mortgage Associates, First National would give me a personal loan for the full purchase price, enabling me to own the entire company myself. I thanked him and said this would be a wonderful company to own, but my very strong obligation was to the Marine Capital shareholders; I had to find a way to complete this transaction for them.

With the help of Roger Minahan, our attorney; Dick Sell, our secretary; and with the support of our directors, especially Virgil Sullivan, we did find a way to make the purchase. We formed a new corporation, Bankers Financial, to buy Mortgage Associates. It was capitalized with $100 from me, and I served as president, with Roger Minahan as secretary. Marine Capital then declared a dividend of $1 million, payable equally to all shareholders of Marine Capital at the rate of about $1.50 per share. Bankers Financial then issued a stock purchase right to the same Marine Capital shareholders, authorizing them to purchase the same number of shares of Bankers Financial that they owned of Marine Capital. The net result was that if all Marine shareholders exercised their rights, they would own all of the Bankers shares, which would then own all of Mortgage Associates. There was one more piece to the puzzle. We needed another $1.5 million to complete the transaction, and it came in the form of a term loan I negotiated with the Chemical Bank of New York, whose officers I met through Virgil Sullivan.

The transaction was completed in 1965. Bill Bunge and his entire management team remained in place, Virgil Sullivan became chairman, and I was appointed vice-chairman. My involvement with Mortgage Associates was limited to board meetings. I understood that Bill Bunge did not want my participation, and things seemed to be proceeding smoothly without any input from me. Earnings were increasing, we repaid our debt to Chemical Bank on a regular schedule, and the stock price went up considerably.

With our base acquisition completed, I turned my full attention to Marine Capital. The entire board agreed that a public SBIC was not desirable, and they decided that our investments should be sold or liquidated and the capital returned to our shareholders. The businesses in our portfolio at that time were Lake States Conservation, Airtek Dynamics, Top Value, Deltox, Great Lakes Homes, and Robin Distributors. We had also purchased Schwitzer Outdoor Advertising and WFOX, a Milwaukee radio station, in their entirety. Schwitzer was acquired from Naegele Outdoor Advertising, a public company on whose board I served. We sold Schwitzer for a gain of almost three times our investment and WFOX at a small gain. The balance of the portfolio was either sold back to the principal owners or liquidated on a break-even basis.

Lake States Conservation was our biggest problem by any measure. Its business was growing Christmas trees at the edge of larger cities, usually on ten- to twenty-acre plots. The trees were maintained during their growing cycle and, when they were ready for harvest, retail customers cut them and carried them away. The concept was to simplify the entire process by combining the three layers of grower, transporter, and retailer in a single operation. In addition, the eight-year cycle had the speculative possibility of land appreciation. What none of us seemed to appreciate was the huge cost of a business that turns its inventory over only once every eight to ten years. The company eventually went through bankruptcy, and we ended up owning it.

Our total investment was $750,000—a huge amount for us, especially in 1965 dollars—but as Virgil Sullivan, a Marine Capital director and ultimately my mentor, said, "Lubar, you must carry a lucky horseshoe in your pocket." We merged Lake States into a small public company in Ohio that was in the business of growing sugar beets. A short time later, after we had liquidated all our other investments, we distributed cash from the sale of the portfolio and the stock from the Lake States merger to our shareholders. The Lake States stock sold for more than the $750,000 we had invested. This was either a miracle, dumb luck, or an unwillingness to give up. You be the judge!

As Marine Capital's other investments went off the books, Mortgage Associates, Inc. became the main event. The significance of this company in my life was enormous; it was through Mortgage Associates that I became an effective manager. Within a year of our purchase of MAI in 1965, things turned very dark, and the company was in serious danger of failing. First, the economy began to sour, and the Federal Reserve Bank raised the prime interest rate to what was then a record high of 6 percent. Next the Fed limited money growth, which, for Mortgage Associates, was like having its blood supply interrupted. This wasn't the worst. Next Bill Bunge, MAI's founder, chairman, and CEO, suffered a heart attack that took him out of management permanently. Shortly after Bill's departure, his chosen successor broke down emotionally and quit, telling me he couldn't take the pressure any more. He spoke to me because I was vice-chairman, and our chairman, Virgil Sullivan, was a Minneapolis resident who didn't get involved

27

in the business. A special meeting of the board was called, and the directors elected me president and chief executive. Virgil resigned as chairman at the same time, and things looked very bad.

When all this occurred at the end of 1966, MAI had a net worth of about $1.5 million and debt of approximately $50 million. That was a lot of red ink in 1966. The worst portion of the debt consisted of commercial construction loans on unfinished buildings, many of whose owners had run out of money. The consumer finance division was operating well, but it was financed by approximately $10 million of short-term borrowing from a clientele of individual private investors. I have never faced such an almost-impossible situation before or since. I say "almost" because we managed to pull the company out of all-but-certain bankruptcy to become a high-performing, very profitable enterprise.

Here is how it played out. On the first day I became CEO, I returned from Minneapolis and met with all the division managers. As it developed, these men were all exceptionally capable, and they were the ones responsible for the company's recovery, expansion, and remarkable earnings growth. My job was to sharpen MAI's strategic direction and shed its problem assets while retaining the confidence of the lending banks and our shareholders. I focused the company exclusively on the origination and servicing of FHA and VA home mortgage loans. Consumer lending was de-emphasized, and construction and commercial lending were eliminated altogether.

The problems we faced as a company were huge, but what no one knew about Mortgage Associates was the high quality, experience, and originality of its operating management. My first actions were to designate Mills Perry as executive vice-president and CFO, Loyal La Plante as general vice-president in charge of branches and mortgage origination, and Ron Huiras as treasurer. Ron worked closely with Mills, while Bob Filla oversaw the branches themselves, which numbered six at first but multiplied as we expanded into new markets. Eric Sundquist and Joe Boulicault handled mortgage sales to both existing and new institutional investors, Dorrance Noonan was in charge of consumer loans, Earl Lillydahl managed real estate, Earl Hill ran the insurance operations, Jim Barden was our general counsel, and John Haering handled all communications.

This was a great team, and, as we shed our problems, the company grew like no other in the mortgage banking industry. For me it was the greatest management opportunity I could ever have hoped for. Our 401(k) retirement plan allowed up to half of each employee's annual contribution to be in the form of company stock. As the value of one MAI share soared from pennies to around $35, almost all of us maxed out the stock portion of our plans.

But it wasn't about making money for most of us; it was about rising from the ashes to become the most respected and profitable company in our industry. Perhaps our greatest compliment came from Terry Murray, the Industrial National Bank officer who was leading his bank's search for acquisition candidates. Terry later told us that, when he was introduced to the various mortgage companies, they almost unanimously said something to the effect that they did all the things Mortgage Associates was doing. Terry then asked the investment banker his bank had retained why, if Mortgage Associates was so good, they weren't talking to Mortgage Associates? So they did, and the result was that Industrial National Bank of Rhode Island acquired us. All our people were retained except me, entirely by my design.

As I look back on the entire Marine Capital venture, it was a great success. The purchase of one share at $15 in 1961 led to the return of almost that much in cash liquidations and the opportunity to buy one share of Mortgage Associates at $1.50 per share. That stock was split four times in three years, giving each original shareholder four times his or her initial holding at a cost of 37.5 cents per share. In 1973, when Industrial National Bank acquired Mortgage Associates, the stock exchange had a value of about $35 per share, or $140 for an original buyer of Bankers Financial. If held longer, the stock would have been worth even more, since the business became part of Bank of America through a series of mergers. Not bad.

Chapter 5

I Go It Alone

In early 1966, when Marine Capital's directors accepted my rec-ommendation to liquidate the company, they also agreed to continue my annual salary of $20,000 through the end of the year, regardless of when I completed the liquidation. It had been thirteen years since I finished college and joined the Marine Bank, and Marianne and I now had four children. As it developed, I still had the Mortgage Associates workout ahead of me, but 1966 gave me my first opportunity to poke my head up and look for an acquisition to make on my own, to be in-dependent. What I most wanted from my career was the ability to sup-port my family as an independent entrepreneur. I remembered what my father would often tell me: "Better to earn one dollar working for yourself than two dollars working for someone else." I got his point and, as usual, he was right.

During my ups and downs at Marine Capital, I had met Bob Moon, who was ten years older than I. Bob had started Lakeside Manufactur-ing, a company that manufactured stainless steel carts, and was doing very well. He was a great help to me during the Marine Capital days, and we often discussed corporate organization and strategy, profes-sional management, employee motivation, acquisitions, raising capital, and a lot of other things now covered by the term "entrepreneurship." Bob asked me to serve on the board of Lakeside, and together we developed the concept of "Professional Ownership," a term that Lubar & Co. trademarked in 2016.

This concept was based on the inability of shareholders, wheth-er individuals or institutions, to interact with the boards of directors of the companies they had invested in. Whether the issue at hand was setting goals, monitoring management performance, truly understand-ing the business of the company, or assessing the impact of conditions beyond management control, the voice of ownership was not heard. It must also be remembered that, in the case of small businesses, the board (if there was one) and the management were most often the same people. The object of most small businesses was usually to fund the lifestyle of the CEO, who was typically the controlling or the sole shareholder.

Over the years, Lubar & Co., my family's business, has built its wealth base by practicing Professional Ownership. Our objectives have all centered on building each of our businesses into ever more sound and profitable enterprises. I can tell you that our transparent motivation and business experience have produced success. In addition to being investors, we consider ourselves coaches, counselors, and cheerleaders. We seek to unite the objectives of owners or shareholders with those of employees and managers so everyone succeeds or doesn't succeed, but we do it together. This concept was the real key to my success.

With the development of Professional Ownership as my guideline, I started to look for a company I could buy for cash, build into a business more significant than the one I had found, and raise the money to do it. At the time my total cash resources amounted to $15,000, but I was undaunted and confident.

I started by visiting the larger accounting firms, law firms, investment banks, and the handful of business brokers in Milwaukee. Everyone listened politely, since by then I had established a good reputation in the local banking community. But as I presented my story of Professional Ownership, I could see it wasn't coming across. I sensed that I sounded too academic. Today what I was describing would be called "private equity," but in 1966 the concept meant nothing to the people I was meeting; I was describing something that just was not being done at the time. After six or eight weeks of this, I was getting discouraged. To make matters worse, the economy was heading into the financial crisis of 1966. My plans and dreams of independence were starting to fade, but I kept at it, even though I was running out of people to talk with.

Things began to change when I called on John Cahill. He was an extremely talented tax lawyer who led his own small firm, Cahill & Fox. I told John my whole story and described what I was hoping to do. He leaned back in his chair and said simply, "That makes a lot of sense." Then he told me that his best client had decided to sell his business and was talking to a potential buyer. The principal owner held 70 percent of the shares and the chief operating officer had the remaining 30 percent. John said, "I am going to introduce you to them, and there is only one caveat. They will answer all your questions, tell you everything they know, provide you with financial statements, and then they will tell you their asking price. At that point you will say 'Yes' or 'No.' There will be no negotiations."

I agreed to his terms, and John got the ball rolling. The business in question was the Sorgel Electric Company, a manufacturer of dry-type electrical transformers on Milwaukee's South Side. Sorgel had revenues of about $4 million and after-tax earnings of $440,000. The first person I met was Fred Koeper, who ran the factory. I really liked Fred. He was a self-taught electrical engineer in his early sixties, and his father had worked at the company before him. I could tell he liked my story, and he really liked the idea that he would be Sorgel's president if I bought the company.

Next I met Bill Sorgel, the founder's son and the majority owner. Bill was about forty-five years old, definitely an extrovert, and focused on sales. He was the one who wanted to sell and enjoy his life without the burden of having all his assets tied up in the company. Bill played the guitar, had a second home in northern Wisconsin, and seemed to be an insider with the Green Bay Packers organization. In summary, he wanted to have fun. When we met, he was in the process of selling the company to an experienced executive in the electrical manufacturing industry. After the sale, Bill would be out. Fred's status in the event of that sale was unknown to me.

I liked everything I saw and everything I learned. I wanted to do this transaction. I made one industry check. I called Dick Zucker, the older brother of my brother-in-law, Donald Zucker. Dick was a graduate electrical engineer who held a responsible position with General Electric. I described the entire situation to him and expressed my interest in buying Sorgel. Dick's response was immediate: "I wouldn't touch it with a ten-foot pole." I asked why, and he said that Sorgel was too small and had no research program, among other drawbacks. GE was then No. 1 in the manufacture of dry-type transformers, Westinghouse was No. 2, and Sorgel was quite a distant No. 3. I thanked Dick and said, "The difference between your view and mine is that you're well-situated at GE while I'm currently unemployed and on the outside looking in."

I called John Cahill and said, "Yes, I want to buy." The asking price was $4.4 million, and that was what I would have to pay. I asked John to put together a purchase contract that was subject only to financing. I felt confident that I could raise the necessary funds; that was my business, after all. The sellers accepted my proposal to pay the $4.4 million on these terms: $2.9 million in cash at closing and the remaining $1.6 million in preferred stock yielding 4 percent currently and appreciating 2 percent a year over a five-year term, for a total return of 6 percent, of which 2 percent would be taxed at the capital-gains rate.

Now I had to raise the money. My first call was to Jim Badger at the First National Bank of Chicago. When I put my proposal to him, he said that if he brought this loan into his committee, he'd probably be fired. Didn't I know the Fed was shrinking the money supply but keeping the prime rate at 6 percent? No, I didn't! My next call was to Bill Brown, vice-president of the First National Bank of Boston. Bill covered Wisconsin, Minnesota, and Chicago for his bank, and I had great respect for him. He eventually became chairman and CEO of the Bank of Boston Corporation. I was calling Bill from Pittsburgh, and I remember how straightforward his reply was: "One, banks aren't making acquisition loans today. Two, this is a loan for a life insurance company. Three, send me a summary of the transaction covering no more than two pages, and I'll be back in touch within two days."

I sent Bill the summary, and in two days he called back to say that he'd reserved a room for me at the Ritz Carlton Hotel in Boston and made appointments with Fred Fedeli at State Mutual Life Insurance in Worcester, Massachusetts, and Don Wheeler at Massachusetts Mutual Life in Springfield. We visited both companies on the same day, and each took $1 million of a $2 million 6-percent subordinated note. Each also received 17.5 percent of the common stock of the new company, which I had capitalized at $100,000. First National Bank of Boston provided the final $900,000 with a one-year loan that we repaid on time. My interest in the new company was a little less than 50 percent, which I paid for with my $15,000 savings and a $35,000 loan from the First National Bank of Chicago.

When the financing closed, Sorgel Electric had $100,000 of paid-in equity, $1,500,000 of preferred stock, $2,000,000 of subordinated debt, and $900,000 of senior bank debt. State Mutual required a "best efforts" letter from an underwriter who would take the company public, which cost 15 percent of the stock for $15,000. My commitment for this potential "best efforts" underwriting was from Loewi & Co.

After closing, I was Sorgel's chairman and CEO, Fred Koeper was president, and the other directors were Bob Moon, Milo Snyder of Loewi & Co., and John Cahill. Nothing could ever work as well as Sorgel did after my purchase. In the next five years, we added two manufacturing facilities, developed new products (including one of the first medical monitoring systems for intensive-care hospital rooms), tripled sales to $12 million, tripled earnings to $1.2 million after tax, and transferred 10 percent of the ownership to the top three executives.

I have characterized the company's performance as pulling the cork out of a bottle of champagne; there was so much pent-up energy just waiting to be released. The difference was that we were running the company to make it a better, larger, more profitable enterprise, not as a source of cash to finance the owner's lifestyle. At the very outset, I told the key employees that I would receive a modest salary and that I would personally pay for my clubs, my car, and any other perks. The entire attitude and demeanor changed. During the first five years, we faced two organizing attempts by the electrical unions, and we won both votes and remained an open shop.

As I have said before, I don't expect to ever create another Sorgel Electric. Absolutely everything worked. The final chapter came with a merger offer from Square D Company, an international electrical equipment manufacturer with roots in Milwaukee but headquarters in Chicago. It is with much pride that I say Sorgel was by then No. 1 in the market of dry transformers, GE was No. 2, and Westinghouse was No. 3. In January, 1971, five years after I acquired Sorgel, we merged with Square D Company for $20 million of Square D common stock, of which my share was 45 percent. I continued to hold most of my stock, and a year or two after the merger I joined the Square D board of directors. Under Square D's ownership and with the help of their strong marketing organization, Sorgel's $12 million annual revenues increased by a factor of ten to twenty times. For me, my ultimate total return was 3,000 times my original equity investment.

Chapter 6

Time Out

All years are important, and each has events that make it stand out from the rest. By any measure, 1971 and 1972 were momentous years for me and my family. The period started with the merger of Sorgel Electric into Square D Company at the end of January, 1971. I continued as president of Mortgage Associates, but the company was running smoothly under the management team I had put in place.

So what was next for me? Early in 1971, Mayor Henry Maier asked me to serve as president of Summerfest for the coming year. Summerfest was a ten-day music festival that the mayor had started in 1968 and that had moved to the lakefront in 1970. In its early years, the event had attracted limited interest and run up substantial losses. In 1970 John Kelly, my long-time friend and colleague at the Marine Bank, had taken over as president, and John saved Summerfest. He consolidated the scattered and multiple events of the first festivals in a single, larger location on the downtown lakefront, and hired Henry Jordan as the director. Henry had been a key member of the Lombardi-era Green Bay Packers. He was an All-Pro, a member of the Football Hall of Fame, and the right man to run operations at Summerfest. The result was success.

I took over in early 1971 and, with the base that John had established, Summerfest grew and was even more successful. However, until the final day of the ten-day event that I was responsible for, no one knew how much of the $750,000 we had committed for talent and other costs would be returned in event revenue. It was an enormous relief to me when the final tally showed we had produced a surplus, or profit, of $150,000. Whew!!

Perhaps the following period, from early September, 1971, to mid-July, 1972, was our most memorable. I have since referred to it as our family's year-long sabbatical; at least it was for me. The idea was planted when our family went on a ten-day excursion to Israel led by Rabbi Jay Brickman. The travelers were all members of Congregation Sinai, and over spring vacation, Jay took us on a wonderful trip through Haifa, Tel Aviv, Jerusalem, the old city of Bethlehem, Jericho, Masada, the Dead Sea, kibbutzes, and every historic place between. From this experience grew the idea that the upcoming year might be the last one we could all spend together as a family unit. Kris was a senior in high school and David a junior; Susan was in eighth grade and Joan in seventh. Very soon our children would be off to college and into their individual lives.

Marianne and I were both of a mind to "re-pot." Exactly when, where, and how were uncertain, but we knew we wanted a change. For my part, I simply wanted to shed the burden of responsibilities I'd accumulated over the years: boards of directors, non-profit groups, colleges, and all the rest. It seemed that everyone had a piece of me and nothing was left for myself. Now the Sorgel merger was a done deal. Mortgage Associates was operating very well, but I was over-identified with the company's success. It seemed like an ideal moment to leave: to cut all ties, lean back, and enjoy life while we were all still young, financially independent, and together.

Out of all this came the plan to spend the school year of 1971-1972 in Europe. We all agreed that the place was to be Switzerland. After an exploratory trip, we decided on the city of Lugano in the canton of Ticino, which is in the Italian-speaking sector of Switzerland. The school all four of our children would attend was The American School in Switzerland (TASIS), which was run by its founder, Ms. Mary Crist Fleming, a most impressive woman.

None of us could have imagined how the year might play out. The children knew they would be attending school in a foreign country with students from all over the world. For Marianne and myself, the extent of our plans were a 1971 SL 180 Mercedes that I had purchased through Concours Motors in Milwaukee for delivery in Zurich and a few clothes and personal items in a small suitcase. For the rest of the year, we would buy and discard as we traveled. Where we might go, how long we might stay, and what we would do when we arrived were all questions we never considered. We had the car, our passports, access to money, and our imaginations.

We didn't spend much time in Lugano. Soon after the children were settled, there was a small reception for parents where I met Ken Lieberman, a fellow member of the Young Presidents Organization (YPO). Ken had established the headquarters for his business in Geneva, Switzerland. He was a bit older than me, but by coincidence, he was also a graduate of the University of Wisconsin-Madison. During our conversation, he asked me what we would be doing when we left TASIS. I told him I didn't know and asked what he would do if he was in our place. Ken didn't hesitate: "I would go to St. Moritz and ski."

Marianne and I liked the idea and, after kissing our children good-bye, we drove off to St. Moritz. We agreed that our plan for the next year was to stay loose and enjoy life. St. Moritz is in the southern portion of Switzerland. The native language is Romanch, which, as you might guess, was brought in by the Romans. To get there from Lugano, we crossed the border into Italy and then crossed back into Switzerland. St. Moritz is a beautiful small town in the Alps. Besides Romanch, the inhabitants spoke English, French, and German.

We went to the central tourist office on arrival, where Marianne inquired about rentals. We were directed to a rather new apartment building over-looking Lake St. Moritz. What we saw was a nicely furnished two-bedroom apartment near the ski lift. The owners were a couple about sixty years old; the husband was an architect. The building was in the center of town, had an inside garage, and was perfect for us. We rented it until March 1, 1972.

We then checked into the Bernasconi Hotel, where we had a great dinner and a bottle of lovely Swiss wine. Yes, life was already very good and getting better. Next day we started on our travels. I had no road maps, visas, hotel reservations, or travel books. With supreme self-assurance, we pointed our car toward Trieste, Italy, and were off. The only guide we had was a one-page travel brochure that had a sketch of Yugoslavia showing, among other advertisements, a road along the Adriatic Sea to Dubrovnik, an ancient Roman city. So that is where we went. From there we traveled to the island of Sveti Stefan, then across the mountains to Belgrade, then to Budapest, Hungary, and Vienna, Austria. We continued to Prague, Czechoslovakia, which at the time was occupied by the Russian army. The governing regime was a puppet of the Russian government.

In Prague we employed a guide who took us through the city. We viewed the notable buildings, the developments on the Danube and Elbe Rivers, and the old Jewish cemetery in the center of the city. You must remember that Prague was the only major city in Europe that was not badly damaged by the fighting in World War II. The cemetery was a type I had never seen before. The burials were piled on top of each other, perhaps six or seven levels deep, and the stone markers were lined up alongside the graves.

After spending two days with our guide, she asked if I could give her some advice. The issue was whether her sixteen-year-old son should join the Communist Party. She told us that to succeed in their country, you had to be a party member. I told her I couldn't tell her what to do, but it seemed that his choices were to either join the party or plan to leave the country. It was a lesson in the realities of the world for both Marianne and myself.

From Prague we drove to Germany, then back to Lugano to be with the children. By this time, it was early November, 1971, and the children had some vacation time. We decided that we would all drive to Rome and spend the holiday there. Virgil Sullivan had suggested we stay at the Hassler Medici Hotel at the top of the Spanish Steps.

Virgil had given me his best knowledge, of which he had plenty, about the hotels, sights, and people he knew in Europe. It was a huge help, but in Rome it was almost life-saving. For a few days before we left, Joan had been complaining of a stomach-ache to Marianne. When we arrived at the hotel, I was unaware of her discomfort and made a dinner reservation on the rooftop for the six of us. When dinnertime arrived, Marianne said Joan wasn't up to going and that she would eat with her in our suite. When we returned from dinner, Marianne said Joan was really sick. Here we were in Italy, we couldn't speak the language, we had a sick child, and we didn't know a soul. What to do? Marianne called the hotel concierge and told him we needed a doctor who could speak English. The concierge connected us with an American doctor of Italian ancestry from Philadelphia who had moved to Rome. He took us to a small hospital staffed by nuns, where an Italian doctor removed Joan's appendix. Marianne stayed with Joan at the hospital and nursed her back to health. As usual, Marianne took care of everything so well that it took me some time to appreciate what a calamity we might have faced without her prompt, decisive action. We didn't see much of Rome on this trip, but there would be other times.

During the children's various other vacations, we traveled to England, Italy, Switzerland, Germany, France, Denmark, Belgium, Norway, Sweden, Luxembourg, Spain, and Portugal. While the children were in school, Marianne and I traveled to Greece, Turkey, Japan, Hong Kong, China, Korea, Thailand, and Jamaica, either on our own or with YPO. During the winter of 1971-1972, we were mostly in our apartment in St. Moritz. Those were great days that consisted mostly of skiing every day and finding good restaurants at night, shopping for food and wine, reading the *Herald Tribune*, and occasionally cashing a check.

Chapter 7

Our Mountains

When we returned from our one-year sabbatical in the summer of 1972, Marianne and I embarked on a search for a ski chalet in the Rocky Mountains—a place where we could enjoy our recent embrace of skiing in the winter, go hiking in the summer, and spend our winter holidays together as a family. It was to be the beginning of a tradition that Marianne and I will continue for the rest of our lives and that our children, grandchildren, and their descendants will, we hope, maintain forever. The 2018-2019 holidays were the forty-sixth year we were all together in Aspen.

To find our Shangri-La, we set off in September, 1972, looking first in Vail, Colorado, then Jackson Hole, Wyoming, and finally Aspen, Colorado—a town we had last visited on our honeymoon in September, 1952. Twenty years later, it was still a small mining and ranching town at its heart, but Aspen was rapidly growing into one of the world's great skiing and cultural communities. In 1952 there had been only one short, single-chair ski lift. Now there were four complete ski areas: Ajax Mountain in Aspen itself, the Highlands, Buttermilk Mountain and, the newest development, Snowmass Mountain. Perhaps most promising for our future, the Aspen Institute and the Aspen Music Festival and School had both started recently. These two institutions became major involvements for all of us, and they were nearly as powerful a magnet as all the wonderful outdoor sports.

With counseling from our friend Stan Kritzik, we decided on the Snowmass Mountain development, purchasing a condominium on the top floor of the new Top of the Village complex. We owned this unit for almost fourteen years, selling it in 1985 when we purchased a home on the west end of Aspen on Lake Avenue. Our home is 100 yards from the Aspen Meadows, the home of the Aspen Institute and the Aspen

Music Festival. Although my skiing days ended at age eighty-five, my interest in hiking is still high. The joys of the mountain trails, the intellectual stimulation of the Institute, and the high quality of the Music Festival draw Marianne and me to Aspen for the summer. In particular, we have attended every Ideas Conference, and I have been a regular at the World Economy Seminar.

Of course, the big attraction of Aspen at the beginning was skiing. In my opinion, the skiing at Aspen is unmatched in the world. Our entire family fell in love with it. Although it was about skiing, we started visiting in summer early on, both for the hiking and for Marianne's interest in Anderson Ranch, a school for ceramicists, sculptors, woodcarvers, and other types of crafts workers. Marianne's ceramics were outstanding. On days when we were alone in Snowmass, Marianne would often spend the day at Anderson Ranch while I went off into the mountains alone, hiking to the top and returning in the afternoon. If bad weather threatened, I would turn around. As an experienced climber once said, "Getting to the top is exhilarating, but getting down is mandatory." When David was available, he and I might do a one- or two-day backpacking adventure. We ultimately climbed most of the trails and mountains in the area, sometimes being out for three nights. Often Joan and Susan would join us.

From the hiking and backpacking we did, the challenge of going higher developed. At about this time, in the 1980s and 1990s, the challenge was to climb the highest mountain on every continent. I had never had that as a goal, and I never spoke of it, but I thought, "Why not give it a try?" And so we did. David, Joan, and I signed up with a mountain outfitter to climb Mt. Kilimanjaro, which borders both Tanzania and Kenya. We flew to Kenya, where our group of about fifteen persons met, and from there we motored to Tanzania. After a few days visiting the game parks and viewing the elephants, giraffes, and other wildlife, we moved on to the mountain. The climb started in the small village of Arusha, which was at sea level. From there to the top of Kilimanjaro was over 20,000 feet, and climbing up and back took six days. The ascent was fun and not too trying. Let's call it a strenuous walk. I learned quite a few lessons on this adventure, the most important being that you should have a good headlamp when you're climbing in the dark.

On the day of the summit, we bivouacked in a hut at 15,000 feet. At this height you are in what is called the "dead zone"; no plants or animals can exist at this very low oxygen level. It is not unusual to develop altitude sickness at this height. Everyone was in their sleeping bags as soon as darkness fell. The plan was to rise about 11 p.m., get our stuff together, eat, and be on the mountain by midnight. The trail was as close to straight up as I had ever experienced. In addition, we were climbing on what is called mountain scree, or volcanic ash. Our guide was a local, and he was using a kerosene lantern to light his way. It wasn't long before the strong winds we were encountering blew his lantern out. I was using a flashlight, which stopped working after about an hour. David had a small flashlight that wasn't much help to me, but Joan had a very professional climber's headlamp. I had no choice but to stay close to Joan, and that meant keeping up with her fast pace.

We three were the first of our group to reach the summit at about 5 a.m. Our guide arrived about thirty minutes later. We were there for the sunrise, but my strongest memory of the climb was trailing behind Joan and gasping, "Slow down, Joan, slow down." She thought she was, but I certainly didn't think so. The next day we hiked out. At the bottom I gave a very good tip to our guide, who was working for a dollar a day, as well as most of the clothes we were using. I can only describe Kilimanjaro as unforgettable.

Our next adventure was to be climbing Mt. Elbrus, the highest mountain in Europe at 18,000 feet and located in what was then Soviet Georgia. The group was made up of David, Joan, myself, John Cahill, and his son. It would be our first climb over snow and ice, so as a warm-up we decided to climb Mt. Rainier, a 14,000-foot giant in the State of Washington. Joan's plans didn't allow her to join us, so she did it later with another group. The Rainier climb took two days, which included a one-night bivouac on the mountain. Our guide was a senior member of Rainier Mountaineers. We spent our first day getting experience on the snow and ice—learning to self-arrest, getting comfortable using an ice axe, wearing pitons, and acclimating to the altitude. Everything went as planned, and we all felt we could do anything. As you might expect, we had a lot to learn.

Since I had arranged the Rainier climb, Cahill wanted to arrange Elbrus. He had some connections with hotel people in Estonia, so he coordinated our arrival in Moscow, hotel arrangements there, travel to Georgia, and the climb itself.

What followed was failure, but it could have been disaster. The only conditions I had given John were that, on the mountain, I wanted guides who spoke English, preferably Americans, and that we would use new climbing ropes, not old and frayed ones. We were met at the airport by two or three of John's Estonians, but not the ones he knew. They piled us and our luggage into a van, and the first thing I noted was that the windows were shaded; you could not see in or out. When I asked what hotel we were staying at, they explained after a while that we weren't staying at a hotel but were going to a friend's house instead. It was 5 or 6 p.m. when we arrived at a large house in a shabby neighborhood. They proceeded to take us to the third floor and said we would have dinner in an hour. First, there was no furniture—just three or four bare rooms and only bed springs for sleeping. When we had dinner, the Estonians told us that the Russians no longer permitted persons from outside the Soviet Union to travel to Georgia, but they had Russian passports for the five of us. I said, "What do you mean?," and they handed out the passports. I couldn't tell whose they were, but the photograph on mine showed a young man. The same was true for the others, including Joan's. I was assured they would work. I then asked about the climbing ropes and English-speaking guides, and they assured me everything would be taken care of, and that I would feel better after dinner.

I can't remember much about dinner, because I was asking myself what I had allowed myself to get my two young children into. After dinner the Cahills went into one room and the Lubars into another. We spread our sleeping bags on the wire mesh of the bed frames and tried to get some sleep. At 2 or 3 in the morning, I got out of my bed, turned the light on, and huddled with David and Joan. I said, "Kids, I don't like anything I have seen or heard. If we leave Moscow tomorrow with these people, we are totally under their control, traveling on someone else's passports, and I have no reason to trust them. It's not what we planned, but what I am saying is we should abort now, when we can."

I next went into the Cahills' room and told John how I felt. He said he would think it over and let me know his decision in the morning.

When we all met the next morning, John said he was going to stay. I explained to the Estonians why we were aborting and asked them to drive us to the Rossiya Hotel in central Moscow, where we had stayed when my father and Cahill and I had come to Russia some years earlier. We stayed in Russia a few nights, did some sightseeing, had a good dinner at the hotel, and got to the airport at 7 a.m. for a noon departure. All I can say is that changing your ticket and going through baggage check and security in Russia is the definition of torture. We just made our boarding time on TWA. I slumped in my seat, drenched with perspiration, and wanted to hug the stewardess when she asked what I wanted to drink. "Double Scotch on the rocks, please." I slept most of the way safely back home. The morals of the adventure for me: You are never too old to learn, and trust your instincts and judgment.

The kids and I did a number of other major climbs. Joan and I climbed Mt. Popocatepetl in Mexico, which is 18,000 feet, and David and I scaled the Jungfrau in Switzerland. I must add that a day or two later David climbed Mt. Blanc in France while I rested. Later I went on an invitational climb of Mt. Powell, 14,000 feet, in Colorado. Perhaps my last adventure was hiking across the Brooks Mountain Range in Alaska with my young friend Bob Kaufman and one of his colleagues. This was a seven-day hike over permafrost for me and 250 miles above the Arctic Circle. Other than the pilot who flew us in and out, we never saw another human. My two colleagues stayed an extra week and traveled by rubber raft as well as on foot. We were up there in early August, and except for a few hours of dusk, it was light for all twenty-four hours of the day. During the hike we saw a few bears in the distance, but none of them threatened us. Besides, I was carrying a .357 Magnum pistol.

Chapter 8

Washington, D.C., 1973-1975

In early February, 1973, before the climbs I described in the last chapter, we publicly announced that Mortgage Associates would merge with Industrial National Corporation, the parent holding company of Industrial National Bank. The *Wall Street Journal* ran a small article on the merger, and about two weeks later I received an unexpected telephone call. It came when our family was spending some time over the 1973 winter break at our residence in Snowmass. Marianne and the children flew out before me, and I arrived at mid-morning on the next day. When I got there, Marianne told me, "The White House called you an hour ago." Not surprisingly, I thought this was a joke. It wasn't!

After some family conversation around our makeshift dining room table—a large packing box from Marshall Field & Co. that had contained the bedding and towels for our new condo—I returned the call. The man on the other end of the line was Allen Parmenter, who was handling recruiting for Richard Nixon. The president had just been sworn in for his second term in January. Mr. Parmenter said, "Mr. Lubar, we understand you could be available to do a job for your country. Are you interested?" I was startled! I was surprised! I said, "Of course. What do you have in mind?" He said, "Commissioner of the Federal Housing Administration; Assistant Secretary, Housing Production and Mortgage Credit, Department of Housing and Urban Development; a director of the Federal National Mortgage Association (Fannie Mae); and executive in charge of the Government National Mortgage Association (Ginnie Mae)." I said, "Let me get a pen and write that down. Meanwhile, I would like to discuss this with my family, and I'll be back in touch with you promptly."

I never did find out exactly how my name came up for consideration. That *Wall Street Journal* story may have had something to do with it, but I think the real connection was John Heiman, an investment banker I had met during my Mortgage Associates days. John had left the world of private finance to work as an assistant to George Romney, secretary of Housing and Urban Development, better known as HUD. He apparently thought enough of me to suggest my name, and Romney apparently thought enough of Heiman to accept it. Interestingly, both men were gone by the time I arrived; turnover in Washington is pretty high every four years. Partisan politics played little if any role in my appointment. I had been a Republican since law school, but hardly an active one.

When I hung up the phone, we all sat around our packing-box table to talk it over. I said, "There are two options: we can stay in Milwaukee and I can babysit the MAI merger, or we can move to Washington, D.C., and embark on a new adventure." There was amazingly little discussion. Kris was at the University of Colorado in Boulder, David was on his way to Bowdoin College in Brunswick, Maine, and Susan and Joan were living with us and attending Shorewood public schools. The unanimous decision was, "Let's do a new adventure." And so we did.

After an interview with Jim Lynn, who was then secretary of HUD, he offered me the job, subject to the FBI background check and other formalities. Much to my surprise, this background check went all the way back to my days in grade school; it was very thorough. Next, I went to the White House to be interviewed by the president's general counsel, John Dean, whose job was to clear me for conflicts of interest and future commitments. I told Mr. Dean that my only commitment was to my father, and that was to take him to visit the hometown in Russia he had left more than sixty years earlier. "No problem," he said. "The State Department will help you."

When all of that was settled, Marianne and I set out to rent a house. We managed to connect on a wonderful house in Georgetown that was being vacated by the former postmaster general, Mr. Red Blount. He wanted to sell us the house, but we wanted to rent. We agreed to a one-year lease, after which he would have thirty days to explore a sale or renew the lease with us for another year. With that taken care of, all that remained was my confirmation by the Senate.

The practice was for White House staff members to first take their candidates on courtesy calls to the chairman and every member of the appropriate Senate committee—the Committee on Banking, in my case. We started with the chairman, Senator John Sparkman of Alabama, a long-serving older gentleman who couldn't have been more friendly. Then again, this was near the beginning of the Watergate matter, and Watergate was in the front of everyone's mind. I had equally cordial meetings with all the other senators except my own, Bill Proxmire from Wisconsin. Senator Proxmire declined to see me, explaining that he preferred to meet me under oath at the hearing. So be it. I wasn't surprised. What did surprise me was the calls I received from Representative Henry Reuss and Senator Gaylord Nelson, both from Wisconsin, who asked if they could escort me to the confirmation hearing. Both gentlemen were Democrats, and their introduction of me to the committee was uplifting and a most decent and civilized gesture. Later I worked closely with both men.

The confirmation session itself was a non-event, and I believe I was unanimously confirmed. After I stated my qualifications, I received only two questions, the first from a young freshman senator from Delaware, Joseph Biden. The future vice-president had just turned thirty years old, and I think this was his first confirmation. The FHA was getting a lot of negative press in those days, and Senator Biden asked what in the world had happened. I replied that I had been on the job all of one week and was still trying to get a handle on the situation. The other question was from Mr. Proxmire, who commented that my financial statement contained no numbers. I replied, "Yes, Senator, and the reason is that the form simply said to list your assets and liabilities, and that's what I did." I had no liabilities, and my assets were listed without amounts. I understand that later forms have required numbers.

Although I went to work immediately, I still had to take the oath of office. This is usually done as soon as possible after the president signs your commission, which he does after Senate confirmation. Later there is a reception for invited guests. I took my oath on Saturday, July 7, 1973, when President Nixon was at his home in San Clemente, California. Marianne and I were at Camp David, the President's Maryland retreat, with Secretary Lynn and his other assistant secretaries and their wives. As soon as the president signs your commission, you are tracked down and the oath is administered. In my case, it was about noon, and I was swimming in the president's pool when a U.S. Marine appeared at poolside with a large towel that he wrapped around me. I was escorted into President Nixon's office, where Jim Lynn swore me in, dripping wet. Quite a beginning. Later there was a second ceremony for family, friends, and colleagues at HUD. Truly a thrill.

It was finally time to officially take over my department. There were 10,000 government employees under me. We had ten regional offices and countless other FHA offices around the country. In every one were framed pictures of President Nixon, Secretary Jim Lynn, and Commissioner SBL.

One of my very first experiences brought back an unpleasant memory. During the Mortgage Associates turnaround a few years earlier, the single largest problem I had to deal with was a construction loan of about $1.7 million for the construction of the Monona Shores Apartments in Madison. At the time I took over MAI, we had disbursed the full amount of our commitment, and the building was only about half-completed. Work had stopped, snow was falling, and there was no roof. The building was being fabricated by U.S. Steel Homes, and they were using a loan that Mortgage Associates was supervising for a fee of 0.5 percent. My first reaction was that there must be a misunderstanding. No lender would take on the risk and effort involved with such a large loan to an undependable borrower for 0.5 percent.

We had to do something, so my first call was to a very experienced real estate lawyer in Milwaukee, Mr. Morrie Levin. When he read the documents, Mr. Levin's reaction was that no one would ever be so stupid as to make this loan. Well, we, meaning Mortgage Associates, had made it. There was no other course of action but to go to Louisville, Kentucky, and deal with the president of U.S. Steel Homes, Mr. Richard Dyas. During a rather unpleasant meeting, Mr. Dyas held my feet to the fire, but he did agree to some additional financing, and he connected us with another builder who finished the job and purchased the building from us. I couldn't believe how fortunate we were, but Monona Shores was not the only underwater apartment loan we somehow shed without much loss.

Fast forward to June, 1973. I had arrived at my sumptuous suite of offices at FHA, and I was starting to get acquainted with my staff. Some time during my first day, I started scanning the staff sheet of the Government National Mortgage Association, which reported directly to me. There on the list of Ginnie Mae's officers was the name of Richard Dyas, executive vice-president. Yes, it was the same man who had hung me out to dry five or six years earlier. My only thought was that this was too good to be true. Retribution would be mine, I thought. I asked my executive secretary to tell Mr. Dyas that I wanted to see him. In a few minutes, he was standing in front of me, the same old Dick Dyas.

The meeting was not what I had anticipated. I had intended to make him stand and wait as I read some meaningless report, but I couldn't do it. Instead I rose with a big smile on my face and give him a hearty handshake. I told him I had major plans for raising the profile and importance of Ginnie Mae in our country and looked forward to working with him and the Ginnie Mae president, Woody Kingman. And this is what we did. By the time I left, we had made Ginnie Mae the principal guarantor of mortgage pools of FHA- and VA-insured loans. This was important if Americans were to access the huge amount of institutional money that could be made available to finance homes. I should point out that these were not the sort of mortgage pools that developed in early 2000 and led to a financial collapse in 2007. Those loans were not underwritten, were usually insured by private companies, and were sold in five or six tranches. The Ginnie Mae pools, by contrast, consisted of federally insured loans that had been soundly underwritten. There has never been a Ginnie Mae default.

As Ginnie Mae blossomed, the Federal Housing Administration was floundering. I arrived in June, 1973, and for the fiscal year that ended on June 30, the FHA showed a loss of $1 billion, which I believe was the first loss in its history. I remember that my first official act in July, 1973, was to sign a note payable to the U.S. Treasury for $1 billion to keep the agency going. That was a very big number in those days.

Like most Americans, I was familiar with the FHA, but a closer look at its history convinced me that it was possibly the single most important stimulant to housing progress the world had ever seen. The agency was created on June 27, 1934, in the depths of the Depression, and it introduced a new and revolutionary housing finance concept: federally insured loans repayable in regular, level monthly installments. Before the FHA came on the scene, the typical home purchase involved very short-term credit—generally mortgages of from three to five years. Second mortgages were commonplace, interest rates were very high, and often the entire principal amount of the loan came due in one huge "balloon" payment when the mortgage matured. No wonder the dream of homeownership was impossible for all but a small percentage of the population.

The FHA changed those conditions practically overnight. When the federal government assumed the risk involved in mortgage lending, the way was cleared for the concept of regular monthly payments to reduce the mortgage loan. Private lenders could now extend credit over a longer period of time, and on far more favorable terms. Because the FHA set minimum property standards for every loan it insured, lenders could also be confident that their investment was just as safe in a home 3,000 miles away as it was in a residence just down the block.

The results of this New Deal program were jaw-dropping. By the time I took over, the FHA had underwritten mortgages on almost 12 million homes in the amount of more than $132 billion, plus another $23 billion in home improvement loans and $27 billion in rental units. FHA programs had helped between 44 and 50 million families improve their housing conditions, often dramatically. They also brought the construction industry back to life and virtually created the vast housing finance industry of today. Best of all, the programs were self-sustaining. Premiums on FHA insurance enabled the agency to repay— with interest—the seed money borrowed from the U.S. Treasury and to set aside "rainy day" reserves of more than $1.2 billion.

So why did this public-sector powerhouse run into trouble? Because in the 1960s the FHA began to broaden its focus from conventional mortgages to programs that served specific populations, from the elderly to displaced families, and specific geographic areas, often inner cities, whose housing markets were in dire need of support. Slowly but surely, the FHA moved away from an economically sound business approach to the assumption of "acceptable risk." The art of determining, in this strange new area, where to locate the line between acceptable and unacceptable had many practitioners but no experts. Without clear underwriting standards to guide the process, "fast buck" operators began to abuse the program by launching projects they knew would fail, and the temptation to cooperate with them proved too great for some FHA employees. The results were financial losses, corruption scandals, and a black eye for the agency.

Here I was with another turnaround situation! In speech after speech to our employees across the country, I said, "FHA is alive and well. It will be better than ever." And that's what we proceeded to make happen. My team imposed stricter underwriting standards that put us back in the black by the end of my first year in office, but there was still a lot of work to be done.

There were plenty of other tasks. I had to manage Housing Production and Mortgage Credit, revise the FHA regulations, and even deal with public housing. My first executive action was to sign the order for the destruction of Pruitt–Igoe, the infamous twelve-building public housing project in St. Louis. I did this with the support of my colleague, H.R. Crawford, assistant secretary, Housing Management.

I was also heavily involved in an all-inclusive study of public housing, subsidized housing, housing needs, FHA-insured housing, and future US housing policy. After four months of the most intensive study and research, the National Housing Policy Review was submitted to President Nixon in September, 1973. One of our principal recommendations was to eliminate public housing as it had previously existed. We described public housing projects as "warehouses of the poor," and in their place we proposed a voucher system. Private units would be inspected and determined to be safe and sanitary, and applicants would be given rental vouchers. The object was to disburse poor persons throughout the community. Some of the best ideas came from the FHA, particularly my deputy commissioner, Dan Kearney, and a group of highly intelligent, unbelievably diligent staff members. Let me add that I have never been part of a group of men and women who worked harder than they did.

The National Housing Policy Review of 1973 served as the basis for legislation that we submitted to Congress. Working with a Democratic Senate and a Democratic House, our department was able to have all our proposals passed as the Housing Act of 1974, which I believe still stands as America's basic housing legislation today. This was accomplished despite the Watergate scandal and the campaign to impeach President Nixon.

The Watergate affair was nearing its conclusion in late July, 1974, when I traveled to Alaska to meet with the North Slope Eskimos (Nuiqsut Inupiats). We flew from Anchorage to Barrow, where the tribe was located. One of the unusual experiences on this trip was drinking a martini on the rocks. The unusual part was that the ice was blue and 10,000 years old, chipped from a local glacier. I then spent the night in one of the Inupiat homes. This small tribe had recently been given approximately 5 million acres of land and $100 million in cash. They were applying for public housing grants. I explained why this was not appropriate or possible. They understood, and we parted as friends. I worried that they were not capable of dealing with the large grant they had received, but they assured me that they would have capable advisors.

I spent the rest of the week with Marianne and our children around Fairbanks, Mt. McKinley, and hiking with David. We departed Alaska on August 8, 1974, the day President Nixon announced his resignation—something I couldn't imagine happening. David stayed behind and embarked on a multi-week solo backpacking trip down the Kenai Peninsula. My FHA director for Alaska, Roger Riddell, drove David to the trailhead, and off he went. It was raining and, as our plane lifted off from the Anchorage airport, I experienced internal panic over leaving David behind. How could I leave an eighteen-year-old alone in the Alaskan wilderness? I should have known he could handle it well, and he did. David surfaced a few weeks later, much to our relief. He proved he could handle it all, but I still can't forgive myself for allowing him this risky adventure.

By the time we got back, Gerald Ford was our new president. My team met with him on August 14. Wonderful man! On August 22, 1974, President Ford signed the Housing Act that Congress had passed, and it became the law of the land—a mighty accomplishment for Secretary Jim Lynn and all of us who had worked so very, very hard alongside him.

It was at about this time that I decided I had done my duty. It had been an unforgettable experience, and we had established entirely new and sounder housing legislation, but we had a new president and it was time for me to go. I could have stayed until the election of 1976, but I wanted to leave, and I did so in December, 1974.

The single most notable thing that occurred before I left was a meeting with Mayor Abraham Beame of New York City and the director of the New York Public Housing Authority. They came to my office to request a $100 million permanent mortgage loan on public housing in New York City, which they had financed up until then with short-term bank loans. I was really put off. I told them that for the past year we had been talking about the multiple failures of public housing and had changed the law to eliminate it in the future. I said we would consider their request, of course, but I couldn't recommend it.

I met with Secretary Lynn to brief him on the meeting and describe my negative reaction. I asked Jim, "What do you want to do?" He immediately said, "This is your decision." I said, "You know what that will be," and he repeated, "It's your decision." The upshot was that I told Mayor Beame "No." In January, 1975, the New York Housing Authority defaulted on some of its loans, which led to cross defaults on their other debt. The New York financial implosion had been detonated.

The most amazing part of the twenty months I served in Washington was not the incredibly long hours, or that every moment of every day of the week was filled, or that I was on constant call. What amazed me was that no one ever contacted me after I left to ask why I had rejected the New York request or to ask whether we had reconsidered it—no one from HUD, no one from New York, nothing! Conclusion: the bureaucracy is sometimes even more dysfunctional than one imagines.

Before I close the Washington chapter of my story, let me talk about the man who appointed me, President Richard M. Nixon. I had met Mr. Nixon only once before I was appointed. It was at a small YPO conference in January, 1968, that was chaired by Bo Callaway, president of YPO, in Washington, D.C. The conference closed with a dinner, after which Mr. Nixon joined us for cigars and cognac, although he partook of neither. We sat around a table and asked him questions. The 1968 presidential election was about ten months away, and Mr. Nixon told us he had not decided whether he would run or not. I asked a question about foreign affairs: "We were told earlier in the day by Dr. Edward Teller that the Nuclear Non-Proliferation Treaty was a bad idea for America. What is your opinion of the treaty?" He answered, "I agree with Dr. Teller, but that won't sell politically, so I have taken no position at this time." I was very dismayed with that answer, but I understood the game.

My next encounter with Mr. Nixon was as a member of his administration. I must tell you that in the operation of government a huge amount of time is spent on the budget. In my case, it began when FHA and our Housing Production and Mortgage Credit arm presented the next year's budget to HUD's secretary, under-secretary, general counsel, assistant secretaries, and various other back-up people. As the head of this department, I made the presentation, but seated behind me were four or five senior directors who were there to back me up, add facts, and provide whatever support I needed. Once this step was completed, the same presentation was made to the Office of Management and Budget, then to the House of Representatives Banking and Housing Committee, and finally to the Senate Banking Committee. The process went on for most of the year and was a true test of the presenter.

In preparation for his State of the Union address, the president would invite his entire cabinet and subcabinet to the White House. Dr. Henry Kissinger, the secretary of state, would begin by presenting our current foreign policy and discussing where things stood around the world. Then the president would present to our body the U.S. budget for the upcoming year. The amazing thing is that he did it without a note. For my department alone, FHA and Housing Production and Mortgage Credit, the process required reams of paper and five backup people, and the same was true for the other assistant secretaries. But here was the president going through the entire government budget for the next year without a piece of paper in his hand! If you weren't impressed, you couldn't have been there. Richard Nixon had a remarkable mind, and yet he had a character defect that, despite his talent, intelligence, and experience, led to his disgrace. I witnessed one of the saddest outcomes ever seen in American politics.

My time in Washington was unique, to say the least. Besides meeting the president, Marianne and I experienced a dinner party on the presidential yacht, *Potomac*, while cruising the Potomac River; use of the presidential box at the Kennedy Center; dinner at the White House; and many, many speaking engagements. Through it all, I often thought of my father's admonition to me as a boy: "Sheldon, remember this: Treat everyone you meet with the same respect, whether it is the president of the United States or the person sweeping the streets." If he were here today, I could say, "I did, and as usual you were right, Dad."

A full account of what I did as commissioner of FHA and assistant secretary of Housing Production and Mortgage Credit would be a book in itself. I can best describe the experience by assuring the reader that I never worked so hard in my life. I mean days, nights, weekends, and then some. At the end, I was proud of what we accomplished at HUD, and I can only say it was life-changing for Marianne, Susan, Joan, and myself in Washington as well as for Kris in Colorado and David in Maine. I was very proud to be an important part of what we accomplished for every American.

Chapter 9

Visiting Russia with Dad

One of my unforgettable experiences as a federal employee was a trip I took to Russia with my father. He turned eighty in 1973, and for the last few years he had been talking about his desire to visit his place of birth: Rossava, a village in what is now central Ukraine. I had tried to arrange this trip a year earlier, but I had never been able to get the necessary visas and clearances to visit this rather remote place. Now, as an assistant cabinet secretary, I was traveling on an official red U.S. passport with State Department clearance and a cable from Secretary of State Henry Kissinger. On October 5, 1973, after we had completed the National Housing Review and submitted our legislative proposals to Congress, my father, John Cahill, and I flew from New York to Moscow.

We were met at the Moscow airport by State Department representatives, who took us to our hotel and then to Spaso House, the U.S. embassy. On the next day I met my Russian counterpart, Y. Rodin Romas, commissar of all civil construction in Russia. It was quite a meeting, and Dad and the commissar exchanged war stories. Both had fought the Germans, although in two different world wars. Mr. Romas did his best to challenge me about the Cold War, blaming it all on the U.S. Fortunately, we spoke through our interpreter, who I am certain softened both sides of the conversation. We did quite a bit of sightseeing in Moscow, visiting the Kremlin and Lenin's tomb and spending an evening at the opera. I recall walking across Red Square with Dad and having to stop almost every twenty yards because of the pain he was experiencing in his legs.

Next day we were off to Kiev, where we met our interpreter, Vladimir Yakovchuk. Early on the morning of October 11, we left Kiev for Rossava by car. The countryside was very pretty in the fall, with rolling terrain that reminded me of Wisconsin. The temperature was pleasant, and later the sun came out. Halfway to Rossava, we stopped for tea and pastries in a town we selected at random. It was 11 a.m., and people were eating a heavy meal, including a thick buckwheat porridge called kasha. By our standards they were poorly dressed, most of them wearing boots and shabby dark coats.

We drove for another forty-five minutes after our break, crossing the Rossavka River, which was actually a very small stream, and finally arrived at a sign that identified Rossava, 102 kilometers from Kiev. Here we stopped and met another car. We thought our driver was asking someone for directions to the village, but it turned out that the Jeep-like auto with three men in it was there to meet us. We followed them to the official building in the city, which also served as the post office, and climbed the stairs to a small office where we shook hands with our three hosts.

The first was Petro Ivanovich, a senior civic official about fifty years old, with blond hair, piercing light blue eyes, and the ruddy face of someone who had spent his life outdoors. Ivanovich had been a soldier from ages sixteen to twenty-four, fighting the Germans and then the Japanese. On the left side of his suit, he wore military ribbons commemorating victories during World War II, including Stalingrad. On the right side he wore a civil medal. Ivanovich had a good face, and he shook all of our hands with both of his heavy, thick hands. Our second host was the head of the collective farm, a man who was thirty-five years old but appeared somewhat more mature. He was an engineer, six feet tall with dark hair and a most courteous and sincere manner. He struck me as an educated, honest man. The third host was a political type who appeared to be over fifty, with a lined face and bulging eyes. He was not very good-looking; I would even call him ugly. He had been an officer in the Red Army for eighteen years and appeared to be a dedicated Communist.

We had been in Russia for about five days by this time, and Dad was picking up and speaking the language fairly well. He was also able to understand a good deal of what was said to him. Cahill could speak and understand a bit, I nothing. We sat down around a small desk with a T-extension, and they started telling us about Rossava, with Petro Ivanovich doing most of the talking. After a short time, we suggested taking a walk around the town. We were not yet aware of how significant our visit was to them. Ivanovich said, "First we talk, and then we will look." He proceeded to tell us that there were no Jews left in the city. Before the Revolution, the White Army, which was church-related and anti-Bolshevik, had come through and killed many of them. The Germans did the rest in World War II. The Nazis occupied the city for three years, and they destroyed the bridges, many buildings, and the Jewish cemetery. Ivanovich, who I believe was born in the area, had never heard the name Lubarsky, our family's name before immigrating to the U.S. Dad asked if he had heard of the Koslov family, and he said "Yes," but no more. Our interpreter, Vladimir, made the conversation quite workable. Dad asked a few questions, and our hosts tried to be as responsive as they could, although there were clearly almost no traces left of what had existed sixty years earlier.

We left the city hall at about 12:30 and drove to the old part of Rossava. Our first stop was at the church, a green building about 300 years old, with an eastern look to it. This was the one thing Dad remembered. Another building we discussed was his former home. He somehow recalled that it had formerly or subsequently been a pharmacy, and our hosts said the building still existed. We walked 100 yards to an old one-story house, large by their standards but a cottage by ours. Dad didn't recognize it.

Forty yards from there, they pointed out what had been the Jewish part of the town. At the time Dad left, Rossava had approximately 2,000 residents. In 1973, despite all the killing, 3,000 people lived here, although I don't think there were more than one or two Jews. The streets in this area were unpaved, and the soil was sandy and dry; it looked as if it would be nice to walk on barefoot. The people stared at us, but they were friendly when given a chance. We met some typical older women and, typically, I took their pictures, and even more typically, Dad wanted to pose with them. He struck up a conversation, and one woman turned out to be the daughter of the blacksmith who had taken Dad in when he broke through the ice on the local lake. He cried.

We then drove to the lake, which now looked like a marsh. Dad said he remembered it being much larger. Petro said that it was, but the bridge the Nazis blew up had also acted as a dam, and since the war the lake had shrunk. On the other side of the lake road was the new Rossava, and beyond it a few kilometers was Mironovka, a city of 14,000 where the dairy and sugar beet factories were located.

From the lake we drove back through the city and continued three or four kilometers into the countryside to the headquarters of the collective farm. It consisted of 3,000 hectares (7,500 acres) and grew sugar beets and wheat and milked approximately 1,000 cows. There were many long, shed-like barns where we stopped. Most of the workers were women dressed in boots, coats, and babushkas. I deduced two reasons for this: one, many men worked in factories and, secondly, there were 20 million more women in Russia than men, thanks to the Germans.

At about 1:45, we went to a building in old Rossava that served as the office of the collective farm. We talked here for forty-five minutes, largely about the farm and how it operated. They explained that it worked as a cooperative, with each worker receiving a share based on exceeding given quotas. That sounded fine, but what the "normals" or quotas were, we didn't understand. The head of the farm was paid 220 rubles per month, and if he made plan, he got a 50-percent bonus. I told him they operated on the same basis as General Motors. They laughed. A ruble was officially priced at $1.43, but it was worth 25 cents in Zurich and 50 cents in the streets of Kiev, so it was clear they were getting a lot of talent for their money.

As our visit ended, Joe Lubar had the best comment of the trip. He looked at his watch, then looked at me, and said, "Well, Sheldon, let's go." It's a good thing we didn't. At 2:15 we left for the farm manager's house and what turned out to be a great surprise for all of us, as well as a genuine honor for Dad. The home was a small but a nice concrete-block structure covered with yellow stucco. There was no landscaping, but the house did have several outbuildings and a little fenced yard. One of the buildings was a one-hole outhouse equipped with a supply of old *Pravdas* torn into quarters and hanging on a nail. The interior of the home was simple but, I am sure, well-furnished by Russian standards. In the main room was a table laid out for a banquet. There was a small bath towel on each chair, and I was told I could wash my hands. I did so in another room, using cold water since there wasn't any hot.

From here on, it was fabulous: cognac and vodka by the bottle and the most delicious Ukrainian food anyone could ask for, including chicken, cabbage with meatballs rolled inside, homemade sausage, pickles, pork, pickled tomatoes, hamburgers *(cotlett)*, with watermelon for dessert. After this we had cigarettes. They then asked me to tell them something about the U.S. and its agricultural practices. I discussed the importance of agriculture both internally and as an export product, and then I broke out my Havana cigars. We continued drinking and having an excellent political discussion. After two or three of my statements, each of which concluded with a declaration of peace, they applauded. The political type was not sold as yet, and then we got into the Middle Eastern problem and why the USSR went into Czechoslovakia. (They insisted it was by invitation.) I asked all three of our hosts if they were members of the Communist Party. They answered "Yes." I asked about the qualifications, and they said there were three: commitment, two sponsors, and five years of probation. I asked if Jews could join. They said that believing in God was inconsistent with Communism, so you could be a Jew, but not believe in God. I asked if they believed, and they unhesitatingly said "No." They asked if I believed.

By the time we left, we were all singing Ukrainian fight songs, and Dad and the political type were dancing together. Through all this merriment, Dad kept asking if he could build a small *dacha*, or summer house, in Rossava for his vacations. The answer was that only Soviet citizens had that privilege. I gave each of the three men an Eisenhower silver dollar that Dad had given me earlier to use as a memento. In private, I gave our host my gold Cross pen. He later presented me with a Red Army statue commemorating the Soviet victory over the Germans. We embraced each other many times. Meanwhile the other men were joined after lunch by their wives. Dad talked to them and told stories of his days teaching bayonet skills and killing Germans during World War I. We left at about 6 or 6:30 p.m. and got back to Kiev at 8:45. It was a truly remarkable day. More than anything, the people we met in Rossava could not get over the fact that Joe Lubar, a man more than eighty years of age, would return from America to see his birthplace after more than sixty years and two monumental wars. We all agreed to see each other again—somewhere.

Chapter 10

Back to Milwaukee and Back to Business

My method of addressing the future has always been to make short-term plans with specific goals that point in a general direction that appears interesting to me. When my service in Washington ended in December, 1974, it was time to start planning again. Marianne was not particularly interested in returning to Milwaukee. Susan and Joan were happily ensconced at Georgetown Day School and, although I had conversations about moving to London to run the office of a prestigious investment bank, I was not thinking in those directions.

Shortly after our Russia trip, my father had suffered a stroke, and about a year later he had a second one. When I came home to see Dad and my mother, we all knew he was nearing the end. I felt I must come back to Milwaukee and be there with him. Marianne understood, and together we developed a plan. I would return to our home in Shorewood in January, after we had all gathered together in Aspen for Christmas and Joan's birthday on New Year's Eve. Marianne and Susan and Joan would join me in Milwaukee at the end of the Georgetown school year. Kris and David were in college. Joseph Lubar died in August, 1975, after a long and eventful life, and I was with him to the end.

Two significant things happened when I came home. First, Virgil Sullivan, my friend, mentor, and the blind trustee of my assets while I was in Washington, asked me an obvious question: "Shel, what are your plans now that you're back?" My answer: "Virgil, I have no plans. What I know for certain is that I am not going to have anything to do with housing or mortgages." He then told me that I should look into the world of energy, and he described current conditions in the industry. Virgil also said that he would ask his old friend, Mark Millard, a partner at Loeb, Rhodes & Co. and the chairman of Apco Oil Company, to elect me a director of the company. Apco was a producer of oil and gas in the U.S. and Argentina, with a listing on the New York Stock Exchange, a good management team, and an impressive board.

I met with Mr. Millard in his elegant New York townhouse, and we had a fascinating conversation. He was truly a class act: very intellectual, a collector of rare books, and a senior member of a highly regarded investment banking firm. He also still had a pronounced accent from some Eastern European country. I must have passed muster because, shortly after our meeting, he invited me to join the board of Apco. I attended my first meeting in the fall of 1975, and what followed was a growing investment of time and money in the world of energy. My involvement with Apco led directly to my acquisitions and board service with Grey Wolf Drilling and Prideco; a merger with Energy Ventures; and major investments in Weatherford, Grant Prideco, EnLink, Star Group, Approach Resources, Ellora Energy, Hallador Energy, and Savoy Energy.

The second significant thing that occurred after my return concerned my very good friend and banking colleague, John Kelly. We had come to know each other when we were both at the Marine Bank, but John and five or six colleagues had left the Marine in 1964 to start the Midland National Bank in downtown Milwaukee. John invited me to dinner shortly after I came home, and he started our conversation by reminding me that, after I went to Washington, he had suffered a serious heart attack and later underwent bypass surgery. He questioned whether the surgery was successful. He also told me, not for the first time, that his father had died of a heart attack at age thirty-nine. John was forty-six, just a few months older than me, and he said, "I am going to die in a few years, and I want you to join me as president and CEO of the Midland National Bank." I said, "John, you are not going to die." He persisted: "I will give you 30 percent of the bank shares, and you name your salary." I told John I didn't want any stock, but that I would think it over and talk to Marianne. After she and I discussed the idea, I decided to take it on for one or two years. I came back to John and said, "You are my friend, and I will give you one or two years of my life. As I said, I don't want any stock or long-term commitments. You tell me what the pay is, but I would work for nothing to help get things straightened out."

As expected, things were even worse than I'd expected. Midland Bank had about $400 million of assets, 30 percent of which were classified or substandard loans. After one month, John came into my office, the one he had previously occupied, and asked, "What do you think?" I said, "Frankly, I have worked on many problem situations, but this is the worst. The only thing that is working well is George Dalton on the fifth floor, who's running operations." The big smile John had come in with disappeared as he walked out of my office. I should mention that George Dalton's activity was ultimately spun off and became what is Fiserv today. It is now an international business serving the financial industry, and in 2018 it earned about $1.2 billion.

While at the bank, I took three important actions. First, I recruited Stu Brafman, who had been the executive vice-president of MGIC Insurance Company, to come in as executive vice-president in charge of real estate loans at Midland. I then recruited David Patterson, vice-president in the commercial loan department of the First National Bank of Chicago, to come to Milwaukee as executive vice-president of commercial loans. But perhaps the most important thing I did was to connect us with Mr. Don Grangaard, the chairman and CEO of First Bank Systems, a large bank holding company in Minneapolis. My connection was through Mr. Conley Brooks, the chairman of Brooks-Scanlon, a successful Oregon timber company whose home office was in Minneapolis. The Brooks and Hollern families—Brooks-Scanlon's owners—were friends of Virgil Sullivan, and through him they had become investors in both Marine Capital and Mortgage Associates. When I left Washington, they invited me to join their board of directors. Conley was also a director of the First Bank system, and he introduced me to Don Grangaard, the system's chairman.

When I was at Midland, Wisconsin banks could not branch, and bank holding companies could not cross state borders, but banks could merge within Wisconsin. Over the course of a year and a half, we negotiated a very successful deal with Don Grangaard and his associates at First Bank, which would later become U.S. Bank. In a nutshell, a subsidiary of First Bank Systems in La Crosse, Wisconsin, acquired Midland Bank and then moved its headquarters to Milwaukee. All the Midland shareholders came out in one piece. It was a real rescue.

By the time of the merger, I was gone, just as I had done in the Mortgage Associates merger. In 1977 I launched my own investment firm, Lubar & Co., and started another career that would last until today. It turned out to be an enormous financial success as well as a stimulating and challenging business adventure. And what was my goal? To put the principle of Professional Ownership into practice in the marketplace. As outlined in Chapter 5, I had developed the concept in long conversations with Bob Moon, who became my good friend and mentor during my Marine Capital days. We both perceived the need for an experienced, sophisticated intermediary between large pools of institutional capital and the many buy-out opportunities I knew existed. We determined that large institutions had neither the ability to identify acquisition candidates nor the talents needed to select, motivate, monitor, and hold management accountable for achieving an agreed-upon business plan. Lubar & Co. was established to fill that void. We developed a brochure that explained our approach to prospective clients, and the basic tenets of that early document are as true today as they were in 1977. This is how it began:

> We are a private investment firm investing our own capital. As principals, we seek to acquire profitable operating companies as well as provide equity capital to proven managers who are acquiring or operating successful businesses.
>
> The principals of Lubar & Co. have proven records in corporate finance, acquisitions, long range planning and professional management. Our basic objective is to build the value of each of our portfolio companies through continued increases in their operating earnings. Our experience has shown that properly capitalized companies with a superior management team, an excellent product or service and a definitive business plan will achieve this objective.
>
> Above all, our prime business principle is to act with integrity and to expect the same from our business partners.

The brochure went on to list our criteria for acquisition candidates —"middle-market companies with fair market values ranging from $10 to $250 million without regard to industry concentration or geographic location"—and specified our investment objectives:

- To build the companies in which we invest into growing, profitable, more successful businesses.
- To invest with, or bring to the business, competent and experienced management teams that operate with well defined business plans to achieve realistic objectives.
- To develop a close working relationship with management in formulating financial and business plans.
- To achieve a superior return on capital.

Most of the capital came from myself and my family. I should mention that shortly after the acquisition of Sorgel Electric, I determined it would be wise and tax-effective to divide all future stock holdings equally among myself, Marianne, and each of our four children—one-sixth each to avoid future inheritance and estate taxes. I had always taken a dim view of tax shelters and that game. I also made the decision to establish a charitable foundation and make constructive charitable as well as tax-effective giving a major part of our family's life plan.

My first task in launching Lubar & Co. was to assemble a team. Many years ago, a young person asked me if one had to be skilled in mathematics and accounting to be successful at business. I said, "You don't have to be a certified accountant, but you must recognize that the language of business is numbers." To lend money or invest intelligently, one must understand the record of a company and whether its performance is headed up, down, or nowhere. Hence, early in my banking career, I became aware of the accounting and auditing firm of Arthur Andersen & Co. My first connection with them was during my early days as a commercial banker at the Marine, when an Andersen partner made a presentation about their new small business division. At the time, I was developing a small business term loan program that would offer term loans to smaller companies repayable out of cash flow over a three- to five-year period. It was something new in our market, and as things developed, it worked well. Arthur Andersen gave me consulting help on the project, and I developed a solid and continuing relationship with them. In fact, they were more than accountants; they handled tax planning and much analysis for me.

Therefore, it wasn't surprising that when I needed someone to handle my personal accounting, income tax preparation, and other administrative needs, I turned to Arthur Andersen. They assigned to me a young CPA named Jim Rowe. Jim grew up on a farm near Dodgeville, Wisconsin, attended a one-room school nearby, and graduated from the University of Wisconsin-Madison with a major in accounting. We hit it off immediately. When I returned from our European sabbatical, I contacted Jim, and he became my trusted assistant and then my partner. Jim had great intelligence, high character in all respects, and a very solid work ethic. He was with me for twenty years until he went off on his own. Together with Jim Rowe and Jeanne Henry, my secretary, Lubar & Co. opened for business in October, 1977. At almost the same time, we formed a small business investment company, 77 Capital Corporation, as our investment vehicle. We rented office space in the new First Wisconsin Bank (now U.S. Bank) and were off and running.

At this point in my life, I wasn't overly motivated toward more investing. I was on the boards of Industrial National Bank, the State of Wisconsin Investment Board, and Brooks-Scanlon, and I was talking with Square D Company and Massachusetts Mutual Life Insurance about joining their boards, which I ultimately did. But Jim Rowe was ambitious. As he put it, "I want to do deals; I am rotting doing what I am doing." So we did!

When we formed 77 Capital Corporation, I viewed it as a low-risk, easy way to make a business out of acquiring control positions in smaller companies, building them into larger and more profitable enterprises, and then merging them into large, prominent public companies through a tax-free stock exchange. The only outside investor we had at 77 Capital was Nick Brady, who by then was president of the prestigious investment banking firm of Dillon, Read & Co. I had stayed in touch with Nick since the Marine Capital days, and he and his chairman, Douglas Dillon, were small investors alongside the Lubars.

Nick Brady to this day is my closest of friends, and how we met is worth describing. It was in the mid-1960s, when I was in the process of selling all of Marine Capital's investments. One of our oldest and largest investments was Racine Hydraulics, a public company in which we had about a 20-percent interest. As the process progressed, we developed several serious, capable buyers for our stock. Then I was contacted by Paul Cameron, vice-president of Purolator, a New York Stock Exchange company that manufactured auto components but had diversified into transporting bank assets and documents. Nick Brady was a Dillon, Read officer at the time, and his father was the chairman of Purolator. Paul Cameron was the guy who searched out acquisitions, and Nick was advising him. Paul asked if I would meet with him and Nick to discuss their interest in buying our position. I agreed, of course. After some pleasant conversation about Racine Hydraulics, Nick asked me straight out, "If you were me, would you be interested in buying this company?" I answered him, equally straight out, "NO. For many reasons, if I wasn't the seller, I still wouldn't be the buyer."

After that they left, without making an offer. I guess my credibility was established. Nick and I have stayed in touch to this day. I have no better friend. When he was the U.S. treasury secretary under Presidents Reagan and Bush, he asked me to be his blind trustee. When that was over, he asked me to join with him in forming Darby Overseas, an investment company investing in South America and later other parts of the world. We are still good friends more than fifty years after we met.

To get back to Lubar & Co., our first investment was the acquisition of 80 percent of the stock of the A.L. Gebhardt Company, a small but extremely well-managed leather tanning company with operations in Milwaukee and Berlin, Wisconsin. The other 20 percent was owned by brothers Art and Bob Gebhardt, the superb, experienced leaders who made this one of our top-performing investments.

At about this time, I met Bill Donovan, who was a junior commercial banker at Manufacturers Hanover Bank in New York. He and the daughter of our attorney and good friend, Dick Van Deuren, were about to be engaged, and moving to Milwaukee was in the cards. I asked Bill to join me as a partner alongside Jim Rowe, and he agreed to come on board. Bill was a graduate of Notre Dame University who had been trained at Hanover Bank, and he was an articulate and analytical addition to our team. In addition, he was our best negotiator.

A short time later, David Lubar, who was an officer at Norwest Bank in Minneapolis, joined us. At Norwest he had specialized in commercial lending in the manufacturing and high technology sectors. David had a bachelor of arts degree from Bowdoin College and a Master of Business Administration degree from the University of Minnesota. His first assignment was managing the Wisconsin Venture Capital Fund, which was organized by Governor Lee Dreyfus and financed by a group of large Wisconsin businesses. This was a highly successful assignment.

As of 2019, Lubar & Co. has three principal activities:
1. Private equity investment. We invest our family funds in acquisitions of private companies that we build and own permanently.
2. Investment management for the Lubar family.
3. Family office for the Lubars, providing accounting, legal, and other advice to our greater family.

Our current team consists of the following individuals:
- Sheldon Lubar, Founder and Chairman
- David Lubar, President and CEO
- Vince Shiely, Partner
- David Bauer, CPA, Partner and CIO
- Dave Kuehl, Partner and General Counsel
- Jean Ellen Trubshaw, CPA, Partner, Managing Director, Family Office
- Mitch Rzentkowski, Investment Analyst
- Cortnie Pfarr, CPA, Tax Manager
- Jamie Ward, CPA, Controller
- Wendy Cartwright, CPA, Assistant Controller
- Jeanne Wallace, Accounting
- Teresa Lee, Executive Assistant
- Seema Talwalker, Executive Assistant
- Holly Games, Administrative Assistant

In June, 2018, we held a conference for everyone associated with Lubar & Co., including the executives of our companies, Lubar family members, and my colleagues in the office. After welcoming and thanking everyone, I told the story of the Rothschild family and its founder, Mayer Amschel Rothschild. He and his five sons are considered the founders of international finance. On his deathbed, Amschel was surrounded by his sons and was giving them his last instructions. He asked one of his sons to go to the fireplace and bring over six sticks of kindling wood. Then he said, "Take one stick and see if you can break it in two." His son took a stick and easily broke it in two. Then he said, "Take the other five sticks and see if you can break these together." He could not. "So," Amschel told his sons, "if you work and stay together ["as a team," I added] you will never lose. You will remain strong." This happened in the late 1700s, and the Rothschild team is still out there winning. "We are a team," I told my colleagues. "I want us all to stay together. We will have ups and downs, but we will never lose if we keep our efforts together."

Chapter 11

My Business: An Overview

What was my business? I could never describe it very well to my children, but in retrospect, I can say that my career since I left college has been banking, investing, and business advising. What follows is a brief case-by-case guide to my business activities over the years and a summary of their results. Some activities predate Lubar & Co.; other companies are still in our portfolio. Every one of them was important, but the most significant are described in greater detail in the next chapter. And so here is a travelogue of Sheldon B. Lubar's business journey:

- Sheldon Erwin & Co. I incorporated this company while working at the Marine Bank. The president and 50-percent owner was my college friend, Erv Plesko, and I owned the other 50 percent. The company was a registered broker, and I sold my interest to Erv to avoid possible conflicts with the bank.

- Marcy Meadows. Erv Plesko and I developed a forty-acre subdivision in Brookfield. My first success.

- Waukesha Fruit Products. This manufacturer of ice cream flavors and toppings was my first acquisition. I owned it all and eventually sold it. No gain or loss.

- Gracious Giving. A packager of Wisconsin cheeses that I eventually sold at my cost. Nothing but experience here.

- Mil-Wis Construction. A bank customer that built roads and bridges. I owned no stock and served only as their financial advisor. It was good experience, and I know I contributed good advice.

- Manchester's. Largest department store in Madison and a bank customer. I served as their advisor. Good experience and fun.

- Marine Capital Corporation. I was CEO. Mortgage Associates made this a great success.

- Banker's Financial Corporation. Holding company for Mortgage Associates. Public company. I was a director and CEO.

- Naegele Outdoor Advertising. I brought this public company into the bank as a customer and served as their financial advisor, restructuring their complex financial structure into a simple large loan with Chase Manhattan Bank. Later I served as a director.

- Mortgage Associates. An important part of my career and a great experience and success.

- Lakeside Manufacturing. Bob Moon's company. Manufacturer of stainless steel equipment that I served as a director. Very success-ful. If I had to name my mentors, they would be Bob Moon and Virgil Sullivan.

- La Maur, Inc. Manufacturer of cosmetics and other products for sale to women's salons. I served at the request of Paine Webber. They were listed on the NYSE.

- Sorgel Electric Corporation. The first acquisition I did for myself, and ultimately merged with Square D Company on the NYSE. This was the base of our family's financial and business success.

- Versa Technologies and Milwaukee Cylinder Company. Con-trolled in partnership with Jim Mohrhauser, who was the CEO. Excellent success. Jim and I owned it equally.

- Maxon Marine. A Lubar family acquisition done shortly before I went to Washington, D.C. This one didn't work. We lost our investment, but the bank was paid in full. No bank has ever lost money with the Lubars. Shortly after we acquired Maxon, I went to Washington, and Jim Rowe handled our oversight.

- Square D Company. After the merger with Sorgel Electric and time spent in Europe and Washington, I was elected to this board and stayed until the company was acquired by Schneider Electric, a large French company. Square D was a double bump after Sorgel was acquired.

- Industrial National Bank. Acquirer of Mortgage Associates. I went on this board after returning from Washington. Industrial National is now part of Bank of America.

- Marshall Erdman & Associates. Marshall was my friend. I was on this board for forty years. After Marshall's death, his son Tim, who became CEO, sold the company to Robert W. Baird and Lubar & Co. Several years later, we sold it to a REIT. A few years after that, Lubar & Co. bought it back, and we own the company today.

- Central Engineering. Lubar & Co. investment. Tom Goulet was CEO. Successfully sold.

- Grey Wolf Drilling. My first energy acquisition, done with Jim Nelson, who was CEO, and Jack McKeithan. Very successful.

- Apco Oil. On the NYSE. Acquired by another energy company while I was on the board. Very successful.

- Racine Hydraulics. A Marine Capital investment. Sold to Rexnord. Very successful.

- United Investors. A New York City REIT. Dan Cowin bought control and invited me to serve on the board. Very successful.

- Stearns Manufacturing. A company we acquired to form Versa Technologies. Very successful.

- Amercargo, Inc. A company formed by Lubar & Co., Bob Hansen, and Joe Cuneo to acquire six oceangoing freighters used for military shipping during the Vietnam War. Modest gain at best.

- Pabst Brewing. Probably one of my most exciting and challenging board experiences. I was invited to join this board to give it Milwaukee representation when the stock was at about $12 or $13 per share. Over the next two years, we had two proxy fights, won both, and acquired another brewery. I was chair of the Finance Committee and was ultimately given the responsibility of selling the entire brewery, which I did. This was my only experience as a broker. I look at the outcome as a huge success.

- Kurth Malting. Lubar & Co. acquisition, ultimately merged with Archer Daniels. Excellent success.

- A.L. Gebhardt. Lubar & Co. acquisition that was later combined with Pfister & Vogel and named U.S. Leather under our ownership. Sold to another private equity firm. This was a huge winner.

- Wisconsin Venture Capital Fund. A private fund conceived by Governor Lee Dreyfus. He asked Lubar & Co. to manage the fund, and David Lubar took on the leadership and made it a great success. Outstanding result.

- Christiana Companies. As described in the next chapter, I was invited on this board by Joe Antonow, who was the company's lawyer and chairman. We ultimately acquired control of this NYSE company, moved its headquarters from La Jolla, California to Milwaukee, settled hundreds of lawsuits, liquidated all its problem real estate, and used the funds to buy Wisconsin Cold Storage, then Total Logistics, and then Prideco. After merging with Weatherford, we ended with large holdings of Grant Prideco (NYSE), Weatherford (NYSE), and Total Logistics (NASD). This was our greatest transaction to date in terms of financial gain. I was chairman and CEO.

- Bradley Trust. This trust came into existence in 1985 with the sale of the Allen-Bradley Company. I served as a trustee from 1996 to the end of 2010. Our investment advisor was Morgan Stanley, and the custodian was Northern Trust Company. My sponsor was Gordon Davidson, and the trust assets were very substantial. This was an assignment that I felt very qualified to take on, and I treated my involvement as a serious responsibility. Every one of the many persons involved with the management of the trust was a professional. It was an assignment I truly enjoyed, and I feel I was a strong contributor to the financial results during my time as a trustee.

- Other corporate boards I served on were Jeffries Group (NYSE), Briggs & Stratton (NYSE), MGIC (NYSE), Fannie Mae (NYSE), Brooks-Scanlon, Brady Co., Darby Overseas, and Nicholas Company (Ab Nicholas, CEO).

- Bank and financial boards I served on were Milwaukee Western Bank, Industrial National Bank (now part of Bank of America),

First Wisconsin (which became Firstar and then U.S. Bank), Midland National Bank, Marine Bancorporation, Pitcairn Trust, and Ixonia Bancshares (president and CEO).

- Perhaps the board I most enjoyed was Massachusetts Mutual Life Insurance Co., a position I held for twenty-five years. This often seemed like a full-time job.

- The two largest boards I served on were Ameritech Corporation (the operator of the telephone systems in Wisconsin, Illinois, Indiana, Michigan, and Ohio, now part of AT&T) and Fannie Mae (a government corporation with trillions of dollars of assets).

- Energy boards I served on were Apco Oil (NYSE), Hallador Energy, Ellora Energy 2, Ellora Energy 3, Star Group, Kestrel, Crosstex Energy Services (now EnLink), Petrosantander, and Approach Resources. All of these investments developed from my friendship with and respect for Bryan H. Lawrence, senior partner of Yorktown Partners, a private energy investment fund in New York. I first met Bryan when he worked for Dillon, Read & Co. As I developed a deeper interest in the energy sector, I approached Bryan with the idea of collaborating on future investments in the field, and we did so with much success. Bryan was and still is the most knowledgeable and astute energy investor I know.

- My current Lubar & Co. boards are Rockland Industrial Products, Zero Zone, Inc., Drilltec, Inc., Lake Express, and Ixonia Bancshares.

Chapter 12

My Business: Some Highlights

I am very proud of all the transactions and acquisitions I was part of over the years. However, there are some that stand out with particular vividness in my memory, and I'd like to expand on them in this chapter.

Emmpak Foods

When Governor Lee Dreyfus put Lubar & Co. in charge of the Wisconsin Venture Capital Fund in 1983, he made us responsible for raising the capital, finding and analyzing investment opportunities, and then working with the target companies to build their businesses, with the overall objective of creating equity value and new jobs. All the Fund's investments were in Wisconsin-based companies. David Lubar took on this project as his first assignment when he joined Lubar & Co. Although we all participated with him, he was the leader, and in time David invested the full $10 million the Fund had raised.

Toward the end of the Fund's life, we received a visit from the president of Emmpak Foods Company. This was a well-known, Milwaukee-based meat-packing business that slaughtered old dairy cows, boned and ground the meat, and then sold it to the makers of hamburger patties for the fast food industry. Prior to our involvement, the business had been sold by the third generation of the founding family to Sara Lee Corporation, who then resold it to a private invest-ment firm. It was suffering from the burden of excessive acquisition debt, which was owed to a large Chicago bank. The loan was in de-fault, and the bank was demanding repayment, under threat of fore-closing and liquidating the company.

Total employment at that time was approximately 1,600 persons, most of them Hispanic and African-American men living in Milwau-kee's central city. Under David's leadership, Lubar & Co. took on the challenge of acquiring the business, recapitalizing it, and formulating a new strategic business plan. It was a difficult undertaking due to the large number of inherent risks as well as several uncontrollable factors that impacted the business. Dairy cows (the raw material) and ground beef were both commodities with fluctuating prices that were unrelated to each other, the production process was both labor- and equipment-intensive, and the business was highly regulated by the USDA.

To assist in formulating a go-forward strategy, David recruited Justin Segel as an investor and a director. Justin was the third-generation CEO of his family's business, Wis-Pak Foods, which made hamburger patties with meat purchased from Emmpak. Later we merged Justin's patty operation into the company to create an integrated meat processor, from the cow to the frozen hamburger patty. The result was a business that grew to employ around 2,200 workers, was soundly profitable, and supported the families of its many employees. Later the business was sold to Cargill, Inc., the large agricultural company based in Minneapolis. By all measures, this was a highly successful investment that saved existing jobs, created many new high-paying central-city jobs, and provided an excellent financial return to the Fund and its other investors.

Zero Zone

Zero Zone Inc. (ZZI) was another investment where we did well by doing good. Lubar & Co. acquired this manufacturer of glass-door merchandising cabinets that were sold largely to supermarkets and convenience and dollar stores. In 1999 ZZI was merged into Total Logistics, and in 2005 Total Logistics was sold to SuperValu, a supermarket chain. About a year later, I received a call from SuperValu's investment banker, who told me that ZZI had lost its largest customer and SuperValu wanted to sell it. He asked if we were interested in buying it back. "Perhaps," I said, "but first I'll talk it over with our team." Based on ZZI's deteriorating financial results, I couldn't get any support from my associates, so I told the banker that we'd have to pass.

About three months later, I was contacted again and told that SuperValu had been unable to find a buyer. If Lubar & Co. was not interested, the chain made it clear that they would shut the company down and liquidate it to stop the losses. I called our team together again. I told them that I felt we had the financial and business resources and the experience to help turn the company around, and that I couldn't live with myself if 200 loyal employees lost their jobs because we didn't step in to assist.

This was a decision from the heart, not the head. It took just over three long years, but ZZI returned to profitability, and every year since then the company has earned three times what we paid for it. Many employees chose to invest with us, and all have been well rewarded. To this day, we are shareholders of Zero Zone. It is a growing business with new products, customers, and plants, and it now employs over 500 people. I love it.

Massachusetts Mutual Life Insurance

I joined the board of directors of Mass Mutual in 1978. My sponsors were Dick Dooley, the chief investment officer, and Don Wheeler, the investment officer who had been primarily responsible for Mass Mutual's investment in Sorgel Electric. (They later told me that their return on the Sorgel investment was the second-highest in the history of the company, surpassed only by McDonald's.) Dick and Don introduced me to Jim Martin, the chairman and CEO, and Bill Clark, president and COO. They were both outstanding men and excellent managers. I was flattered to be asked to join such a prestigious board.

When I asked how often they met, I believe they said quarterly, but they also wanted me to join the Executive Committee, which met at 7:45 a.m. on the first Wednesday of every month. I reminded them that I lived in Milwaukee, Wisconsin, and they were in Springfield, Massachusetts, which would involve a bit more travel than I had anticipated. "Shel," they explained, "our board is loaded with CEOs of big, important companies. We have plenty of those. What you bring to the board is an impressive knowledge of investing in both securities and real estate. These decisions are made by the Executive Committee, and that is where we need you."

My service on this board was like a job, but I loved every minute, and I felt my contribution to their growth was significant. When the Sorgel acquisition was completed in 1966, Mass Mutual was a company of about $2 billion. Today its revenues are $642 billion, including those of subsidiaries such as Oppenheimer, which was acquired during my service. To the best of my knowledge, my quarter-century on the board was the longest term in the history of the company, which was founded in 1851.

Harley-Davidson

Among the bank boards I joined was the Marine National Exchange Bank's. I was pleased to serve as a director of my old employer, but I resigned from the boards of both the bank and its holding company when management proposed selling a major ownership interest to a group of Middle Eastern investors. I strongly disagreed with the plan, which I felt was not in the interests of the bank's future or its existing shareholders.

Shortly after my resignation was made public, I was invited by Hal Kuehl, the president and CEO of First Wisconsin Bancshares, Wisconsin's largest bank holding company, to join their board, and I did. I presume that because of my deep experience, I was also invited to join the bank's Executive and Loan Committees. At my very first meeting, the Loan Committee considered a crucial request from the Harley-Davidson Motorcycle Company. Simply put, Harley had been owned by American Machine and Foundry, and about a year earlier AMF had sold the company to a group of employees led by Vaughn Beals, the CEO. Mr. Beals had an excellent reputation and was highly capable. My recollection is that almost all of the purchase price had been borrowed from one of New York's largest and most prestigious banks. Harley was on the hook for $100 million, and now the bank was calling its loan. Of course, Vaughn was searching for financing, and he was doing it during a difficult economic period. What he presented to our bank was a request for $10 million. He had a commitment for $90 million from a Chicago commercial finance company, but it was contingent on getting a local Milwaukee bank to take a $10 million loan participation. If we granted his request, the refinance would be complete at $100 million.

Remember that this was my first meeting, and the other members of our committee were all older, very successful people, almost all with extensive manufacturing experience. I heard all the reasons against approval: the loan was too risky, the economy was too bad, and lots of other negatives. Then our chairman, Hal Kuehl, spoke up. He reminded the committee of the large work force at Harley, its almost 100-year history, and its overall significance to the community. I had been a listener up to this point and was as skeptical as the others, but Hal changed my mind and I said so. Then, one at a time, the rest of the committee came around. We made the loan, and Harley was given a second chance.

What happened next was that President Ronald Reagan placed a tariff on imported motorcycles. Harley's product quality, brand strength, and efficiency soared, and it went from near death to great success. The story of the loan has never been made public, but I believe all the persons involved have now passed away. In August, 2018, I read that Vaughn Beals had died. He was eulogized in a *Wall Street Journal* obituary. Hal Kuehl deserved the same.

Christiana Companies, Inc.

In 1987 I received a phone call from Mr. Joe Antonow, a well-regarded business attorney from Chicago. He had been connected in the past with Dillon, Read & Co., a company I knew well through my friendship with Nick Brady, its former CEO. We had previously purchased two companies that Joe represented in the Chicago area, neither of which were successes. Hence, when Joe explained that he was now the chairman of the Christiana Company and invited me to join its board of directors, I told him that I was already overcommitted and couldn't take on another board. He said the company was listed on the New York Stock Exchange, and its stock was selling for four or five dollars per share. I again declined, but Joe persisted. He said, "Let me have Ray Logan, the operating head of the company, come to Milwaukee and explain why it's a value beyond the price of the stock today." Finally, to get Joe off the phone, I agreed to see Ray Logan.

Ray was a tall, good-looking man in his mid-fifties. He knew the real estate management business, and he explained the company's history and present situation to me and Jim Rowe. Christiana was formed after World War II in Delaware by a group of prosperous investors for the purpose of investing in oil properties. It operated with modest success and moved its headquarters to Denver after a few years. At that point, new management thought the company should change its focus to real estate development, and the headquarters was moved again, this time to Los Angeles. Christiana enjoyed some real success with their development of Huntington Harbor, the last home and ocean marina development on the West Coast. Then they moved their headquarters again, this time south to La Jolla, a lovely oceanside town just north of San Diego.

What followed turned out to be almost fatal. The company bought a large tract of land near San Diego from the U.S. government and proceeded to build and sell over 400 residential condominiums. The Christiana people knew this property had once been a military firing range, but it had been swept numerous times by the government to remove unexploded artillery ordnance. Then came a tragedy. Two young boys who were playing in a canyon on the property discovered an unexploded shell, and they apparently pounded on it with rocks until it exploded, killing them both. Litigation followed, but the case was ultimately settled.

Next, heavy rains in the area caused the soil to subside, causing a lot of cracked foundations in the development. The owners of the condos sued, and eventually, after much litigation, Christiana's insurance companies were forced to buy back almost all of the condos, which they then deeded to Christiana. This is where things stood when we came into the picture.

I should add that, despite all of these issues, the company had not lost money and in fact was operating modestly in the black. Christiana had no tax losses, no debt, and it owned other real estate scattered throughout southern California. To add to the confusion, control of the company was held by two "brain-dead" savings & loans in Texas that were being taken over by State of Texas regulators.

At this point, I thought one would have to be a certified fool to get involved in this mess. I refrained from throwing Ray out the door and asked, "What is your plan?" In his slow drawl, Ray proceeded to tell us the following:

1. He was in negotiations to sell some of the company's land to the State of California for about $11 million.
2. He had brought in an engineering firm whose people were confident they could remedy the soil subsidence problem, repair the buildings, and resell them for more than their initial sale price.
3. He thought the S&Ls would sell their stock if they had a cash offer.
4. The company owned another oceanside parcel south of Huntington Harbor that might have considerable value.

I thanked Ray and told him we would think it over. Jim Rowe and I discussed it and decided we would buy in if the stock of at least one of the savings & loans was available. Jim was able to negotiate the share purchase, and for about $12 million, we became the controlling shareholder of a New York Stock Exchange company. What followed may seem like the stuff that business novels are made out of, but it all happened.

After we bought the first block of Christiana stock, I joined the board of directors. Shortly after that, Joe Antonow left the board, and I was elected chairman and CEO, with Ray Logan as president and COO. Our game plan was the one Ray had discussed with us, and we proceeded to carry it out exactly as he had described. Over time, we settled the many outstanding lawsuits, sold land to the state, completed the soil engineering, rehabbed the condos, and sold them for even more than Ray had initially expected. Now the challenge was to take this shell and use the money we had generated to grow Christiana.

The first step was a shareholder rights offering at a bit below the market value, which was then four dollars per share. Since we had no investors or brokers following the stock, there was little interest in the shares, and, as I recall, Lubar & Co. bought most of the offering. At this point we bought out the other savings & loan, so now the Lubars owned 60 percent of Christiana.

Our first acquisition for Christiana, completed in 1989, was Prideco, Inc., a company that manufactured and heat-treated heavyweight pipe for oil and gas drilling. Jim Rowe found Prideco, which Willy Chunn and Don Morris had started a few years earlier. A year after that, we bought a mothballed manufacturer of drill pipe. Christiana's sales soon went from $5 million to $50 million and our pretax earnings from zero to $5 million. How did we do it? We had experienced, high-grade management with Ray Logan running Christiana and Willy and Don at Prideco.

In 1992 we added Wiscold, a Milwaukee company that operated four cold-storage facilities. Again, the key was excellent management, this time from Gary Sarner, a man we all knew and respected. Early on, Gary told us that to be a real player in the cold-storage business, you had to have logistics capability, which means refrigerated trucking and all of the technical back-up needed to support a multi-state truck fleet. In 1994, Christiana acquired 100 percent of the TLC Group, Inc. and combined it with Wiscold. The merged company was renamed Total Logistic Control, Inc. and, under Gary's direction, it grew internally and prospered well beyond our expectations.

Meanwhile, as Prideco grew, our largest competitor, Grant, which was about twice our size, started a lawsuit claiming patent infringement. Grant was a subsidiary of a company called Energy Ventures, whose president was Bernard Duroc-Danner. I arranged a meeting between myself and Bernard in Denver. After we shook hands and sat down, I said, "Bernard, you know as well as I do that we are not infringing on any of your patents. Why do you want to waste your money and ours playing games with us?" He said, "I know, but I want to slow you down." I said, "What we should be talking about is merging our companies and dominating the drill pipe market." Bernard said, "I agree with you, but my directors are cool to that idea. Why don't you go to New York and persuade them?"

So that is what I did. I met with their lead director, Bob Millard, a partner in Lehman Brothers, and in 1995 we merged with Grant to form Grant Prideco, taking Energy Ventures stock in exchange. We bought even more stock from an unhappy Prideco director and ended up owning about 12 percent of Energy Ventures, which was also listed on the New York Stock Exchange. Up to this point I thought I had been successful in business, but the final story of Christiana developed in a way I could never have imagined.

First, Energy Ventures acquired a large oil service company named Weatherford and changed its corporate name to Weatherford, Inc. Management then decided to focus on technology. They felt that Grant

Prideco was simply ordinary heavy manufacturing, so they spun the company off as a separate business. I stayed on the Weatherford board, joined the new Grant Prideco board, and held shares in both. When Grant Prideco was created, combined earnings before tax and depreciation was $15 million. In 2001, when I left that board because of age, we were earning $700 million EBITDA as the result of growth and acquisitions. At the same time, for many reasons, I decided to leave the Weatherford board, so I could sell all of my stock, which had also appreciated mightily. What was left of Christiana was Total Logistics, and in 2005 a SuperValu Company representative approached us, and his firm ended up acquiring the company for cash. The graph below was in the Weatherford board of director's book at the last meeting I attended. One graph is worth a thousand words.

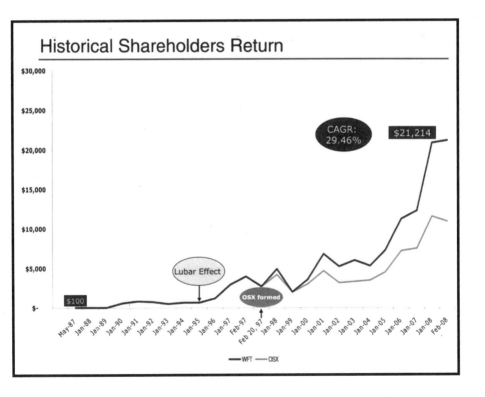

Ixonia Bank

Perhaps the last boards I take on will be Ixonia Bank and its parent, Ixonia Bancshares. In early 2012, our country was in the midst of a financial crisis that fell heavily on the banks, large and small. Many banks lost all of their capital. Many others were taken over by larger, better-capitalized banks. Smaller banks found it very difficult to raise needed capital.

It was in this period of time that I decided to invest in banking. It had been forty-six years since I left the Marine National Exchange Bank. Since that time, I had actively served on the boards of several banks, including some of Wisconsin's biggest. It was a business I knew and understood. Perhaps most important, it was a business I could step in and run myself. I wanted a vehicle that I could guide and build that would provide direction for our family's assets and help in the development of small and mid-sized businesses. I concluded the best vehicle would be a small bank with a very professional trust department that could continue for years to come, theoretically in perpetuity. Because of the problems in the industry, I knew prices would be low, and we had the capital to invest. I would teach my bank colleagues all I knew of the concept of Professional Ownership.

Everyone I spoke with about my idea of buying a bank thought I was, let's be kind, losing my mind. Except Marianne. She said simply, "You have always loved banking. You know it, so do it." So I did. We retained Lorrie Keating Heinemann, who had been secretary of the Wisconsin Department of Financial Institutions under Governor Jim Doyle, to guide our search, and we probably considered twenty possibilities. In June, 2012, after a year-long search, we picked Ixonia Bank. We liked Ixonia because of its 100-year-old charter, its good deposit base, the high household incomes in its market, and its location in the Milwaukee-to-Madison corridor. The bank had lost all its capital, so we recapitalized it and went to work.

The bank employees I can describe as everyday, hard-working, real Americans. I just plain liked them all. At my very first meeting with Ixonia's employees in 2012, I described my vision for the company —"soundness, profitability, and growth, in that order"—and I explained my own role. "I am not a passive investor," I told them. "I am a coach and if called upon a player. I will be available to you always. I will encourage your continued education. I will help you when I can contribute to a solution, and I will certainly be your mentor and cheerleader as we move ahead together."

Before our transition was completed, we recruited Dan Westrope, a very experienced banker, to be Ixonia's CEO. We have worked together successfully since then. Five years after buying the bank, we had solved most of its problems. We added high-quality, experienced people to build a team I'm proud of. We were on our way to an asset base of $1 billion from the $270 million we inherited. We were growing our earnings and planning to expand in our geographic market. Ixonia Bank will be a proud example of Professional Ownership at its best.

Success in Business

I have heard other persons say that I am "a great investor" or that I have "the Midas touch." Those characterizations of me are not correct. I am sure I am much like any other person. I buy a few stocks, and some go up and some go down. What I am good at is business. And what makes success in my business? First and foremost, I have relied on my knowledge and above all on my judgment. I stay in close touch with what is going on currently, and I do my best to look ahead and try to determine what the future developments might be in the world, in the U.S., and in my state of Wisconsin. That means constant reading, discussion, questioning, and becoming more informed on everything that interests me. I made sure that I had good background knowledge—always.

From good knowledge comes good judgment. I determined early on that my judgment, after studying, examining, and discussing an issue, was far better and much more reliable than that of any committee. A committee is political, and acceptable decisions are driven by compromise. If there are three paths to follow—the correct one, the wrong one, or the one that combines the two, which is the political or compromise path—I always sought the right one. Hence, I operated without partners. I built a team, but I was always the majority. I sought and accepted input from others, but I always made the final decision alone. My decisions proved to be correct in terms of meeting my objectives. The few times I was wrong, I was able to work my way out. It was the same when I was a boy, riding my bicycle across the railroad bridge over the Milwaukee River. I always knew where I would jump if I met a train headed toward me.

I believe I am a person of high character, integrity, and honesty. I have never intentionally lied. I have not always been right, but I never lied, and I always showed respect for the other fellow.

My motivation was never about money. I never thought about money. Money simply followed the commercial ideas I developed and the way I developed them. I did what I determined was right. When it came to my first job, I thought long and hard about where I could learn the most. Who would I be most proud to be associated with? And I remembered a conversation I had with my father early in my life. He said, "Sheldon, I am going to give you the same advice my father gave me." At this point he dug into his pocket and pulled out a Russian gold coin. "This is all you need," he said. "All you need is enough." I never forgot that. If I determined that my wife and child and I could live on $4,000 per year in 1953, that was enough. I never asked for a raise. I believed pay, wealth, what I needed, would follow if I engaged in productive activities that made me proud of my accomplishments.

I worked for a bank, and as I progressed and became more productive, they paid me more. Would I become rich? No, I knew that to become rich, you had to own something—a business, real estate, or something else that would increase in value for the many reasons that certain assets do appreciate. Usually this means an enterprise that steadily creates more income and therefore becomes more valued—or, in financial terms, develops a higher price-times-earning (PE) value. I believed in these principles without ever doubting that if I simply stuck with them, success was certain to follow. And that is the way it worked. I have been successful in building smaller companies into much larger and more profitable companies.

No one does it alone, of course. If there is one characteristic running through my career, it is that I have been a good judge of people and business talent. I always associated with people who were serious, honest, and hard-working. I always looked at the management of our companies as my team, and I avoided politicization. We must all succeed together or suffer together.

I often think back and wonder how I did it all—how I kept all my business dealings straight and usually maximized each company's value. The answer is that I worked hard, I loved what I was doing and, in all modesty, I knew how to do it.

I also had what I would call the luck of genetics. My parents' wisdom, practical good sense, and decency were guiding and inspirational to me.

I have often thought of how fortunate I was to be raised by my mother and father. The best way my father had of making a point or establishing a principle was to start with a story. I often do the same thing. There is no doubt in my mind that I acquired this manner from Dad.

The Wheat Story is the one I remember best and the one that I have retold most often. As the story goes, my grandfather and his two principal employees were on horseback in the countryside around Rossava, Ukraine, visiting farmers whose wheat they would buy and then grind into flour for sale. They had stopped their horses on the top of a hill that overlooked a dirt road. Coming toward them was a caravan of two or three wagons. My grandfather turned to one of his men— let's call him Peter—and said, "Ride down there and see where they are going." So Peter rode to the first wagon, talked to the driver, came back to my grandfather, and reported that the wagons were headed to Kiev.

My grandfather then turned to the other man, Vladimir, and said, "Now you go down and check." So Vladimir rode down, stopped at the first wagon, talked to the driver, then rode to the second wagon, talked to that driver, and after a long conversation came back with his report. "These people are farmers from twenty-five kilometers east of us," he said. "Their wagons are filled with wheat, and they are on their way to sell it in Kiev. The owner of the wheat is in the second wagon, and his wife is very sick. After talking to him, I offered to buy all his wheat at a 30-percent discount from the Kiev market price, so he could turn around and go home. He said, 'Yes, it's a deal.'"

My grandfather said, "Go back and make the buy." Then he turned to Peter, who for the last few months had been complaining because Vladimir earned so much more money than he did. My grandfather looked into Peter's eyes for a moment and then said, "That's why." And that's how the Wheat Story was born.

Inspirational stories, good judgment, and in-depth knowledge have all been important contributors to my business success, but I also want to stress the importance of physical fitness. You have only one vehicle to carry your mind around, and that's your body, so keep it in shape. I started jogging when we lived in Shorewood, where our next-door neighbors were Pat and Mary Louise Gorman. Pat headed advertising at the Schlitz brewery, and he was a serious runner before almost anyone I knew. At this time joggers were very rare. In fact, there wasn't any such thing as jogging shoes on the market. When I started, I would jog in thin-soled tennis shoes, which resulted in very stiff feet the next morning, but I am getting ahead of the story.

In 1962 I was thirty-three years old and working very hard in my assignment as president of Marine Capital Corporation. I was about fifteen pounds heavier than I am today or, I should simply say, fat. On a lovely day in early summer, I was sitting on our front porch going over business papers with my shirt off, enjoying the sun. Pat Gorman was at his kitchen sink washing dishes, I believe. I heard him say, "That's disgusting." I replied, "What's disgusting?" He answered, "You. A young man like you shouldn't be so out of shape. You ought to start jogging or stop eating!"

That hurt, but I knew he was right. A few days later, I walked over and asked Pat to help me start. He didn't compete in races, but on the weekends he would typically run eight or more miles. I was wearing my tennis shoes, and Pat said, "Let's go now." So off we went. The first leg was about four blocks, and I did the first three without a stop. The next block took us to Capitol Drive, and we stopped again. Then we turned right to St. Robert's Church, and again I stopped every block. I think we had logged a mile by the time we were back home. I remember feeling as if someone had put a blowtorch down my throat. A few days later, I had recovered enough to get out on my own, and I ultimately built up to doing four miles at least four or five times a week.

I told myself that I had to run. I had to do it without thinking. I couldn't tell myself the weather was bad, even if it was raining or snowing. I just had to dress for the weather and get out. After a few years, I would take my running gear with me wherever I was traveling. I have jogged all over the world, usually getting out at 6 a.m., and I've seen things I never would have if I hadn't been running. I did this until I was in my early eighties.

I don't think of myself as being competitive—just competitive with myself—so I never raced. However, after my daughter Joan started running, I decided I would do a marathon. I bought books, worked on running schedules, and ultimately got up to about twelve miles without stopping. Then I developed plantar fasciitis, a very painful condition.

My doctor told me to stop training and let my feet rest, which I did. After a few months the problem was gone, but so was my desire to run a marathon.

Today I still swim every day when I'm in Milwaukee, using an indoor pool we built at our River Hills home in 1976. I also walk and hike frequently. My favorite sport was downhill skiing, which I learned during our one-year sabbatical in Switzerland and which I continued in Aspen until 2014. I was eighty-four when I quit, and I still miss the snow, the mountains, and the graceful sensation of gliding down the mountain.

I'd like to close this chapter by quoting some basic rules of business and life that have been especially meaningful to me:

1. Peter Drucker: "In business, everything is a cost until you make a sale."

2. Bob Beyer (managing partner of Touche Ross): "Profit is your first expense."

3. Virgil Sullivan: "It is amazing what you can accomplish if you don't care who gets the credit."

4. Roger Fitzsimmons (with SBL): "Soundness, Profitability, and Growth—in that order."

5. Ronald Reagan: "Trust, but verify."

6. Mohammed: "A person's true wealth is the good he or she does in the world."

7. Jesse Livermore: "Throughout all my years of investing, I've found that the big money was never made in the buying or selling. The big money was made in the waiting."

8. William Shakespeare:
   "Who steals my purse steals trash; 'tis something, nothing;
   'Twas mine, 'tis his, and has been slave to thousands;
   But he that filches from me my good name
   Robs me of that which not enriches him,
   And makes me poor indeed."

9. Paul Volcker (Federal Reserve chair): "We can cure inflation, but the issue is what threshold of pain the American citizens can handle: 10 percent? 15 percent? 25 percent?" (He pushed it to 20 percent and broke the inflation trend.)

10. Robert Maynard Hutchins, 1949: "It is the task of every generation to reassess the tradition in which it lives, to discard what it cannot use, and to bring into context with the distant and intermediate past the most recent contributions to the great conversation."

11. J. Hawes: "You may be whatever you resolve to be. Determine to be something in the world and you will be something. 'I cannot' never accomplished anything. 'I will try' has wrought wonders."

12. Lao Tzu: "When you are content to be simply yourself and don't compare or compete, everybody will respect you."

13. From the French: "The madness of liberty is never cured."

14. Leonardo Da Vinci: "A life spent in the pursuit of learning."

15. Frank Lloyd Wright: "What a man does, that he has."

16. SBL: "Think! Then do what you know is right."

17. SBL: In business it's always about management."

18. SBL: "Learning from failure."

19. SBL: "Hit for singles, but swing for the fences when you get a soft pitch."

20. SBL: "Be humble."

21. David Lubar: "Diversify."

22. SBL: "Keep it simple."

23. SBL: "Get paid for taking risk, but do not be afraid to take risks."

24. SBL: "Stay away from the crowd."

25. Cicero: "A life well spent."

26. Henry David Thoreau: "The world is but a canvas to our imagination."

Giving Back: Public Service

During my life I have devoted an important part of my time and wealth to public service and philanthropy. I did it because I truly believed I had an obligation to give back both time and money. Simply said, it was the right thing to do, and we had the necessary resources. To me, the two main ways of giving back are public service and philanthropy, and I'd like to discuss them separately in this chapter and the next.

My first experience with public service occurred in 1967. We were living in the village of Shorewood, and one of our live-wire neighbors, John Haering, asked me to chair a citizen's committee he was organizing to study the need for a middle school in the Shorewood school system. At that time the village had a high school that covered grades 7 through 12 and two grade schools, Lake Bluff and Atwater, that covered kindergarten through 6. After a careful study, we made the case to have the elementary schools serve grades K to 5, build a new middle school for grades 6 to 8, and have the high school serve grades 9 to 12.

We submitted our proposal to the school board, who agreed to consider it, subject to the approval of a village referendum. When the issue was put on the ballot, our committee went to work, talking to as many villagers as we could. The referendum passed. The middle school was built on the campus of the high school, and the Shorewood system continues to be one of the best anywhere.

A couple of years later, my focus shifted to higher education. In early 1969, Governor Warren Knowles created the Wisconsin Commission on Education and appointed Bill Kellett, former president of Kimberly-Clark, as its chairman. I was asked to serve as one of nine Executive Committee members. Our charge was to examine all aspects of public education in Wisconsin, from K-12 to colleges and universities. It didn't take long before the newspapers started referring to us as the Kellett Commission. Bill Kellett was a proven, successful executive. He was full of ideas, had an endless capacity for work, and was a man of the highest integrity.

Bill directed us in an effort that included hundreds of others, but it was the Executive Committee that was responsible for the final report to the governor. We submitted it to Governor Knowles in 1970. The report contained numerous recommendations, the last of which was the creation of the University of Wisconsin System. The System was to be governed by a Board of Regents appointed by the governor, and it was to consist of the University of Wisconsin-Madison; the various extension schools; the entire statewide University Extension System, which had offices in every county in Wisconsin; and the twelve former State Teacher Colleges, which would be raised to the status of universities.

At about the time we completed the report, Governor Knowles announced he would not seek re-election. Our proposals were inherited by Pat Lucey, who won the 1970 gubernatorial election. In 1975, finally, Governor Lucey implemented one of our core recommendations, and the University of Wisconsin System became a reality. The first president of the System was my good friend, Jack Pelisek. In 1991 Governor Tommy Thompson appointed me to the Board of Regents, and in 1997 I was elected president of the UW System. My seven-year term as a regent was a wonderful experience. As an alumnus with two earned degrees, I felt both ownership and commitment. As a citizen, I was convinced that this educational system, which opened the doors of advanced learning to all Wisconsin high-school graduates, was the most important institution in the state of Wisconsin. I have always believed that the wealth of people and nations is directly measured by their level of advanced education, not money.

In Chapter 8, I wrote about my service in the Nixon and Ford Administrations. In 1979 I was invited to take on a second assignment on the national level. Some time after Jimmy Carter was elected president in late 1976, Senator Gaylord Nelson of Wisconsin approached me. Gaylord was then the chairman of the Senate Subcommittee on Small Business. He was working with President Carter to affirm the importance of small business by analyzing its impact on the economy and seeing what the government could do to further its development.

They had agreed that the effort would start with a White House Commission on Small Business, and Gaylord had proposed my name to the president as its chair.

President Carter was not enthused about putting a former Nixon appointee in charge, but he did appoint me as the sole Republican on his commission, and I chaired the section on capital formation. We organized a conference that drew more than 5,000 people to Washington, including 1,682 official delegates, for five full days in January, 1980. After weeks spent digesting those proceedings and continuing the discussion among ourselves, my fellow commissioners and I submitted our report to the president in April. We pointed out that small businesses, defined as independent enterprises with fewer than 500 employees, provided an astonishing 86.7 percent of the nation's new private-sector jobs. We described the sector as America's "birthright economy," the nation's purest and most powerful expression of "the freedom to take our lives into our own hands and pursue prosperity by our own lights." But small business, we maintained, was being held back by federal policies that tilted unfairly in favor of big corporations, discouraged productivity by placing too much emphasis on demand, and put the private sector in a straitjacket of regulation. "Small companies," we concluded, "are aggrieved by a policy of neglect that has inadvertently imposed obstacles and inequities that seem to thwart efficient business operations at every turn."

We submitted a long list of recommendations, sixty in all, that called for a more equitable tax burden, a lighter regulatory touch, small-business incentives, technical assistance, and a host of other reforms. Although most of my fellow commissioners were Democrats, we had no trouble agreeing on the quote that introduced our report. It was the ideal of federal authority expressed in Thomas Jefferson's 1801 inaugural address: "... a wise and frugal government, which shall restrain men from injuring one another, which shall leave them otherwise free to regulate their own pursuits of industry and improvement, and shall not take from the mouth of labor the bread that it has earned."

And what were the results? Did we move the needle of support for small business? I have to conclude that we did not. The American people had other things on their minds in 1980, including runaway inflation and the Iran hostage crisis. Jimmy Carter proved to be a one-term president, and small business was not one of his highest priorities. But the White House Commission planted a seed that would sprout in the years that followed.

The other public bodies I have served on were all closer to home: the State of Wisconsin Investment Board, the Governor's Commission on Taliesin, the Governor's Commission on Small Business, and several others over the years. One of my later public-service projects resulted in a major downtown building. Milwaukee had been talking about a new convention center for years. Why couldn't the city attract larger and better gatherings? Some said Milwaukee wasn't big enough, others said there weren't enough hotel rooms, and still others said the old Auditorium was too small. There was widespread agreement that we needed a new convention center located in downtown Milwaukee.

The first I heard of these plans was from Gary Grunau, a contractor, a builder, and an idea person. He had been discussing the matter with Mayor John Norquist, who took office in 1988. Between the two of them, they decided to ask me to lead the effort, which would mean bringing the city, county, and state together and also obtaining the financing for the building.

After discussing the idea further with Gary, I told him I would take the chairmanship if Governor Tommy Thompson, County Executive Tom Ament, and Mayor Norquist would all assign their administrative chiefs to the committee. They agreed, and we moved ahead, determining the convention center's location, source of funding, and governance structure. A bond offering underwritten by Bear Stearns & Co. in New York provided the necessary funds, and we convinced the Wisconsin Food and Beverage Association to agree to a sales tax to pay the money back. We took our final plan to the governor, the mayor, the county executive, and then the Wisconsin legislature. Everyone signed off, and the result was the Wisconsin Center, a beautiful facility on the west side of downtown that was dedicated in 1998.

Another local project was just as interesting but much more frustrating, and that was the State Task Force on Milwaukee County Finances. I co-chaired the group when it started in 2006, and I continued when the effort moved to the Greater Milwaukee Committee.

After operating relatively well for decades, Milwaukee County government had slipped into a period of dysfunction marked by incredibly poor communication between the county executive and the county board. I once said that the system wouldn't work "even if Jesus was the county executive and Moses chaired the Board of Supervisors" —a line that was quoted quite frequently. The county also faced a fiscal crisis rooted in an irresponsibly generous pension package, and there was needless duplication of services with other units of government. It all amounted to a drag on Milwaukee's progress.

"How can we keep up," I asked the Milwaukee Rotary Club in 2008, "when we're bogged down with glaring redundancies and inefficiencies in a government that works with the speed of a horse and buggy in the age of the satellite?" I proposed a "devolution" of county government, a radical restructuring that would include delegating specific services to other public bodies (including independent transit and parks authorities) and replacing the existing county board with a fiscal oversight board that would have responsibility for approving all expenditures. Progress on those proposals to date has been, shall we say, slow.

My interest in public policy also led me to found or co-found a couple of institutions that bring independent research to bear on the issues of the day. The first was the Wisconsin Policy Research Institute (now the Badger Institute), which I co-founded in 1987 to deal with some of the big questions facing our state. The Institute has made a major contribution that favorably affects the future of Wisconsin. Our studies in education, welfare, crime, and business have helped make Wisconsin a leading state in the formation of better public policy, and they have contributed a free-market perspective to the discussion. I served as WPRI's president for the group's first seven years, and chairing those board meetings was like moderating a public television panel discussion. Everyone had a viewpoint, but they always challenged WPRI to be its best.

More recently I have become involved with the Marquette University Law School. Working with Joe Kearney, the Law School dean, Marianne and I endowed and created the Sheldon B. Lubar Center for Public Policy Research and Civic Education in 2017. It focuses on issues affecting the Milwaukee community. The Center was inspired by another quotation from Thomas Jefferson, whom I consider one of our greatest Americans. "If you hope to live in a free country whose people are uneducated," said Jefferson, "you want something that never has been and never will be." I look forward to the Lubar Center raising the level of public awareness and thoughtful debate in Milwaukee.

Let me end this chapter by discussing one more area of public service, and that is speaking out on matters of public interest. I have never been afraid to express my opinions, whether in speeches, guest editorials, or some other form of communication. Over the years, I've called for greater civility in state and national politics, greater tolerance of diversity, and a more enlightened approach to governing. One of my most passionate stands concerned "the fog of war." As I look back over my life, it seems there were only a few years when our country wasn't engaged in a war. World War I ended about eleven years before I was born, and World War II started ten years later. While I was a student at the University of Wisconsin, we became involved in the Korean War. As you'll recall from Chapter 2, I planned to join the Air Force, and I was disappointed when I wasn't called up. I was young and patriotic. I have since learned that wars don't accomplish anything for either side.

At the tail end of John Kennedy's administration, we became involved in Vietnam. Our initial engagement was largely as an advisor, but under our new leader, President Lyndon Johnson, and his secretary of defense, Robert McNamara, our participation grew until we took the conflict over as our war. This war was unpopular, especially with young men who were being drafted and sent into the jungles to fight and die against an enemy whose only crime was fighting to maintain a Communist form of government for their country. There were demonstrations and riots on campuses over our entire country. Our nation split into two hostile groups: those who approved of the war and those who despised it and were risking their lives in hopes of ending it.

At that time, I was a very outspoken critic of our involvement in Vietnam. Friends of mine would ask, "How can you be in Milwaukee with no special knowledge and think you can determine a strategy so different from our leaders?" My answer: "Only an acclaimed genius can mislead the majority of the country, and Robert McNamara is such a man, but his policy will be disastrous." I predicted that the effect of the division in our country would take ten years to heal. I was wrong. More than fifty years later, we still aren't together. As if this wasn't enough, we have had Iraq War I, Iraq War II, the war in Afghanistan, and now the war against ISIS.

For all the blood and money that has been spent on this long list of wars, we could have rebuilt our country's infrastructure, provided a free college education to every high school graduate, and avoided a national debt that is now over $30 trillion and growing. Even worse, the spread of nuclear weapons and the increasingly sophisticated means of delivering them have put the entire planet at risk of destruction.

Can't we get smart? Can't we see that these wars bring only pain and unimaginable costs? Worst of all, they divide us. Nothing good comes from war. I have come to believe that, instead of individual armies, there should be only the United Nations army, made up of soldiers from all member nations. When a country has broken the law, as determined by the UN, its leaders would be considered war criminals and subject to appropriate punishment.

As an interesting postscript, I once met Robert McNamara at an Aspen dinner party. I made it a point to visit with him. We talked of several things, but not the Vietnam War, and I realized that he was just a man—not an evil man, but one who was so confident of his own judgment that he couldn't see himself as anything but right. Mr. McNamara later wrote a book that was made into a 2003 documentary film entitled *The Fog of War.* He explained the mistakes made by himself and our government, and concluded, "We thought we were fighting a war against Communism, and they thought they were fighting a civil war." The results of that fundamental misunderstanding were disastrous.

Giving Back: Philanthropy

Over the course of six decades, Marianne and I have contributed many millions of dollars to various Wisconsin universities and colleges, many large and small visual and performing arts groups, many community and Jewish charities, and a number of women's health efforts. What we did gave us great personal gratification. Giving a helping hand to students, universities, and other institutions in our community, and doing good work for persons in need, has been joyful, but perhaps even more gratifying to me is the commitment and involvement of Marianne and our four children. They have each contributed huge amounts of their time and their money in many different areas of philanthropy.

I want to highlight a few of our family's most important causes in this chapter. First of all, we believe nothing is more important in this world than education and the arts. The latter receive almost no government support, and the former not enough. What a wonderful world it would be if we spent nothing on war and very much more on education and the arts.

Milwaukee Art Museum

After my return from Washington to Milwaukee, I was asked to succeed Bob Krikorian, a leading industrialist, as president of the Milwaukee Art Center. At about this time, the director of the center was leaving, and I asked if I could start my term after a new director was selected. The board agreed, and then asked me to head the search committee. Our committee embarked on a national search, and we ended it by hiring Mr. Jerry Nordland, who was at the time director of the San Francisco Museum of Modern Art. Jerry was an art scholar, a writer, and a brilliant director. He did an outstanding job, managing the accreditation that elevated the Art Center to the Art Museum, enhancing the collection, and especially adding many talented people to the staff. I assumed the presidency when Jerry started and served for three years, retiring in 1980.

Jerry's successor was Russell Bowman, who had been chief curator. He led the effort, along with Marianne, to build the Calatrava addition. This world-class building on the shores of Lake Michigan has in many ways become a symbol of southeastern Wisconsin. The cost was originally estimated to be $40 million, but it rose to $50 or $60 million and ended up at $135 million.

When the building was completed, I was recruited to close the gap between the $100 million already raised and the $35 million we still owed to the banking syndicate. This wasn't something I wanted to do, but I thought to myself, "If not me, who?" I will shorten the story by simply saying that I did it. The only real help I received was from the new director, David Gordon. Together we found multi-million-dollar donors, which included Marianne and me. We paid every penny of principal and interest, and the museum is now debt-free. The lesson here is that nonprofits cannot safely borrow unless they have monies committed in advance. When the debt was paid off, I was again recruited to serve as president and then chairman for another few years, and now I serve as a life trustee.

Education

During my life, I have been closely involved with several Wisconsin colleges and universities. I served as a trustee of Beloit College from 1971 to 1973. In 1980 I joined the Board of Trustees of Marquette University, and in 1991 the governor of Wisconsin appointed me a regent of the University of Wisconsin System. After serving as vice-president for three years, I was elected president of the Board of Regents in 1998. The System consisted of thirteen degree-granting universities, thirteen two-year campuses, and the UW Extension, whose services are available to all citizens in every county in Wisconsin. A high percentage of Wisconsin's high-school graduates find their way to one of the UW schools every year. I believe it is the most important institution in our state. I next served two six-year terms—the maximum allowed—as a trustee of the Medical College of Wisconsin, from 1999 to 2011.

As you might surmise, I believe strongly in continuing education. It is the pathway to an exciting, informed life. I know my life wouldn't have been what it was if I hadn't practiced what I have continually preached: education is ongoing for life.

While in Milwaukee, I became involved with the University of Wisconsin-Milwaukee. I lectured from time to time at the School of Business, and Marianne and I became major benefactors. The Business School eventually became the Sheldon B. Lubar School of Business, which was truly an honor.

Over the years I have received three honorary doctor's degrees:

- Honorary Doctor of Commercial Science, University of Wisconsin-Milwaukee, 1988
- Honorary Doctor of Humane Letters, University of Wisconsin-Madison, 2009
- Honorary Doctor of Science, Medical College of Wisconsin, 2010

Marianne has also received honorary doctorates, from both the Medical College of Wisconsin and the University of Wisconsin-Milwaukee. Recently we funded a program at Alverno College: the Marianne Lubar Scholarship Fund.

David Lubar and I recently worked with UW-Milwaukee to create and endow the Lubar Entrepreneurship Center at that university. Being an entrepreneur—owning all or part of a business and participating in its growth—is a benefit for both the entrepreneur and the community. It was what my business life was built on, and I loved the freedom and independence that it brought me. The center is being funded by Marianne and myself. I have strong feelings that entrepreneurship can be learned and developed through education.

Lubar Institute for the Study of the Abrahamic Religions

We feel just as strongly that tolerance and respect can be learned, and one of our efforts, the Lubar Institute for the Study of the Abrahamic Religions, was designed to promote those values. Let me tell you how it came about. First as an undergraduate and then as a Law School graduate, I gained much of my initial base at the University of Wisconsin. I had been considering for some time what I could do financially for the university that would be meaningful. Marianne and I had been generous to many nonprofits in Milwaukee and elsewhere, but I asked myself what I could do that would have the potential of bringing about positive and meaningful change.

And then it happened. I mean 9/11 happened, and I was in Manhattan when it did. For as long as I was a director of Massachusetts Mutual, the insurance company sponsored the U.S. Open Tennis Tournament in New York. In most years, Marianne and I would come out for the last weekend of the event, watching the women's finals on Saturday and the men's finals on Sunday. In 2001 I also chaired the Audit Committee of Weatherford, Inc. For my convenience, Weatherford had scheduled a meeting of that committee in New York on the Tuesday after the U.S. Open, which happened to be September 11. We were slated to meet at 4 p.m. in the American Express Building, which was directly next to the World Trade Center.

On the Monday morning after the tournament, Marianne decided that she didn't want to hang around New York for two days, so she flew back to Milwaukee. I planned to attend my meeting and follow her on Wednesday. On the morning of 9/11, I got a phone call from the Weatherford chairman's office, informing me that his flight from Houston had been diverted to Alabama and that everything was uncertain. Up to then, I knew nothing about the disaster going on in lower Manhattan, so I turned on the TV just in time to see the second hijacked jet crash into the Twin Towers. What followed was the horror of the Towers' collapse, the destruction of the American Express Building next door, the grounding of all aircraft in the country, the sealing off of all automobile and train traffic into and out of New York, and the deaths of 3,000 people. By nighttime there were no cars on the streets of Manhattan.

On Wednesday, some trains were running, but I could not get a seat. The bridges into New York were closed, and I couldn't rent a car. All I could do was go over to the office of my friend and business associate, Bryan Lawrence, and hang out with him. Thank heaven for Bryan. On Thursday, I heard that LaGuardia Airport was open again, and I got a seat on an airplane leaving at about 5 p.m. I got to the airport an hour early and checked my bag. Shortly thereafter came an announcement that all flights had been canceled and that the airport was closing. It turned out to be only a scare, but there was nothing to do but get my baggage and leave.

As I was accepting my fate, a friend from Milwaukee, Marian Brill, came up to me and said, "Why don't we rent a car and drive to Milwaukee?" I told her I had tried to rent a car on Wednesday and failed. "I'll try again," I said, "but I am not optimistic." Well, I picked up the direct line to Hertz and asked if they had a car available for a trip to Milwaukee. The lady on the other end said "Yes," and a half-hour later we were on our way home.

We left at about 6 p.m.—Marian, me, and another woman who had heard me calling and asked to go with us. We drove straight through the night, and by 9 the following morning, we were at Mitchell International in Milwaukee. As I went to check out, the ladies said they wanted to share the cost, but I said "No." When I got the final bill for the trip, I reminded the check-out lady that I had been promised there would be no drop-off charges, and she agreed. Much to my shock, the total bill was less than $100. It was good to be home in Milwaukee.

Of course I was never in danger, but 9/11 left a deep impact on me. In the months that followed, the terrorists were identified as Arab Muslims, and America's resentment of the attack turned to hate of all Muslims. If you are Jewish, I think you are extra-sensitive to group hate. My thoughts again turned to a desire to do something meaningful at UW. I conceived of an institute devoted to the highest possible level of collaboration among the three religions that trace their roots to Abraham: Judaism, Christianity, and Islam. This, I thought, could be the link. If we could establish a venue where academicians of the highest caliber could come together in a civil setting to work toward understanding, peace, and civility to all, perhaps we could plant the seeds leading to a better world. Just think of what the prophets of 2,000 years ago accomplished.

I discussed my thoughts with the chancellor of UW-Madison. He agreed that this could be something big, something meaningful. He took our idea to the University Committee, which was made up of key faculty persons, and they enthusiastically endorsed our proposal for the Lubar Institute for the Study of the Abrahamic Religions.

The university chose Professor Charles Cohen from the Department of History to lead LISAR, and we were in business. The Institute's stated goal was to "advance mutual comprehension by mingling scholars with the general public, clergy with laity, and members of different faith communities with citizens of Wisconsin, the United States, and the world." For more than a decade, LISAR did just that, and we were proud to have our name associated with all its efforts.

I want to close this chapter with the story of a philanthropic project that was just plain fun. In 2008 I was attending a regular meeting of the Greater Milwaukee Committee. Sue Black, director of the Milwaukee County Park System, was giving her report to the GMC's Quality of Life Committee, of which I was a member. Sue advised us that Bradford Beach was closing because the county would not fund lifeguards. I couldn't believe it. I knew that thousands of citizens and children depended on the beach for summer recreation. After I asked Sue a few questions, I volunteered to fund the lifeguards for 2008 and later for 2009. The gift turned out to be a catalyst for the rebirth of Bradford Beach. With new restaurants, new volleyball courts, and even tiki huts, that scenic stretch of sand on Lincoln Memorial Drive recovered its appeal as a destination. In 2016, much to the surprise of everyone, myself included, a *USA Today* reader's poll ranked Bradford the third-best urban beach in America.

Our Family Today

On Saturday, August 31, 2019, Marianne and I celebrated our sixty-seventh wedding anniversary. My memories of that day in 1952 are still clear. We were both very young, but nothing seemed beyond our abilities and our reach. We created a close family over the years. Our four children are married and have given us eleven grandchildren and so far two great-grandchilden.

Kris is married to John MacDonald. She is a graduate of the University of Colorado and later received a master's degree from the University of Wisconsin. John is a graduate of the University of Montana. Kris has three children. The oldest, John, is a graduate of Colorado College. He spent four years as a mountain guide and then earned his master's degree from the Kellogg School of Business at Northwestern University. Maddie received her bachelor's degree from Connecticut College and later her master's degree from the Fletcher School of Diplomacy at Tufts University. Joseph graduated from the University of Arizona, majoring in business, and he's now pursuing a master's degree at the University of Minnesota.

Our son David graduated from Bowdoin College and later received his master's degree in business from the University of Minnesota, earning it while he was working at what is now Wells Fargo Bank. Today David is the president and chief executive officer of Lubar & Co. His wife, Madeleine, is a graduate of both Marquette University and Marquette University Law School and practiced law until their second child was born. Their three children are Joseph, Hannah, and Patrick. Joseph was a junior at the University of Denver in 2011 when he lost his life in a skiing accident—a loss that is with us always. Hannah is a graduate of Brown University. Patrick graduated from the University of Wisconsin-Madison and is now an officer at Ixonia Bank.

A few years back, I promoted myself to chairman and founder of Lubar & Co., and we elected David as president and CEO. He has continued to build our team, the company, and our family. In addition to the boards of the companies in our portfolio, David serves on many outside boards, including the Milwaukee Brewers Baseball Club, Northwestern Mutual Life Insurance Company, BMO Financial Corporation, Greater Milwaukee Committee (president), Nicholas Company, UWM Lubar School of Business (Advocacy Council, president), and numerous non-profit boards.

Next in chronological order is Susan. She is a graduate of the University of Vermont and worked in marketing at Xerox Corporation before returning to school to earn her master's degree from the Kellogg School of Business at Northwestern University. At Kellogg she met Oyvind Solvang, who graduated in the same class. Oyvind was born in Norway and came to the USA on a skiing scholarship at the University of Utah, where he received his undergraduate degree before proceeding to the Kellogg School of Business. They married, moved to Milwaukee, and have three children. Simen graduated from Northeastern University in Boston and is now in the world of music. Isabelle graduated from Syracuse University and then taught school before going to work in Minneapolis. Sonja graduated from the Maryland Institute College of Art and is now a designer in California.

Our youngest daughter, Joan, graduated from Colorado State University with a major in nutrition. After working for the Milwaukee Health Department, she returned to school and earned her master's degree in exercise physiology at the University of Wisconsin-Milwaukee. Joan's first husband, Jeff Siegel, died in 2002 at the age of forty-seven of stomach cancer. She later married Dr. John Crouch, a heart surgeon. Joan's two children are Isaac, who graduated from the University of Colorado, and Charlotte, who is in her second year at Emory University.

Marianne and I are exceptionally proud of every one of these persons. They are intelligent, honest, and ethical individuals who every day continue to contribute to their families and communities. We love them all.

As this account of my life nears its conclusion, I want to address a message directly to our grandchildren. I am ninety years old at this writing. Your grandmother is eighty-six years old. We have created much wealth and good will in our community. We have seen that each of you shared in these accomplishments. We have many current interests, but none is more important than helping each of you travel the path to a happy and meaningful life. Now it is a question of sharing our lifetime of experiences to help you make meaningful lives for yourselves and those you love. Your grandmother and I are very proud of each of you. In fact, what I am most proud of in my life is our entire family and every one of its members. From first to last, it was always about family.

I am well aware that there are beginnings and endings, always. In my lifetime I have experienced tragedy only once, in the death of our grandson, Joe Lubar, on February 11, 2011. I felt the even deeper pain of that loss as I saw my son David, his wife Madeleine, and their children, Hannah and Patrick, endure it. Joey was only twenty-one at the time of his fatal skiing accident. He had spent the fall semester in Geneva, Switzerland, studying and working as a copywriter and editor for an international online magazine, along with traveling through Europe on the weekends. He had a limitless life ahead, with interests in politics, academics, and business as well as climate change. I could even include sports, because Joey was a truly outstanding baseball pitcher in high school and at Denver University. David and Madeleine have honored his memory in many ways, especially by establishing the four-year, full-tuition Joe Lubar Scholarship at his high school, University School of Milwaukee, for a gifted student who otherwise might not consider attending the school. They also sponsor the annual Joe Lubar Day baseball game with the Milwaukee Brewers. Joey is in my thoughts every day.

Thankfully, there are also beginnings. On February 7, 2019, Marianne and I learned that we had become great-grandparents. Kris's daughter, Maddie, and her husband, John McElhenny, announced the birth of their first child, a son, Reid Lubar McElhenny. Then, on July 8, 2019, Kris's son, John, and his wife, Elaine Yang, had their first child, a daughter, River Yang Thomson. Young ones, we look forward to seeing you and welcoming you into the family.

The Character-Driven Life

I will conclude this memoir by trying to answer a simple question: what single thing led to the success I was able to achieve in business, public service, and philanthropy? What enabled me to climb my mountain? Certainly, native intelligence is part of it, but almost everyone I know and work with seems to have a comparable IQ. Is it about hard work and giving it your all? Yes, but many persons do that as well. Perhaps it's about good luck or providence. No, I don't believe in luck; I believe we each make our own luck.

My conclusion is that it's about the character-driven life: integrity, decency, truthfulness, honesty, curiosity, and respect for others. It is about delivering what you promise. When I acquired Sorgel Electric, why did Massachusetts Mutual Insurance and State Mutual Insurance each invest $1 million with a young man whose only capital was $15,000 of his own equity? And at the end, why did the First National Bank of Boston lend me the final $900,000 unsecured? Simply put, after checking me out, they were persuaded that I would deliver what I said I would. I was credible. It was all the result of the high principles my loving mother and father instilled in their children.

That's been the "secret" of my success, and it's a secret that everyone can use. If you are a person of high character who builds a reputation for doing what you promise, every mountain, large or small, will be yours for the climbing.

My family has **roots in Europe.**

The Lubars are from Rossava, a small village in what is now Ukraine. My father, Joseph Lubar, is highlighted on the right.

Joe Lubar came to the U.S. in 1913. Four years later, he was back in Europe, fighting as an American soldier in World War I.

My parents wanted only the best for their children.

Charlotte Stern Lubar, a lovely woman and loving mother known to everyone as Lottie

Joe Lubar, a two-fisted man's man and a very hard worker

If I excelled at anything in **my early years**, it was at being normal.

A wide-eyed three-year-old

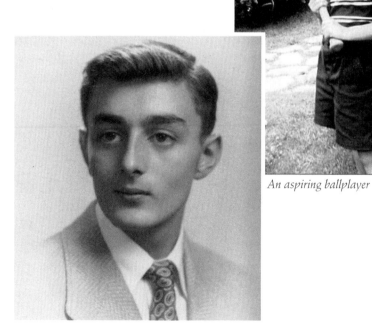

An aspiring ballplayer

Whitefish Bay High School, Class of 1947

The **University of Wisconsin** gave me a great foundation for both work and life.

In my ROTC uniform outside the Pi Lambda Phi fraternity house with Paul Meissner

Making like a fountain during my sophomore year

It was at UW that I met **Marianne.**

I was waiting on tables in her residence hall when I met Marianne Segal, a lovely freshman from Kenosha. We soon became a couple. Here we are at a fraternity dance.

Marianne and I were married on Aug. 31, 1952.

Our first home was an apartment in this house on Wilson Street.

The Ford came with Marianne in our marriage.

My business career started at the **Marine Bank.**

I reported for work at the old riverfront office in 1953 ...

... and stayed through construction of the glass skyscraper that covered the same block in 1961.

Eliot Fitch (r.) and then Jack Geilfuss ran the Marine. They were both true gentlemen.

Our family grew along with my responsibilities at work.

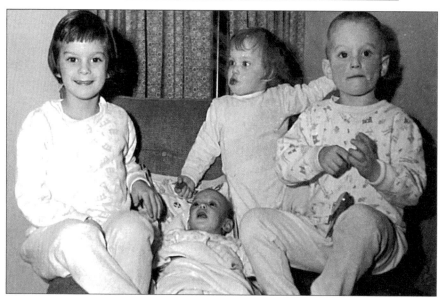

Four "little ducks" all in a row (l. to r.): Kris, Susan, Joan, and David

The same quartet a few years later

Venture capital became my professional passion.

In 1959 I started a small business investment company inside the Marine. It proved to be my first step toward independence.

I acquired Sorgel Electric on my own in 1966. Nothing could ever succeed like Sorgel. It was the base of my family's success.

In 1971 the Lubars crossed the ocean for a **European sabbatical.**

After merging Sorgel with Square D, we took a year-long time-out. Marianne and I made St. Moritz our base and learned to ski there.

We toured the continent with our kids during their breaks from the American School in Switzerland. Lunch was often served on the hood of our car, with a map close by.

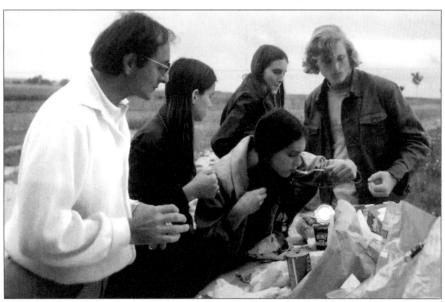

Mountains have been a powerful constant in my life.

At the top of Mt. Kilimanjaro with
David and Joan—our first major climb

Climbing Switzerland's
Jungfrau with David
(directly behind me)

On Mt. Rainier with John Cahill,
my good friend, business associate,
and climbing partner

129

Mountaineering became a family affair.

Especially since buying a home in Aspen in 1972, I've had "peak" experiences with Kris ...

... with Susan in the mountains ...

... with Joan (on Mt. Sopris)...

... and, of course, with Marianne.

Here we are in the Canadian Rockies.

My family attended my formal swearing-in as assistant secretary of Housing and Urban Development and head of the Federal Housing Administration. Marianne and three of our kids are on my right, my parents and her mother are on my left.

Dan Kearney, my superb deputy commissioner

132

. . . to work in the Nixon Administration.

In the Oval Office (fourth from left) with President Nixon

I finished my service under President Gerald Ford.

I went to **Russia with my father** in 1973.

One benefit of government service was helping my father fulfill a lifelong dream of returning to his hometown.

The trip's highlight was a day in Rossava hosted by an official Soviet delegation.

Joseph Lubar and John Cahill posed under a portrait of Lenin.

We came **home to Milwaukee** in 1975, this time for good.

Marianne and I moved into the River Hills home that has been our residence ever since—with plenty of improvements.

Running the **Midland Bank** was my first job after returning.

Midland was established in 1964 by John Kelly, a good friend from my Marine Bank days, but it was in trouble when I arrived.

With John's full support, Midland was acquired by the First Bank System to the benefit of all shareholders and employees.

Bob Moon, who helped me develop the
concept of Professional Ownership

Virgil Sullivan, a true mentor   Getty Images

Gary Sarner, CEO of
Total Logistic Control

Eric Schenker (l.), dean
of the Lubar School of
Business at UWM, and
Jack Pelisek, my old friend
and fellow UW regent

138

I've had great **mentors and colleagues** over the years.

Hal Kuehl, head of the
First Wisconsin Bank

Jim Nelson, CEO of Grey Wolf Drilling

Nick Brady,
former U.S.
Secretary of the
Treasury and
one of my closest
friends. Here
he poses with
a portrait of his
earliest predeces-
sor, Alexander
Hamilton.

In 1977 I founded **Lubar & Co.**

Twenty-four years after entering the business world, it was time for me to put the principles of Professional Owner-ship into practice.

The firm's early partners were (l. to r.) Jim Rowe, David Lubar, myself, and Bill Donovan.

The same group on the slopes of Aspen

We acquired and started a great **variety of businesses** over the years.

At the wheel of Total Logistic Control, part of our Christiana holdings

Acquiring Ixonia Bank took me back to my business roots.

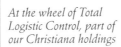

The Lake Express Ferry offers high-speed service across Lake Michigan.

Ken Szallai (l.), CEO, is standing with David and me.

Giving back has always been an important part of my life.

As an alumnus, regent, and devout believer in education, I've backed numerous University of Wisconsin System initiatives, including the Lubar School of Business at UWM...

Staking Our Claim
Innovation and

... and the Lubar Entrepreneurship Center on the same campus.

UW-Madison awarded me an honorary degree in 2009.

At Marquette University, I helped fund the Lubar Center for Public Policy.

I led the campaign to pay off the debt for the Milwaukee Art Museum's Calatrava addition —a significant number.

I didn't forget my old high school, helping to build the athletic stadium at Whitefish Bay. "Once a Blue Duke, always a Blue Duke."

The Lubar family came together for an awards ceremony at the Woodrow Wilson Center in 2011

For Marianne and me, it's always been about **our family.**

The immediate Lubar family gathered in our kitchen in 1992: (l. to r.) me, Kris, Joan, David, Marianne, and Susan.

The same group with their spouses in 2010

With my big sisters, Dorothy and Esther

The Lubar clan in 2018

Our grandchildren have been the lights of our lives.

On the trail with "Johnny Boy" Thomson

Maddie and Joseph Thomson

Patrick Lubar and Isaac Siegel

Sonja Solvang

Joey Lubar on his 21st and final birthday.
We miss him every day.

Simen Solvang

Izzy Solvang

Charlotte Siegel

Hannah Lubar

As often as not, **Lubar family gatherings** take place outdoors.

On the road in Norway

Hiking in the Colorado Rockies

Skiing at Aspen

*Rafting on the
Colorado River*

Marianne once said that she and I make **a good team.**
I realize that more every day.

*We're both true-blue
University of Wisconsin Badgers.*

*On the plane to Arizona
in our usual poses. I am on the right.*

*Congratulations
to each other
at Marquette
University
– 2018*

The **Lubar & Co. team** gathered in 2019.

I couldn't be prouder of the legacy I've created. As Henry David Thoreau put it, "The world is but a canvas to our imagination." I've done my best to live by those words.

Part Two

On the Record

Selected Speeches of
Sheldon B. Lubar

Part Two
Contents

Introduction

This section of *Climbing My Mountain* is a coequal companion to Part One. It consists of speeches I've given on various topics over the years, going all the way back to 1972. Some of the speeches might be of purely historical interest, but they all express what I was thinking at the time I gave them, and they're another way to communicate my principles and values.

The speeches are grouped into five sections and arranged chronologically within them. The first section, "The Life of an Entrepreneur," is the most autobiographical. It describes what I've done throughout my career and offers some guidelines that others might follow if they want to enter the same field. "The Importance of Education" highlights a theme that has been central to my existence. It includes a number of commencement speeches, including some I gave when I was a regent of the University of Wisconsin System. The third section, "The U.S. Economy," takes a higher-level view of the economic environment in which I've operated for many years, through bad times as well as good. "Milwaukee and Wisconsin Issues" gives my perspective on some of the problems facing my home city and state, particularly Milwaukee County's ongoing challenges. Finally, "Housing in the 1970s" includes just a few of the many talks I gave during my term as head of the Federal Housing Administration.

Chapter 1

The Life of an Entrepreneur

The New Entrepreneur
University of Wisconsin-Milwaukee
Oct. 31, 1972

Let me start by asking you a few questions. How many have heard the word "entrepreneurship"? How many know what it means? The classic definition of an entrepreneur is someone who is an employer of productive labor, someone who undertakes to carry out any enterprise. I think of an entrepreneur as one who provides the leadership to create the new and different.

The fifty years before World War I might be called the Age of the Entrepreneur. It was then that the big businesses of today were founded, in steel (Andrew Carnegie), automotive (Henry Ford), electricity (Thomas Edison), and many other fields. In the fifty years since World War II, the emphasis or premium has been on management. Not that entrepreneurship has been lacking, but the great need was for the productive organization of people to do something that was relatively well-known.

As you all know, we are in a period of dynamic, world-wide change. This change is not just technological; it is social and political. It means we are again entering an era which will emphasize entrepreneurship, since we won't be able to continue doing things in the same way. Entrepreneurship will be necessary for successful survival.

However, it won't be the entrepreneurship of a century ago, which meant the ability of a single man to organize a business he could run and control. We need men who can operate as entrepreneurs and build enclaves of new entrepreneurship on the foundations of the past fifty years.

I would like to illustrate how this could work, and the opportunities and personal satisfaction it can afford, by using our company, Mortgage Associates, as an example. We are an intermediary between large financial institutions—banks, insurance companies, savings & loans, pension funds—and the consumer who is seeking to purchase a home. We originate loans through sixty-plus loan officers working in twenty-two branches. We then sell those mortgages to large institutions but continue to service them. We provide the administration—interest, principal, taxes, insurance, inspection, collection—on 60,000 loans, a process that depends on computerization.

Our expansion since 1967 has been dramatic. We have grown from $200 million to $900 million in the loans we service. Our annual production has grown from $40 million to $260 million. We have expanded from eight offices to twenty-two. Along the way, we have organized ourselves into eight divisions and nine departments, plus those twenty-two branch offices, which means that we have thirty-nine entrepreneurial centers—in effect, thirty-nine separate businesses.

Our managers all know the goals and objectives of the corporation and what portion of them they are responsible for. From that point on, they are individual entrepreneurs determining their own paths to their portion of these goals. If they succeed, the company succeeds.

We give our entrepreneurs a variety of incentives. Some are material—good salaries, stock ownership, and profit-sharing—but they can also take pride and personal satisfaction in creating and knowing they are effective. Each of them has a sense of independence, and you can't put a price tag on that.

I have spoken of entrepreneurship in business, but we need it in all aspects of today's society. First of all, we need entrepreneurs in government. Our political procedures preclude most entrepreneurs from ever trying for an elected office. Our civil service is also a system that discourages entrepreneurs, since it's not based on merit. The result is a noticeable lack of leadership and an unwillingness to take risks, innovate, or discontinue anything that the government is involved in. We also need entrepreneurs in our institutions, including our schools and hospitals. The leaders of those institutions must perform—not just for their clientele, but for the community and society.

There are five thoughts I want to leave with you:
1. Don't do things you don't believe in.
2. Concentrate your efforts; don't do many things.
3. Think first, but then do something. You can't spend all your time thinking. Don't postpone.
4. What counts is performance, not intentions.
5. Always think of yourself as an entrepreneur.

Venture Capital:
Is It a Business for Today's Women?
TEMPO Milwaukee
Jan. 20, 1983

First, the answer to the question in my title is "Yes, of course. Why not?" All you need is a capacity for hard work, intelligence, patience, a sound business background, a command of the big picture, and the ability to put off gratification for years. If that sounds like you, a bright future awaits you in the field of venture capital.

But let's begin by talking about what venture capitalism is. Capitalism itself is an economic system characterized by private or corporate ownership of capital goods, by investments that are determined by private decision rather than by state control, and by prices, production, and the market distribution of goods that are determined mainly in a free market.

A person who has capital invested or to be invested in a business —spare money—is called a capitalist, naturally. Venture capital is commonly taken to mean any and all forms of investment in business enterprises of a high-risk level. Venture capital is not speculating, but it is investing today based on what one perceives the future to be.

Bernard Baruch, the great financier, wrote that, to invest capital successfully, three things are necessary:

> First, one must get the facts of a situation or problem.
> Second, one must form a judgment as to what those facts portend.
> Third, one must act in time, before it is too late. I have heard many men talk intelligently, even brilliantly, about something only to see them proven powerless when it comes to acting on what they believe.

For our purposes today, it is essential to distinguish between investors who specialize in real estate, building development, wholesale/retail operations, franchising, oil and mineral exploration, and other activities and companies like ourselves—Lubar & Co.—who seek to be a part of creating high-growth manufacturing or service businesses by emphasizing high levels of technology. No other investors become as closely involved with their companies and their managements as we do, or stay involved as long as we do. Ten years is not unusual.

Let me describe how we operate at Lubar & Co. Our objective is to create the maximum total value of an operating company in which we have a meaningful investment. We do this by creating high-quality, reliable products, growing earnings, and eventually achieving a strong financial position. Once we are involved with a company, we try to participate in all activities, strategies, and judgments that go into achieving the objective of creating maximum value. The only thing we don't get involved in is operating, day-to-day management, which is the responsibility of the CEO of the company and his team.

As venture capitalists, our approach has several steps:

1. We determine the business, industry, or area of activity we want to be involved in.
2. We identify opportunities, which usually means solving someone else's problem.
3. We determine the appropriate method of investment, which could mean buyouts or growth financing. We structure the "right" side of the balance sheet, and management is responsible for the "left." This applies to both the acquisition and operation of the business.
4. We select management and create accountability. Everyone performs best when they are responsible to someone they respect. We choose the CEO, establish standards (typically return on assets and rate of growth), provide incentives (stock ownership, simple bonuses), and review management performance.
5. Together we establish the business strategy and objectives. Management takes the lead in making the game plan, and we collaborate by offering our view of the big picture. The variables in our strategy usually include balancing internal and external growth, targeting the rate of growth (run, walk, or wait in the shade), and setting the level of capital expenditures.

I call what we do "professional ownership," which doesn't exist in most companies. Businesses without "professional ownership" often become bureaucracies. They are run by politics and seniority; management is secondary. Small companies are often owned and managed by the same persons, and their temptation is to become non-objective and confuse their personal goals and lives with the goals of the business. We take an objective approach instead, determining when to buy, hold, and sell; choosing the degree of risk to be assumed; establishing the relationship of net worth to debt; deciding the number of stock shares outstanding; and setting dividend rates.

And what has worked for me as a professional owner? We have had multiple successful buyouts of manufacturing companies that had experienced executives we could work with closely.

My worst failure was working with someone not experienced in the business we bought. We have also developed and built our companies through innovation. Every successful company is a different one after five years from what we acquired. Innovation means developing new products, adding people who bring new and special talents, adopting new technologies, and turning on management by giving them ownership and challenging them to build and create to their level of ability. In our approach, they have no one to blame but themselves.

Let me sign off by leaving you with two thoughts. First, there are more opportunities available to motivated people today than ever before. Remember that in every problem lies a unique opportunity. Second, small is beautiful, and bigness is clumsy. Just look at the government, major corporations, unions, and gigantic institutions. Going small avoids the structural adversaries that waste the time, money, and energy of business, to wit: government, unions, special interest groups, and all those others who are in business to be your opponent. So stay lean and mean.

The Role of the Venture Capitalist
Professional Dimensions
Nov. 9, 1988

My subject tonight is the role of the venture capitalist. After thirty-five years, this is a subject I should know something about. First, what is venture capital? It is early money. It is high-risk, equity-type capital invested in the early, unproven stages of a business. Its uses can be for development, research, capital equipment, or working capital. It is by its nature speculative.

Why would someone take on high risk and be a speculator? Modern usage has made the term "speculator" a synonym for gambler and plunger. That is not a good connotation. Actually, the word comes from the Latin *speculari*, which means to spy out or observe.

Bernard Baruch defined a speculator as a man who observes the future and acts before it occurs. To be able to do this successfully requires four things:

1. One must get the facts of the situation or problem. You must do your homework or due diligence. In my business, we do this thoroughly and on a large scale.
2. You must interpret the meaning and impact of what those facts will lead to. I think I have been fortunate to have seen opportunity in situations where others have seen only problems. An example is Mortgage Associates. The company was insolvent, but we gained time, shed marginal activities, and focused on residential mortgage originations and sales. In twenty years, the company has gone from nothing to one of the biggest mortgage bankers in the world
3. Besides the facts and the analysis, you need good instincts. Call it intuition, or call it perception.
4. You must act in time before it is too late. Opportunity waits for no one.

Let's talk about the venture capitalist as a personality type. I have heard some describe us as a breed between a riverboat gambler and a mother hen. I prefer to think of a venture capitalist as a systematic risk-maker and risk-taker. I have always been this. I do it. We create situations that in turn create businesses, generate jobs for others and, if successful, yield profits and capital gains for ourselves and those involved in the business with us.

Let me give you the four key characteristics of a venture capital firm:

1. It invests its capital as an equity or co-owner in a high-risk and often untested business. It is not a lender. The goal is appreciation of equity, and make no mistake about that.

2. It is an active, not a passive investor. It is involved in planning, strategy, and often technical advice. It holds management accountable for the mutually agreed upon plans and goals.

3. Its principal objectives and management's are identical, namely to develop and build the company.
4. It has a long-term view of its position as an investor—at least five to ten years.

My firm, Lubar & Co., puts venture capital to work in basic start-ups, in product development, and in leveraged buyouts of operating companies. The niche where we have created our greatest successes to date has been the acquisition of small and medium-sized companies, which, along with management, we build and develop into better, more profitable companies than the ones we started with.

Very often we seem to invest in slow-growing companies in mature industries. In these situations, we seek to be innovative and encourage management to be innovative, with the goal of building market share and earnings growth by:

1. Introduction of new products.
2. Reduction of costs through more modern equipment and technology. We reinvest and automate to be the lowest-cost producer.
3. Improving operations by means of the most advanced computerization.
4. Better marketing and distribution.
5. Efficient capitalization. This is our design. The objective is simplicity and the lowest cost of capital.

If we are a success at our efforts, then five years after acquisition, the company doesn't look like the one we acquired. Let me give you the example of Sorgel Electric, a manufacturer of transformers here in Milwaukee. On the operations side, we automated transformer winding and moved to computer design of transformers. In distribution, we went from selling through manufacturer's reps to stocking national distributors. We also introduced new products, notably heart-monitoring equipment for hospitals.

To illustrate the significance of venture capital in the economy, let me quote from two studies made in the late 1970s. The first, done for the Congressional Ways and Means Committee, concluded that, for every dollar invested by a venture capital firm in a small company, five years later that company will begin paying an average of 35 cents each year in federal, state and local taxes, allocate 33 cents to R&D expenditures, and generate 70 cents in export sales.

Figures compiled by the Government Accountability Office—the GAO—are even more astounding. They found that $209 million invested in seventy-two companies between 1970 and 1979 produced 130,000 jobs, $100 million in corporate tax revenue, $350 million in employee taxes, and $900 million in export sales. It is important to bear in mind that the GAO did a random-sample survey. We have every reason to believe that similar benefits are accruing today, where billions of dollars are at work in venture capital. Compare this with the billions spent on government programs and the modest results they produce.

On a more current basis, I can tell you that over the past ten years, small companies (those with under 500 employees) have created more than all of the net new private jobs in the country. This means large companies have shed employees on a net basis. In fact, since 1980 the Fortune 500 companies have shrunk by a total of 3.1 million employees. During this same period, small companies have created 12 million jobs. Last year 700,000 new companies were created in the U.S., compared with 300,000 in 1975.

I hope that some of you are now asking yourselves if venture capital is a business for you. Anyone can do it, as long as you're willing to put in seventy hours a week, focus your intelligence and curiosity, develop both constructive skepticism and patience, and put off gratification five to ten years into the future. Some might also add that a dash of hedonism will improve the recipe; we are all human. If you're made out of this kind of stuff and have a bit of luck, you will make it as a venture capitalist.

Venture Capital: What and Why
UW-Milwaukee Financiers Roundtable
Mar. 1, 1989

It's good for me to be here with you today. Actually, my partners at Lubar & Co. think that I spend all of my time at UWM as the chairman of the UWM Foundation and president of the Business School Advisory Council. I was also a member of the Fine Arts Advisory Council. Now if this isn't love, it will have to do until the real thing comes along.

I want to talk about venture capital today—what it is, what it does, and why it's important. Venture capital, from whatever source, is the lifeblood of new and developing businesses. The key to the venture capital process is the entrepreneur who starts his or her company. The venture capitalist assists the entrepreneur with the money and expertise necessary to make that company a success.

Venture capitalists generally have a number of characteristics in common. First of all, they finance new and rapidly growing companies. This money is often categorized by the stage of development of the business:

1. Seed money used to develop a business plan or idea. This is usually done by non-professional investors, often friends or relatives.
2. Start-up capital to develop a product, which means creating a business from the beginning. We have done this in software, medical equipment, food, and a number of other businesses.
3. First stage, provided after the business is going, but probably not yet profitable.
4. Second stage or Mezzanine, when a company is profitable but needs expansion funding for inventories, receivables, or new plant.
5. Bridge financing, which carries a company over until it can secure public financing. This is used for acquisitions and a variety of other things.

6. Another type of venture capital is money invested in ailing or mature companies. The challenge here is to revitalize the company by developing new products, better marketing, and using the most advanced technology to create a growth company from what was a mature company. At my firm, we have successfully done this by buying companies in mature industries and then working to make them into growth companies.

Another quality of venture capitalists is active participation. Unlike other investors, the venture capitalist is actively involved, usually on the board level. He provides management with his experience, contacts, and broad business view, hopefully enabling the management to make fewer mistakes.

Venture capitalists also take higher risks with the expectation of higher rewards. Their investment is always equity-oriented—not like a bank's. Failure is always around the corner. As someone once said, "You may be disappointed if you fail, but you are surely doomed if you never try."

Finally, venture capitalists have a long-term orientation. They look down the road five or ten years and sometimes more. The process requires patience if it is to develop properly. If the business is successful, the gains grow and compound geometrically. To have a long-term orientation, one must be able to look ahead. As hockey great Wayne Gretzky said, "I don't skate to where the puck is, but where it will be."

There's nothing particularly new about venture capital. It is as old as America itself. Virtually every company in existence today was started with some form of venture capital, and every one of them started small. There was no alternative. Think about it.

It was after World War II that the venture capital business developed in its modern form. The first computer was created at the University of Pennsylvania on February 13, 1946. Called ENIAC, it consisted of 18,000 vacuum tubes, 70,000 resistors and 10,000 capacitors. It weighed thirty tons, filled an entire room, and consumed so much power that the lights of West Philadelphia dimmed whenever it was turned on. At this time, the first professionally managed venture capital firms were established, including such names as J.H. Whitney & Co. and Venrock. Many of their ventures were related to computers and other electronic devices.

A new development for venture capital at the same time was the formation of American Research and Development. This company raised $5 million through a public offering, the first ever for a venture capital firm. It was headed by General George Doriot, a professor at Harvard Business School. The firm's most renowned investment was made in 1957, when they put $70,000 into Digital Equipment. At one time that investment was worth more than $500 million.

In 1958 the Small Business Investment Company Act was passed by Congress, and a whole new group of professionally staffed, publicly owned venture capital firms were established. I ran one of them. In 1959 I spearheaded the formation of Marine Capital Corporation, which later raised $10 million of capital. Let me just say it was the experience of a lifetime and all kinds of fun.

For the time being, I think I have said enough about venture capital to give you a beginning idea of what it is all about. Now I would like to comment on a related subject: money. So what is money? In itself it has no intrinsic value. Money is simply a means of facilitating business and exchange. The early Phoenicians are said to have invented it, but almost all civilizations have adopted it. The American Indians used shells or wampum as money. Early French Canadians used furs, and early Americans used tobacco. Money is an advance over barter as a means of exchange.

Wisconsin's own Thornton Wilder said, "Money is like manure. It's not worth a thing unless it's spread around." It has to be spent. This is the venture capitalist's view. My father had his own take on the subject: "All you need is enough." The point is that money is not an end unto itself. In my judgment, it is not a worthy object in isolation. Rather it is a means to create wealth, to build businesses and a better society.

Presently, we seem to be passing through a period of extreme greed. Ivan Boesky, the Wall Street arbitrageur, said, "I think greed is healthy." Michael Douglas in the movie *Wall Street* shortened that to "Greed is good." I don't believe that. What I believe in is motivation and incentives, but I don't think greed is good. I think being a part of creating or building a business that serves a legitimate public need is good.

Finally, how do you make money? I can talk at least about what has worked for me. First of all, you must own something. In a private-ownership, capitalistic society, the most certain path to wealth is to own something and see it appreciate. It could be a business or part of it, i.e., stock. It could be real estate, like a farm or a home, or it could be some other type of tangible asset.

This doesn't mean you can't make money by earning a salary or fees. Consider the executives of very large companies or top sport stars or famous entertainers. However, the most doable way for most of us is to create value in a business we are working at.

Once you own something, you must build it; you must add value. To do this, you should concentrate, focus all your efforts on executing your plan. You should also have patience. Let compound interest work.

I hope by now that some of you are asking yourselves, "Is venture capital a business for me?" The answer: Why not? All one needs is a commitment to work seventy hours a week, intelligence, curiosity, constructive skepticism, and patience—as well as a sense of urgency, the ability to see the really big picture, and a willingness to defer gratification of today's efforts for five to ten years into the future.

The Christiana Story
Association for Corporate Growth
Feb. 8, 1991

What I will be talking about today is the Christiana Companies, a New York Stock Exchange firm that I serve as CEO. In 1987, when the Lubar Group came on, Christiana had a pretax loss of some $10 million, no direction or management, a discredited reputation and, worst of all, no plans for the future. The company has come around to one that, in the first six months of 1991, had pretax income of $16.6 million, a focused management, and an ambitious vision for its future. This is the beginning installment of the story. You will have to ask me back in five or ten years for the ensuing chapters.

As background, let me tell you a very little about Lubar & Co.: what we do, what our guiding principles are, and how we became involved with Christiana. Lubar & Co. was formed in 1977 by myself and Jim Rowe. We have three principal activities: management buyouts (where we are essentially backing management), venture capital, and managing our own assets.

The firm consists of nine persons, five of whom are partners. Everyone participates. The companies we have acquired are often in mature industries, and our challenge has been to make these companies grow. This means taking market share from a competitor by means of higher technology, lower costs, better systems, and, we hope, a more motivated management. Management always has a meaningful ownership stake in our investments. I describe what we do as professional ownership. The people we work with are professional managers.

In the past, we have been investors or owners in industries such as electrical distribution equipment, hydraulics, gears, food-processing, computer software, molded silicone, shipbuilding, financial services, energy production, telecommunications, leather manufacturing, and a number of others.

Now let's talk about Christiana. Christiana Oil Corporation was formed in 1953 by a group of investors in Wilmington, Delaware.

They were Martin Fenton and George Weymouth, of Laird & Co., and Thomas Brittingham, a notable benefactor of the University of Wisconsin. They began by investing in oil and gas production and later invested in gold mining. The company was headquartered in Denver until the late 1950s, when they moved to Beverly Hills, California. I believe the move had to do with their acquisition of a 40-percent interest in 7,300 acres of land within thirty minutes of downtown Los Angeles.

By 1960 Christiana had sold its oil and gas holdings, purchased several title companies, plus an interest in a broadcasting group, and were full-scale into home-building. Their home-building and land development efforts were very successful. In 1962 they started development of Huntington Beach. On 878 acres of undeveloped tidal marsh, Christiana developed over 5,000 homes, several marinas, access to ocean boating, and numerous amenities. Today's value would certainly be in the billions of dollars.

Their other large home-building success was Tierrasanta, a 1,600-acre development in San Diego. In 1969 Christiana purchased 2,600 acres from the General Services Administration that had been a portion of the Navy's Camp Elliott. Fully 1,600 of these acres were marked for development, and by 1982 Christiana had constructed and sold 3,200 homes.

Other developments were taken on, but none with the success of Huntington Beach and Tierrasanta. In fact, if the company had focused on only these two developments, its history would have been quite different; its success would have been substantial. Instead the company meandered into airplane leasing, computer leasing, commercial real estate development, title insurance (in Arizona and southern California), magazine publishing (*Venture* magazine), investment management, ownership of F.A.O. Schwarz (a toy retailer), retirement housing (Remington Club), condominium conversion (Cross Creek), and mortgage banking (in Texas).

All of the above were losers to greater or lesser degrees. The amazing thing is that, despite these losses and distractions, the excessive overhead the company carried, and the 22-percent interest rates of the late 1970s and early '80s, Christiana kept moving along in a marginal sort of way. Annual income was usually around $750,000, but it reached $4.2 million in 1979 and $2.5 million in 1980. However, after 1980 it was all downhill.

The company fell so hard and so fast that in 1985 stock control (48 percent) of the business was sold to two Texas S&Ls. Fortunately, they didn't have the time or opportunity to get too involved with Christiana, and by 1986 both S&Ls were being run by the FSLIC and the State of Texas. The board seats they had held were given up, and a caretaker chairman, Joseph Antonow, a director and the company's general counsel, took over as chairman.

In December, 1986, 1 was contacted by Mr. Antonow. At this time Joe was about seventy-one. He was a highly respected lawyer in Chicago, and we knew him from acquiring two of his clients. Joe called and asked if I would buy out the holdings of the two brain-dead S&Ls. Jim Rowe and I batted the situation back and forth. At this time Christiana was involved in over 100 lawsuits resulting from a class action for construction defects, but it appeared to have a good asset base of real estate. At the end of the day, I asked Jim what he thought. He said, "Let's do it." We purchased the stock of one of the S&Ls, amounting to about 12 percent of the total, and bought an equal amount of newly issued shares from the company, so we went in owning 24 percent. Two years later, we bought the other S&L shares from what was now the FHLBB or FSLIC, for 80 percent of what we had offered earlier. In the interim, the company had a rights offering to raise new capital, which the Lubar Group in effect underwrote.

In fall of 1987, I took over as chairman and CEO. With some reluctance on his part, Jim took over as chief financial officer. Our program to resurrect Christiana was simple. First we settled the lawsuits. We settled or litigated to conclusion over 100 of them, so those costs and the drag they entailed are behind us. Worst of all was a wrongful death lawsuit, which was settled. Next we cut overhead. We went from forty people in San Diego to two in California, plus Lubar & Co. in Milwaukee. What NYSE company has two people?

Then we went on to liquidation. We extracted ourselves from the multitude of private investments that had been accumulated over the years. Remington Club was sold for $2 to $3 million, FAO Schwarz for $5 million (plus a lease), Gordon Ranch for $1.3 million, and various others for significant amounts. We also sold real estate, bringing in $13.3 million for a tract on Interstate 52, $1.7 million for a shopping center, and $3 million for fifteen houses that sold for about $200,000 each.

We also raised capital to grow with, including $11.4 million from a rights offering. In 1989 Christiana bought 60 percent of Prideco, a manufacturer of heavyweight pipe for oil and gas drilling. Prideco has grown by 100 percent in each of the past three years. This year's sales should be over $30 million, with earnings of over $2 million.

What is Christiana's future? This year we had big earnings from land sales—over $13 million in the first six months. We now have approximately $37 million of cash. Prideco is growing, and we see it continuing to grow into a $100 million business. We are studying the best strategic course of action regarding the 365 condominiums we own in Tierrasanta in San Diego. They are carried on our books for $11.9 million. A recent study leads us to believe they would retail for a total of $45 to $50 million. This could be our capital bank for the future.

Our strategy for growth is to acquire and build sound operating companies. We have a good start with Prideco. We have the knowledge to expand further in the energy industry. Our highest priority is a major acquisition that will truly have a major impact on Christiana.

So what guides us? Making acquisitions is a hard way to make a living, and we have survived by following a few basic principles:

1. We seek to associate ourselves with management people who have integrity, experience, and a commitment to work hard.
2. We want management to own a share of the company that is meaningful to them so that their goals and objectives will be identical to ours.

3. We don't like overhead. Buckminster Fuller said, "Less is more." He was talking about overhead and its effects on profits.

4. We believe in reinvestment in our companies as a creator of value. Our policy has always been to bring the highest level of usable technology to our companies. This is the road to being a low-cost producer.

5. Our idea of effective marketing starts with producing the highest-quality products and offering our customers the best service.

Though business conditions and opportunities change, we don't think these guiding principles will.

Let me close by discussing how I manage and what has worked for me. In its most basic form, my management approach has the characteristics of small scale. It is paternalistic, personal, opportunistic, and flexible. It does not follow the traditional pattern of bureaucracy and professional structure we typically see in U.S. business. Ten years ago, Peter Drucker did a study that showed GM to have fifty-two levels of approval. That is the antithesis of what I believe. I get sick thinking about it. For me, the best organization is the flattest.

Charles Handy, the Irish management thinker, describes the organizational approach I seem to follow as federalism. It implies a variety of individual groups allied together under a common flag with some shared identity. Federalism seeks to make it big by keeping it small. What I have is a circular organization with me, and a very few other people, in the center and our operating companies on the outside. Information and ideas flow both ways. The work is not being done in the center, but the center makes sure it knows how the work is going. The center chooses who runs each organization. It concurs or approves of new investments. It can only function if it is respected by the outlying organizations and in turn respects them. To use Handy's language, it is a 'tight-loose" organization.

Is this the model for the new corporate organization? I don't know but, as I said, it works for me.

Practicing Venture Capitalism
The Economic Forum
Oct. 16, 1996

I am very pleased to be with you today. I am aware of the many distinguished speakers who have been with you before. My subject today is venture capital. I hope to give you some insights into this mysterious business, at least the way we do it at Lubar & Co.

First of all, what is venture capital? It is high-risk, equity-type capital invested in the early, unproven stages of a business or in any high-risk business transaction. Its uses can be for development, capital equipment, working capital, or acquisitions. It is by its nature higher-risk and speculative.

Venture capital is as old as America itself. When entrepreneur Christopher Columbus convinced Queen Isabella of Spain to back his innovative idea—a faster route to the riches of the Far East—that was the spirit of venture capitalism. He used the capital he raised to buy and provision the *Nina, Pinta* and *Santa Maria,* and off he went. The result of this investment, which never did accomplish its goal of reaching the Far East, was still untold wealth and the rise of the Spanish Empire over the next centuries. I am afraid C.C. never got his fair share of the deal.

Until World War II, venture investing was primarily done by wealthy families or syndicates organized by investment bankers such as J.P. Morgan or the Rothschilds. Eli Whitney was able to develop the cotton gin through backing from his wealthy friends. This was also the case for Henry Ford in the development of his automobile, although he later resented the participation of his investors. The railroads and canals in the United States were largely financed by British and Scottish venture capital, and the returns were handsome.

Virtually every business in existence was started with some form of venture capital, since every business has its roots in a small business. In 1911, a group of wealthy investors combined three companies to form the Computer-Tabulating-Recording Company, which later become IBM. I learned, much to my surprise, that an early leveraged buyout happened in the early 1920s, when Coca-Cola, then a small soft drink company, was acquired by Robert Woodruff and financed by his family and friends. He built it into today's giant. Venture investments by Laurence Rockefeller in 1938 and 1939 started Eastern Airlines and McDonnell Aircraft.

Let's move on to the practice of venture capital. I said that it is by nature high-risk and speculative. Although I don't think of myself as a gambler or speculator, I am a risk-taker. In understanding myself, I realized I liked the feeling of doing something chancy and succeeding. As a very young boy, I liked to ride my bicycle across a narrow railroad trestle that crossed the Milwaukee River in Estabrook Park, but I always knew where the train was and what I would do if it surprised me. Most people think climbing a mountain is risky, but my mountain experience has never left me feeling I was risking life or limb.

Staying alive in the venture business requires adhering to a few basic principles. Assuming you have a business opportunity that looks interesting, this is how you would proceed:

1. Get all of the background and facts. This means understanding the business, industry, people, financial information, and the particular situation. Then check it again. As the sign at the Chicago Press Club reads, "If your mother says she loves you, check it out."

2. Next you must interpret the meaning and impact of where those facts lead. Most important, you must recognize a business opportunity even it if is camouflaged. You need good instincts or perception. You must act in time, before it is too late. John Hancock said: "Many men have good thoughts, good plans, good intentions. Precious few put them into action." Opportunity can rarely be put on hold.

And how does our venture capital perform? The real business of a venture capitalist is to be the systematic risk-maker and risk-taker. We create situations that in turn create businesses, jobs for others, and, if successful, profits and capital gains for ourselves and those involved in business with us. Let me talk about the characteristics of our firm:

1. We invest our money in some form of equity and expect to become a meaningful shareholder. We are not lenders; we are partners. We provide more than money; we hopefully bring wisdom and ideas as well.

2. We are very active, not passive, investors. We are involved in planning strategy and often in locating people. We hold management accountable for the plans and goals we mutually agree upon.

3. We have a long-term view of our ownership position. In fact today we consider our positions permanent. This differentiates us from other venture investors who are investing money from funds they have raised, usually from large institutions. Their incentives are to get in and out in the shortest possible time so as to achieve the highest annual rate of return. We are different.

4. I characterize our firm as professional owners. The concept developed from the traditional inability of ownership to interact with the boards of directors of the companies in which they'd invested. Whether it involved setting goals, monitoring the performance of management, or truly understanding the business of the company and the impact of conditions outside of their control, the voice of ownership was not heard. We insist on being heard in every investment we make.

Lubar & Co. has been involved in basic start-ups, in growth investing, and most often in buyouts of operating companies. The niche where our best successes have come from has been buyouts of small or medium-sized companies, which ideally, together with management, we build and develop into better, more profitable companies than the ones we started with.

Very often we invest in companies that are in mature, slow-growing industries. In these situations our challenge is to be innovative and create a growth company. We do it by:

1. Developing new products.
2. Reducing costs by converting to the most modern equipment and technology, which enables us to become the low-cost producer.
3. Accelerating computerization.
4. Efficient, simple capitalization, rather than high-yield debt, excessive fees, or other common practices.
5. Reinvesting cash flow to reduce costs, develop new facilities and products, and reduce debt. We don't pay dividends.

If we are successful, we achieve growth, usually at the expense of our competitors. Let me conclude with a quote from Albert Einstein. He wasn't a venture capitalist in the true sense, but for me he captured what is required:

> I believe in intuition and inspiration.... At times I feel certain that I am right while not knowing the reasons.... Imagination is more important than knowledge. For knowledge is limited, whereas imagination embraces the entire world, stimulating progress, giving birth to evolution.

My Four Guidelines
UW-Milwaukee
Executive MBA Commencement
May 14, 2004

I am honored to be with you tonight, and I want to offer my most sincere congratulations to each of you graduating and receiving your Executive MBA. I have been around this program from the beginning, and I have some sense of the work, sacrifice, and sleep deprivation you have all experienced to reach this point. I also want to congratulate the support groups who helped get you here: your spouses, parents, children, friends, family, and the faculty.

Finally, let me commend your employers—those fine persons who allowed you the time and financial support that you needed to do what you have done. I expect that the person who returns with his or her MBA will be a different employee from the one who embarked on this program two years ago. Perhaps the challenge for your employers will be to direct the energy, confidence, and maturity you have developed so as to gain the maximum positive input for your company.

Having said that, I thought it might be useful if I were to spend my time by simply sharing with you four guidelines that have served me in my career, and hopefully will be of help to you in yours. These are principles that I have developed through my experiences:

First, be an innovator. An innovator is someone who sees what everyone else is seeing, but thinks what very few are thinking. An innovator seeks change. Let me bring this closer to home. Most businesses, if judged fairly, would be considered to be in slow-growth, mature industries. For example, consider warehousing, construction, manufacturing, and banking. Most of you, like me, are probably involved in mature industries, and yet it has been my experience that the best-performing companies are those in mature industries whose management focused their efforts on growing their company by bringing new ideas and new technologies to their mature markets. They are innovators. They changed the status quo.

I speak with conviction about the potential and the profitability of innovation in mature companies, because I have built a career and business on doing just that. Our firm, Lubar & Co., has participated with various managements in making growth businesses out of companies engaged in such prosaic activities as leather-tanning, malting, hydraulics, transformers, refrigerated warehousing, metal-machining, contract oil and gas drilling, and many other equally ordinary businesses. I can't tell you that every one of our investments was a growth success story, but I can say that many of them were. I can also tell you that five years after our acquisition, the successful companies didn't look like the companies we had acquired. We had changed them by upgrading equipment, developing new products, new customers and suppliers, and new systems. The innovators in the business had caused the changes

Number two, be a builder. Take the long-term view, and act as though you personally owned the company where you work. Conduct yourself as though every dollar the company spends and earns is yours. When I become involved with a company, my mindset is that it is a permanent holding and that my single objective is to see this business develop an ever-growing and high-quality stream of earnings. Our approach is to reinvest all earnings to develop the people, products, technology, and systems of the business. Although I have short-term plans, they exist only within the context of a long-term plan and strategy. I think I always know where I am trying to go, even if I often get lost along the way. By taking this approach, I establish common and unified goals with each person in the company. By unified goals, I mean that the single thing all of us in the company have in common is to build the business to the maximum we are able.

Third, always remember that defeats and failures are inevitable, but they are temporary. If you are an innovator and a builder, by definition you must be a risk-taker, and risk-takers don't win them all. Remember the turtle makes no progress until it sticks its neck out. I love the challenge and thrill involved in strategizing, analyzing, and risk-taking. I can tell you I also know the pain and embarrassment of failing. It's a price I have been willing to pay for the joy of seeing something work and of confirming my judgment, and ultimately enjoying the fruits of winning. Perhaps Thomas Aquinas put it best when he said, "If you take no risk, you suffer no defeats, nor will you enjoy any victories."

It's probably not necessary to remind you of how many times Thomas Edison failed before he developed a light bulb that worked, or of the multiple failures of Alexander Graham Bell before he created the telephone. So I say: Aim high, don't be afraid to fail, and when you do, pick yourself up and move ahead.

My fourth and final guideline is to put something back. I speak with confidence when I say that people with your education, living in this great community in the greatest country in the world, are going to be successful. The greater your level of commitment and effort, the greater will be your success. As this happens, I urge you to give some of this success back to your community and your university. Like the farmer who holds back some of his corn as seed for the future, remember that we all have a debt to the system that made it possible. Giving some of your time and money can be as rewarding to you as it is necessary to those following you in the years ahead.

Thank you for listening. Good luck, and be well.

Six Big Decisions
Harvard Business School Club of Wisconsin
Milwaukee Journal Sentinel
Business Leader of the Year Award
May 3, 2005

I am grateful and humbled to be chosen as Wisconsin's Business Leader of the Year. I want to start with some thanks, first of all to the *Milwaukee Journal Sentinel*. I have read the *Journal* or *Sentinel* or both almost every day of my life. (See what it does for you?) I remember the Green Sheet, the Pink Sheet, and all else. There was a time when it was fashionable to love or hate Milwaukee's only newspaper. I assure you that today I love the *Journal Sentinel* and respect their place in our community.

I also extend my thanks to the Harvard Business School Club of Wisconsin. One must have enormous respect for Harvard. It is the first of now many business schools. As a school, it has led the way in making business a profession. It is or should be the role model for every business school. I have great admiration for Harvard and what it stands for.

I want to thank my family: Marianne, my wife of almost fifty-three years, my partner, my critic, my best fan; and my children:

David, who is my friend and business colleague and son; Susan, a ray of sunshine; Joan, an undeniable winner; Kris; and their spouses. They are all my best supports.

I thank my business colleagues from Lubar & Co. and Darby Overseas who are here. No one can do it alone. And I thank my good friend and colleague Bernard Duroc-Danner for being here this evening and talking about the world of energy. I have focused most of my business efforts for the past thirty years on the business of energy—the oil patch. No one in the world understands this subject as well as Bernard, and no one strategizes it better. I can only describe Bernard as a driven genius. He is nonstop. You don't start from zero and build a $20 billion company without being driven. I am fortunate to be associated with him, and hopefully he feels the same.

Finally, but equally important, I want to thank all of you, my good friends, associates, and people who have helped me along the way. Thank you for being with me today. It is very meaningful to me.

On any occasion such as this, it is not unusual to look back at a career of more than fifty years and ask yourself what you did that made a difference in your outcome. I believe there are only perhaps a half-dozen decisions in one's lifetime that truly make a real difference. If I might be permitted, here are my six:

1. Above everything, education. That includes college, advanced degrees, and continuing, never-stop education. You must always read, ask, and listen.

2. You must know yourself. Early in the game, I realized that I am an independent person. I don't like people telling me what to do. I like to be at the head of the pack. And though I admire leaders of large companies, I knew I couldn't pay the price of being a small cog in a large organization until a chance at the top was possible. Better to be a big fish in a small pond. Steering my own ship was a necessity, a priority for me.

3. It's crucial to pick the right spouse. Life is too short and your focus is too important to cope with a tumultuous home life. I know I did that right. My heart bleeds for children who have never had a father in their home. My advice to a young person is to graduate from high school, hopefully go to college, and marry before you have children.

4. I have been fortunate to choose wonderful CEOs. In my numerous business and civic involvements, I have been able to ally myself with good, honest people who are proud of what they do—people who can be motivated. Really, that was my job. I am a coach, but, perhaps more important, a cheerleader. Remember, none of us can do it alone. We need the support of our colleagues. As Hillary Clinton said, "It takes a village."

5. I have trusted my instincts. At the end of the day, I did my homework and knew what to do. My mistakes occurred only when I allowed myself to be persuaded to act against my instincts and judgment. I have tried to preach this to my children: Think for yourself.

6. Finally, longevity is important. I believe we can all affect this. In terms of productivity, I have had a huge advantage over the successful executive whose company has mandatory retirement at age sixty-five. I can keep playing as long as my health permits. So my final advice is stay healthy. Run, walk, climb, swim, bike, stay active. Even play golf. Certainly, eat lots of broccoli!

From the bottom of my heart, thank you and God bless you.

My Own "Great Journey"
University of Wisconsin – Milwaukee
Golda Meir Library
Sept. 25, 2006

I am pleased and honored to be with you this evening as the first speaker in this wonderful series about "Great Journeys." Fifty years ago, I was sitting where you students are now. If some of what I have experienced and learned can be of help to you, I will consider this evening a success.

I grew up in Whitefish Bay, Wisconsin, graduated from Whitefish Bay High School in 1947, then from the University of Wisconsin-Madison with a Bachelor of Business Administration in 1951 and a Bachelor of Laws in 1953. My remarks tonight concern some of the critical lifetime decisions I have made so far during my seventy-seven years. In my judgment, there are no more than a very few decisions that really determine what you will be and where you will go—certainly no more than ten. However, they collectively direct your course and determine your fate.

The first is education. All of my early life, my parents talked of the value of education and the importance of doing well in school. Going to college was not a decision for me; it was simply assumed that if you wanted to be anything serious, then graduating from high school and college was a given. From education comes knowledge, and from knowledge and experience come wisdom. Wisdom is respected and gives you the power to lead.

I recently read a lecture given by one of my favorite and most respected authors, David McCullough, who spoke of one of our great Americans, Thomas Jefferson. In the Declaration of Independence, Jefferson wrote of "life, liberty and the pursuit of happiness." What he meant by "happiness" wasn't longer vacations or more material or consumer goods. He was talking about the enlargement of the human experience through the life of the mind and the life of the spirit. And he knew that the system of government he and his colleagues were setting up—democracy—wouldn't work if the people weren't educated. Jefferson wrote, "If a nation expects to be ignorant and free, it expects what never was and never will be." Just consider that for a moment. To be a player you must be educated.

Commitment to lifetime education is first and foremost in my judgment. Education can never cease. You must be a listener, a questioner, a reader, a viewer, and finally a thinker. Education is Decision One in a successful life. Pursuing it is a lifetime assignment. If you stop, you stop. I have never stopped. I am always reading, listening, questioning, and thinking.

The second decision is marriage. Very few of us can do it alone. I know I couldn't. (Isn't that right, Marianne?) So choose the right person to be your lifetime mate, collaborator, partner, parent of your children, supporter after your inevitable disappointments and defeats, and cheerleader for your successes. How do you know you're making the right choice? It's all about character: integrity, sharing high values, integrity and more integrity with each other. Life is not easy; we all need a real partner.

Career comes third. As a teenager, it seems that I was always trying to find a job and earn money for myself. It wasn't that I had to help support myself, but I wanted to be independent, to not ask for money. Besides, I liked working. I cut lawns, shoveled snow, and caddied at Ozaukee Country Club in summer. By the time I was sixteen, I could get a summer job in a factory. I worked at Cutler-Hammer, A. O. Smith, and a local tannery. I quickly learned all the things I would never want to do.

Once I was in college, I discovered that my guiding principle was spelled out by Henry David Thoreau. I read his words and have kept a copy of them in my wallet for fifty years: "Go confidently in the direction of your dreams. Live the life you have imagined." He is telling us to pursue our passion. Your passion will undoubtedly change, since the world itself and everything around you is constantly changing, but whatever you are doing, pursue it with all your energy.

I am a great believer in looking ahead and planning. We do it in business, you do it when playing chess, so why not do it in your life and career? Today's buzzword is "thinking outside the box." Wonderful, but first think ahead. What is your next move? And yet I don't think of myself as a long-term planner. I try to know generally where I am going, but because I am opportunity-oriented, I move ahead with a series of constantly updated short-term plans. Vince Lombardi captured the idea when he said, "Run to daylight." As circumstances change, so do my views and plans, but not my long-term goals.

So what were my goals? At the university, it was simply to graduate, then it was to graduate law school, then it was to receive a direct commission in the Air Force in the Judge Advocate Group. If I did that, I wouldn't have to think of my future. It was a four-year enlistment; I would learn the law, gain experience, and be paid more than I was worth. I viewed it as a four-year vacation with pay. But, as I said, conditions change, and a few weeks after graduation, and after I had been sworn into the Wisconsin Bar early, I received a letter thanking me for my interest in joining the Air Force and advising me that, with the end of the Korean War, my program was terminated.

My moment of reality had arrived. Here I was, a married man. Marianne and I were expecting our first child, I had no job, and I knew I really didn't want to practice law. I wanted to learn about big business, not small business, and I determined I could best do that if I could get a job at a downtown commercial bank. I am really not sure why I came to that conclusion. Perhaps it was because in my last year of law school I won a statewide contest for estate planning sponsored by the Wisconsin Bankers Association.

I told myself that my first job was to find a job that would enable me to learn and grow. I interviewed with the downtown banks in Chicago and Milwaukee. I can't say the banking community was clamoring for my talents, but I did receive a number of offers from the Chicago banks and one offer in Milwaukee from the Marine National Exchange Bank. Marine was smaller than M&I or First Wisconsin. It was exclusively a commercial bank and trust company. I wanted to be in Milwaukee, not Chicago. The pay was less than in Chicago, but money was not a consideration. It was enough for our young family. I had made a critically correct decision that would positively affect the future direction of my business career and life.

At the Marine, I was the only lawyer on the commercial banking side. I progressed from tax analyst to credit analyst to commercial loan officer. Then I helped form a bank holding company, formed an SBIC (a vehicle for venture capital), ran the SBIC, and ultimately became a venture capitalist myself. It was a time for change, for shifting gears. I loved the bank and I was proud of my association with it. I loved my work and looked forward to it every day. I worked very hard. I was doing fun things, helping companies and, in my mind, playing in the big leagues. Some of my customers were large companies such as Allen-Bradley and Briggs & Stratton. Some were almost start-ups, some were just growing businesses. I was doing worthwhile things, I felt. I wasn't making much money by today's standards, but we had enough and we were happy, "we" being Marianne and our four children. I did this until the mid-1960s.

But after ten years, people change, institutions change, and I am sure I changed. I wanted independence. I wanted to be my own boss. I wanted to be a principal acting for my own account, not an agent. Based on my experience in banking and venture capital, I had developed a concept that I called "Professional Ownership." It was about how professional investors should work with professional management. I felt my technique was a new system for private investing that separated ownership from management but combined the skills of both and aligned their objectives. I determined I would become a "Professional Owner." It was a way to buy a smaller company and build it into a larger, better one. I have done it twenty or more times and, with only a very few exceptions, I have done it with great success.

We don't have the time, nor is this the place, to examine all of the aspects of Professional Ownership, but I can tell you that it has worked beyond my expectations. I will save that discussion for a course in corporate growth strategy. What I will say is that venturing off on my own was certainly a life-changing critical decision. It could also have been a failure.

I know that it isn't always you alone that makes something happen. Some say it can be good fortune or luck. "Wasn't Lubar lucky to find that electrical engineering and manufacturing company and have it grow exponentially?" However, I prefer to think that you largely make your own luck, that the harder you work, the luckier you get. But I have also learned the value of an original idea.

What I haven't talked about in this journey is dealing with failures. I assure you that they are inevitable if you are out there in the competitive world. You will have failures. I have, and I know the pain they bring. Nor have I touched on giving back—public and community service and all of our obligations to those who need a helping hand in getting their lives together. I now spend more than half my time on community and nonprofit projects. Nor have I talked about the time I spent in the Nixon, Ford, and Carter Administrations. Again that is for another time.

My final thought is that we are all so fortunate to live and grow up in the United States and particularly in Wisconsin. Opportunity is out there for the taking. It requires only hard work and diligence. You have a great life ahead of you. You have every reason to be optimists. Don't ever forget that what happens is in your control. You may have to make lemonade out of lemons, but ultimately you determine what happens. I envy you the exciting years that lie ahead for you.

Knowing Yourself
University Club of Milwaukee
June 25, 2014

I have spoken many times regarding my career, my life in business, about housing and government, about Wisconsin and Milwaukee County government, but I have never spoken on why I believe that in my long business career I have been successful. By most measures, things have worked for me beyond anything I might have expected or intended. I say this in all humility. Money was never an objective. My father told me all you need is enough. For me, it was about independence.

I will talk about that with you this morning. I will try to make this a conversation, eliciting your questions, responses, statements, and experiences. My object is to share and provoke, to be helpful and constructive.

I start with the belief that most of us are not much different from each other. In other words, most of us start out very equal. It is through our life experiences that we develop, but everyone is different. Some persons work harder, study harder, and become more disciplined. Some understand that honesty is the only way to live. Others don't, and they usually pay a heavy price. Some realize that good habits are necessary, and all of these habits make up your character. An example is poverty. I learned in Washington there are many causes, including family background, disease, or physical and mental conditions.

In my life, I was the youngest child. I had two older sisters, and my parents felt their job was to educate their children and provide for them. As the only boy, I was special in our family. No doubt this was undeserved. The result was that I developed a level of confidence and self-assurance probably beyond what I merited, but it has been extremely important throughout my life. It never occurred to me that I couldn't do any task or job. From that basic platform I would plan.

When I was a boy, I would ride my bicycle to Estabrook Park over a railroad trestle, confident I could avoid a train coming at me. I knew where I'd leap off if I had to. When I worked at the Marine Bank, there was never an assignment that, given the opportunity, I didn't jump at. If asked to take on something new, I always said "Yes." In fact, that led me to always welcome the next assignment, the next challenge.

The result was that I did a great many things. I took a great many risks and never considered that I couldn't do them. I never said "No" to anything. "Fail" is still not in my lexicon. If something doesn't work as planned, I make a new plan.

That was my self-description. Let's now talk about getting to know yourself. For most people, work is something that is required to receive pay that will provide support for yourself and your family. For me, my work was fun. Last week I spent five days fishing in Canada. I had a great deal of fun, but I must confess it was WORK—dealing with rain, dealing with gear, and so on. When I returned to Milwaukee late Tuesday afternoon, my mail and my emails were at my home waiting for me. I started what some people would call work and what I call the most gratifying part of my life, second only to my family. That is me.

Getting back to my initial inquiry: getting to know yourself. It took many years for me to understand myself. I am a loner. I do things that I can control. I am a good delegator, but I don't see myself as a team player. My most important goal in business was independence. In business, I very early concluded that I didn't want partners. I ask questions, I get other information and opinions, but at the end of the day, I make the decisions. Is this the best process? For me, the answer is "Yes."

Any questions of me before I ask some of you? Do you know yourself and where you are going?

Our Future Together
Ixonia Bank Employee Retreat
Oct. 12, 2015

It's great to have us all together. I look forward to these opportunities of everyone being together and discussing the future plans of Ixonia Bank and also Ixonia Bancshares, our holding company. We are all united in this investment—you with your careers, me with my time and capital. We are all teammates on the Ixonia Team, as I will discuss shortly.

Let me explain my role at Ixonia. Officially, I have been elected by the shareholders of Ixonia Bancshares as a director of the Ixonia Bank and the president and chief executive officer of Ixonia Bancshares. But my true function is as a Professional Owner. This term and how it functions are based on a concept I developed with the collaboration of a wonderful man, Bob Moon, more than fifty years ago. Since then I have based my career on this concept of Professional Ownership. I can tell you that it has worked.

This concept recognizes two kinds of corporate governance. One is the relatively small business where the controlling shareholder is also the CEO, or the boss. Generally speaking, this person's objective is to have the business pay for his (or rarely her) lifestyle: cars, trips, and anything else that could be charged to the company. In effect, this boss (and often majority shareholder) is accountable only to himself. This has generally worked to create a modest enterprise that gives the boss a satisfactory lifestyle.

Then there is the (usually) larger company that almost always has public shareholders, who in almost all cases are passive. These shareholders are satisfied as long as their dividends continue to grow and their shares appreciate, but generally they don't feel they can do much if the company starts to perform poorly except sell their stock.

Now in my case, the case of the Professional Owner, our object is to build a bigger, better, more profitable business—a business that will produce the best results for the shareholders and all employees. The Professional Owner takes little or, in my case, nothing in cash compensation. Our compensation is in the value created from a dynamic, profitable business.

My functional job is to work with the CEO of the enterprise, in our case Dan Westrope, to plan the future, help grow the company, and see to it that this strategy, if successful, satisfies the goals of shareholders and employees. The objective is to make sure that all succeed together or, if things don't work, we all feel the pain together.

Let me review what has happened in the past three years. In Phase I, we recapitalized the bank. By 2012 Ixonia had lost virtually all of its capital. The challenge for Phil Holland was to find an investor. He did—the Lubar family and Mr. Selig, who is now a director of Bancshares—and together we invested $27.3 million to buy 83.6 percent of the unissued stock of the bank in 2012 and 2013. Perhaps 90 percent of the investment capital came from Lubar. I wanted to get back into banking, and Ixonia was my choice.

Phase II began in June, 2012, and our goal was to collect marginal and sour loans, sell off bank-owned real estate, restore our balance sheet, and end the Memorandum of Understanding with the FDIC that was hanging over the bank and regulating most of its actions. There was also Federal Reserve Bank oversight. Both were eliminated in June, 2015, when the FDIC raised our rating, which three years previous had been Number 5, to Number 2. We are now free to grow and focus on profitability.

Now we are embarked on Phase III: Profitability, Vision, and Mission. Remember my opening words to you three years ago? I said we would focus on Soundness, Profitability, and Growth, in that order. Those are our marching orders. No matter what happens, they will always be the same.

Let me emphasize that a business cannot be successful unless it has a plan for what it intends to do and a team of employees who are capable of executing that plan. The greatest business results, or innovations, come not from a single person, or by solving problems from the top down. The great successes come from everyone working together, from each person understanding what he or she is responsible for and working as a member of the Team to execute a particular part of the plan. It is always the Team, and everyone on the Team executing his or her assignment.

It is about the Team! Team! Team!, which is as important as soundness, profitability, and growth. Vince Lombardi ran the Packers that way, Steve Jobs ran Apple that way, and that is how we must run Ixonia Bank and its parent, Ixonia Bancshares. Everything we do must be a collaborative effort involving every one of you in ways that Dan Westrope, CEO of the bank, will be explaining to each of you and working with all of you to execute as we move forward.

Our overall objective for the bank, as well as the holding company, is to go from where we are today—a $300 million bank in the "Lake Country" of Wisconsin that is earning a modest profit—to a much larger, more diversified financial enterprise earning a targeted return on its equity capital of 15 percent. We can do this with the collaboration and commitment of each of you, and we will do it.

The future for the bank and the holding company is based on new as well as established activities. Let me outline generally what I see ahead, first for the bank:

1. We will improve our processes and our systems and reduce our costs.
2. We will continually build and expand our commercial lending to mid-sized and small businesses, and we will grow our home mortgage business. These efforts are happening now, and we can see we are gaining momentum and have great opportunities ahead.
3. We will be involved in wealth management on a greater scale than the single-person effort we currently have at the bank.
4. We will strive to be market leaders in particular market segments, including mid-sized and small business, women business leaders, and elderly persons in need of trust and wealth management services.

5. We will acquire trust powers that will enable us to act as an executor of estates, a trustee of trusts, and generally take part in all fiduciary activities. Ken Krei was recently added to the Bancshares board. He previously ran the M&I trust and money management business. Ken is an excellent addition for us, and his experience will help guide our efforts in this business.

We also have big plans for our holding company:

1. An investment fund making higher-risk debt and equity investments in mid-sized and small companies that need more equity–type capital to be bankable. I have extensive experience in this field, as do my colleagues at Lubar & Co.
2. Sale of insurance products. Most banks have an insurance agency, and at some point I hope we can too. We'll probably start with an acquisition, but we will explore and consider all possibilities.

That's the outline of what we are thinking. I am pleased with where we are after these past three years, and I am proud of all of you.

Chapter 2

The Importance of Education

Into the 21st Century
UW Extension Conference
Oct. 3, 1995

As we look ahead to the twenty-first century, I would like to make a few general background points:

First, as a businessman, I can tell you that in my forty-two years in business here in Milwaukee, the outlook for the economy of our entire state has never looked better. We are on a path of steady, maintainable growth. I see no excesses in inventory build-up or construction over-building. Things are in balance. Unemployment in the state is at a record low of 3.1 percent. Our banks are sounder and more liquid than they have been in the last twenty-five years, and they are eager to lend to business. This will drive businesses. It just doesn't get any better.

That's the good news. The not-so-good-news, regrettably, is that I see our society developing into two tiers. Not rich and poor, not young and old, but effectively educated and trained or uneducated and untrained. If you fit into the first category, you will participate in a prosperous economy the likes of which the world hasn't seen before. But if you are uneducated and untrained, your lot will be to compete with the working population of the Third World at low wages. This is sad but true. It is globalization, and it is happening; you can't hide from it. That is why I believe our state's highest priority should be education and training.

UW Extension represents the ultimate in the Wisconsin Idea, which is that "The borders of the University are the borders of the State." The people of Extension have made it their educational mission to teach young and old, full-time and part-time, people with families and people seeking new careers. They are there for each of our lifetimes. What they are doing is important to all of us. They are preparing our citizens to be more productive, prosperous, and happy.

The Board of Regents is in the process of a planning study to help to determine where the University of Wisconsin should be in the twenty-first century. At this time, we have defined five key topics as our focus:

1. Access and affordability
2. Future funding and revenue structures
3. Mission and roles: Capturing the synergies of the system
4. Program array
5. Instructional technology and distance education

These are broad, all-encompassing subjects, and I see strong roles and contributions from UW Extension in all of them. I hope this tells you that we at UW are working to help all of our citizens learn, and to help them better help themselves. I want to thank everyone at UW Extension for what you are doing and assure you of my continued support.

Wisconsin's Two-Year Centers
UW Center-Rock County Commencement
May 18, 1997

We are gathered here today to celebrate the positive power of family, community, and learning. I am honored to join with you in congratulating the members of the University of Wisconsin Center-Rock County 1997 graduating class. Today, I bring greetings and congratulations on behalf of the UW Board of Regents, as well as from the UW four-year institutions in which many of you will enroll next fall as juniors, well-prepared for continued success and academic achievement.

Our two-year centers have a very important mission in the UW System. Statewide, the centers offer exceptional quality, value, and access to thousands of students who might otherwise never have the opportunity to earn a university four-year degree. I might add that, with today's technology, future students will be able to earn a full four-year degree without leaving their centers.

U-Rock is succeeding in its mission for two important reasons: the dedication and exceptional quality of the faculty and staff and the ongoing support of Rock County. County taxpayers and elected officials provide the funding support for the buildings and classrooms that comprise this campus. In no small way, it is their investment that has made this day possible. The Board of Regents is dedicated to ensuring that the state's role in this important partnership with Rock County remains strong for the Class of 1998 and all that follow.

To the Class of 1997, I offer a brief observation and a challenge. Graduation from this institution is a rite of passage that will take you from one stage of life and learning to another. You take with you into your next phase of education a superior preparation. You leave behind teachers who care deeply about you, and who have worked hard to prepare you for both the academic and life challenges you will face.

As you leave this place today, I challenge you to do three things:

1. Nurture and reinforce the values of determination and hard work that got you this far. By necessity, the pure force of societal pressure and the rapidly changing workplace will insist that you work hard and be creative and flexible.

2. Be positive in the face of adversity. Every day we both succeed and fail. Draw upon your inner strength. Learn from your mistakes. And keep smiling.

3. Find your passion and pursue it, whether it is studying marine biology or designing computer software, whatever. If you love your work, you will have a happy, successful life.

You're off to great places. Best wishes to each of you.

Not to Multiply but to Add
UW-Milwaukee Commencement
Dec. 21, 1997

It is a privilege for me to be with you today, to share in this moment in the life of UWM and in the lives of the Class of 1997 and their families. I am honored to bring greetings on behalf of the Board of Regents of the University of Wisconsin System. My colleagues and I wish you, the graduating class, much success, joy, and accomplishment as you move forward in your lives and careers.

Speaking personally, I want to say that I am no stranger to your university. I have deep roots in Milwaukee, and I recognize with great pride and affection UWM's important past and its potential for the future of our city and state. For many reasons, certainly not the least of which is the quality of its graduates, UWM is recognized among an elite grouping of American urban universities. Because of its urban location and the business and industry that stands at its front door, UWM is a vital force in Milwaukee and throughout southeastern Wisconsin. An important reason for this is that approximately 75 percent of its student population is from this region, and almost the same percentage of its graduates stay in the Greater Milwaukee Area, contributing enormously to the economic and social strength of our communities.

We forget that the university is one of the world's most ancient institutions. The first true university was founded at Bologna, Italy, in the eleventh century. No city can be great without great universities. I believe that there is no other single institution or organization or force that has a more important influence on the continuing economic and cultural well-being of the Greater Milwaukee Area than the University of Wisconsin-Milwaukee. The sheer volume of graduates who stay in the community, to live and work here as taxpaying citizens, proves my point.

But it's more than that. I believe that excellence breeds excellence. On that note, UWM graduates figure prominently among the Milwaukee area's most influential and visionary leaders, teachers, entrepreneurs, managers, and innovators.

You graduates have that very same potential—to contribute excellence. And so, within the context of all of that UWM has given you, the one additional thing I hope you take from this place is this: When you are alumni of UWM, and representing it as teachers, technicians, or managers, I hope that you will look around yourselves each day, see the unmet needs of humanity, and act in good conscience. Act and be involved.

I hope that you do not come to learn, as did Marley's ghost in *A Christmas Carol*, too late, that "humanity" is your business. It is everyone's business. The Book of Psalms says it this way: "To whom much is given, much is expected."

After today, you are a matured investment—to your parents, to yourself, to society. You are our human capital. You are our best and our brightest, trained in an exceptional institution. You are what has made our country great. Society is now looking to you for its dividends, its return on its investment—its payback, if you will.

I urge all of you to go forth, not so much to multiply as to add— to add value and excellence in all that you do. The goal of UWM was to provide each of you with an education that would enable you to become broader in perspective, more literate, intellectually more astute, and ethically more sensitive. It is now time to see if this goal was met.

Congratulations, God bless all of you, and good luck!

Building Diversity
UW-Milwaukee Commencement
May 10, 1998

Soon my seven-year appointment to the UW Board of Regents will conclude. I must tell you that serving as a regent of the University of Wisconsin System has been a challenging and rewarding experience, one that has brought me to an even stronger conviction of the enormous contribution that UWM makes in Milwaukee and throughout southeastern Wisconsin.

Let me also say that the stature and reputation that UWM enjoys is a reflection of Chancellor John Schroeder's dedicated efforts and leadership. I am certain that John's decision to return to teaching and writing will further enrich UWM in a new and significant way. In fact, I told him that I was intending to become one of his students.

As president of the board this year, I helped the regents focus on two major priorities: nurturing excellence and designing a new, more effective diversity program. Today I would like to talk a bit about diversity. Diversity is a fact of American life, and it is a concept we must all embrace. The only issue is how to successfully achieve diversity in our own lives and on our campuses. Over the past year, the Board of Regents, with the input of staff, faculty, students, and citizens, has undergone the most in-depth effort it has ever undertaken to redesign the system's diversity program. I believe we have created the most effective and accountable program of its type in the country. I also believe that great universities must lead if they are to be relevant. We are leading. Our program is based on fairness, self-motivation, and personal improvement.

This is not an affirmative action program. It is about developing the potential in our young people of color. It is about offering a hand to help these people participate in our country's growing prosperity through higher education. It is about motivating them with more financial grants and scholarship funding and therefore less reliance on loans.

I am personally very proud of what the Board of Regents has done and optimistic about what the results of this undertaking will be in the future. It is a program whose success will require new efforts from parents, students, the K-12 schools, school boards, the Department of Public Instruction, and each of our universities. Success will require all to share responsibility. It is a bottoms-up program that will be tailor-made to fit the unique characteristics and situation of each of the thirteen Universities, the UW Extension, and the thirteen two-year colleges that together make up the system. This program can make a big difference.

Finally, you have worked hard and sacrificed to reach this point, and so have the people beside you—your parents, spouses, children, friends, family, and teachers. God bless all of you, and good luck!

Pursuing Excellence
UW-Madison Commencement
Ph.D. and Professional Degrees
May 15, 1998

It is a privilege for me to be with you today, to share in this moment in the life of UW-Madison and in the lives of the Class of 1998 and their families. I am honored to bring greetings on behalf of the Board of Regents of the University of Wisconsin System. My colleagues and I wish you all much success, joy, and accomplishment as you move forward with your lives and careers.

Speaking personally, being here today at the commencement for Ph.D. and Professional degrees is very meaningful for me and closes the loop on some unfinished business. Forty-five years ago, in June, 1953, to be exact, I missed attending the commencement ceremony for my Law School class. It had something to do with the Korean War, but I won't ponder that. I hope you agree with me: better late than never.

Longer than the six years and several summers I spent at UW-Madison in undergrad and Law School studies have been my seven years as a regent of the University of Wisconsin System. As president of the board this year, I have helped address two of our highest priorities: furthering excellence and creating a new diversity plan. Last Friday, the regents approved a new diversity program that I believe will lead the way for universities in the rest of our nation. I am very proud of what we have done.

Today I would like to briefly talk about excellence. As background, be aware that I have spent most of my business career as a venture capitalist, building small companies into larger ones. Needless to say, the miracle of Silicon Valley in California, the cradle of the electronics and computer industries, was enormously impressive to me. Many of the engineers, scientists, and businesspeople who have created this miracle are Stanford University graduates. So it only was natural that a few years ago I asked a business associate of mine who had earned his Ph.D. degree in electrical engineering from Stanford, "How did this happen? What do they do at Stanford?"

He responded by sending me a paper by Professor Fredrick E. Terman of Stanford Engineering School entitled *Strategy for Excellence*. Professor Terman wrote, "The quality of the academic program of a college or university is determined primarily by the quality of its faculty and the extent to which this faculty is grouped into 'steeples of excellence.' It is significant to note that impressive buildings and expensive equipment are not primary factors in determining quality. While a faculty needs space and equipment to carry on its work, space and equipment do not by themselves produce excellence!"

Professor Terman goes on to explain that excellence costs money. It doesn't cost a great deal more, but a marginal amount more for the faculty stars than the average of their peers in the university world. UW-Madison is a great research university. To maintain it, to enhance it, to assure its excellence we will need more money. To accomplish this, UW-Madison must receive more freedom than it has now and more than the other universities of our system. UW-Madison is different. This university requires independence to set its own tuition levels and to motivate all of its supporters to provide higher levels of private support so it can compete to hold and attract the best of faculty. To you graduates, whom I shall call the "best of our best," I hope you will be aware of the unmet needs of your university and, when you are able, join with so many of your fellow alumni to provide for these unmet needs with your own support. Let's call it paying back.

Finally, let me congratulate every one of you graduates for the work and sacrifice you have put forth to reach this point. I want to also congratulate your support groups who helped get you here—your parents, spouses, children, friends, family, and faculty. God bless all of you and good luck.

Making Your Luck
Whitefish Bay High School
National Honor Society Induction
May 19, 2008

It's good to be back in Whitefish Bay. Most important, I want to congratulate each of the inductees on their past accomplishments that have gained them membership in the National Honor Society. You and your families should be very proud of your achievements and this recognition. Your challenge in the years ahead will be to continue on the path that has led you here tonight, namely excellence in scholarship, service, character, and leadership.

I come to you tonight as someone with a common bond with each of you: I too am a graduate of Whitefish Bay High School. I can assure you that the educational base which has served me so well as I continued my studies at the University of Wisconsin-Madison and went on into the world will do the same for you. Although I was not a member of the National Honor Society at Whitefish Bay, I did earn membership in the Freshman Honors Society at UW—much to my surprise. I can also tell you that I was much more serious in college than I was in high school. You are all fortunate to move on to the next phase of your life with the solid foundation from your days at Whitefish Bay.

I also want you to know how impressed I am with the Whitefish Bay Class of 2008. I asked for a list of inductees into the Honor Society, and I was given the names of eighty-four of you, with the possibility that one or two names might be added. I don't know how large the class is, but for eighty-four members to qualify is extraordinary. What a great class!

Now for tonight. I am well aware that no one remembers in later years what a speaker at an event like this said, so I am going to simplify my message to all of you. I want to leave you with a particular thought that I hope you will consider as you go forward with your education and then your careers.

I want to talk about luck. Last week I had the honor of co-chairing a dinner sponsored by the Woodrow Wilson Center of Washington, D.C., which is named for our twenty-eighth president. The institute is a very highly regarded think-tank focusing on international issues and known throughout the world. They came to Milwaukee to honor two of our prominent citizens for their past achievements and community efforts.

Both of these fine men spoke of their early beginnings, their dreams, their work, and the luck that brought them to the high positions they had attained. And yet, as I later reflected on what they said, I don't think they really meant it was luck or good fortune that brought them the success they have achieved.

I must tell you that I don't believe in luck. I believe we all largely make our own luck. I don't consider that it's good luck that enables Ryan Braun or other baseball professionals to step up to the plate and hit a home run. What does it is years of training, years of practice, and finally concentration. It isn't luck that has made Yo-Yo Ma the world's greatest cellist. It is years and years of never-ending study and practice at a profession he loves. And from my own experience, I can tell you that whatever success I have enjoyed in the world of finance and business hasn't been luck; it's been education, continued learning, hard work, and loving your subject so much that when the opportunity presents itself you are prepared and able to grab it.

You have made your own luck. Equally important to remember is that if you fail at first, don't be discouraged. Simply pick yourself up, reflect on what you have learned, and try all over again. Don't forget that Thomas Edison tried well over 1,000 experiments and attempts before he created the electric light bulb.

Perhaps the best description of what I am saying is something you have all undoubtedly heard before: "The harder you work, the luckier you get." Think about it, and please never forget it.

With that I will say to each of you inductees, your parents, families, friends, and, of course, your beloved teachers, good night and good luck—the kind you make for yourself.

Aiming High
Medical College of Wisconsin Graduation Dinner
May 20, 2010

I am delighted to be here with you this evening discussing a few thoughts with you on behalf of my wife, Marianne, and myself. It is a privilege for us to share this moment in the life of the Medical College of Wisconsin and the lives of the Class of 2010 and their families.

Marianne and I salute you and recognize the work and sacrifice that went into your achievements and earning your new title "Doctor." I also want to include in our congratulations your parents, wives, and husbands, and the rest of your support group, because we know they also have a substantial investment in this effort. And finally, let me commend the faculty of this wonderful Medical College who have spent their energies sharing their wisdom, their knowledge, and their values with you.

I believe I can relate to some of the concerns and uncertainties you must be experiencing as you look ahead and plan for your careers. I graduated from the University of Wisconsin Law School in 1953. Marianne and I were married a year earlier and were expecting the first of our four children. In the fifty-seven years since then, I have been a banker, venture capitalist, entrepreneur, and chief executive of a number of public and private companies. In addition, I have held appointive government service positions under three American presidents and served on numerous profit and nonprofit boards of directors. My wife and I have traveled the world and come to know world leaders wherever we went. It has been an exciting, gratifying life for us. My hope is that each of you will have an exciting, gratifying life for yourselves as you move on.

I can assure you that there is a challenging and exciting world out there waiting for you. It will require you to work hard and aim high. I truly believe this will produce success. But I will also caution you that along the way you will experience frustration, defeats, and failures. This is inevitable for anyone who is working and moving ahead. I can also tell you that I know the pain and embarrassment of failing as well as the pleasure of succeeding. Failing is a price we all must pay for the joy of making something worthwhile happen and ultimately enjoying the fruits of success.

Finally, as doctors you join a select group of citizens who will with certainty be the leaders of our state and country in the years ahead. In that role, I would ask you to consider the words of Judge James G. Jenkins who, shortly after the death in 1908 of William Vilas, a great Wisconsinite who left his considerable fortune to the University of Wisconsin for scholarships, professorships, and buildings, had this to say in memorializing Mr. Vilas before the Wisconsin Supreme Court:

> The man of study, the man of science, who reserves the knowledge acquired for mere personal use and enjoyment, comes short of the correct standard of life, and is of little value to the world. It is by spending that one can save. It is by giving that one can have. By this is not meant indiscriminate distribution, but that wise, practical spending and giving which benefit humanity and enrich the spender and the giver in those things which make for character and worth.

So if I could leave you with a final thought, let me say in addition to aiming high and not being afraid to fail, consider sharing and giving back as you are able. Again, let me extend our most sincere congratulations and wish you God's blessing.

The Role of UWM
University of Wisconsin Board of Regents
June 10, 2010

It is almost exactly twelve years, to the day, that Mike Grebe and I retired from the Board of Regents. You have our regard and respect, I am sure. Let me outline a few things that are already well-known to yourselves:

1. The Milwaukee metropolitan area is the largest in the state of Wisconsin. It is still this state's manufacturing and commercial center.

2. The Milwaukee Public School System spends about $15,000 annually per student and is still competing with Detroit for the lowest graduation rate in the country; less than 50 percent of MPS students graduate from high school. We also have the highest percentage of special education students in the U.S. By almost any measure, MPS is a failed system. It needs help. I should add that most of its teachers are graduates of one of the thirteen universities of the UW System.

3. Too many of our problems in Milwaukee relate to a central city community where about 80 percent of the children are born to single-parent homes and where the unemployment rate for males is over 40 percent.

Clearly we have serious problems here, and that means our entire state has problems. For the state to succeed, its largest metropolitan area must succeed. If you don't believe that, look at Michigan, where the demise of Detroit is sinking what was one of the leading industrial sectors in the world.

Yet all is not lost. According to a very current survey, Milwaukee businesses are expecting to hire at a solid pace during the rest of the year. In fact, the survey says our pace will rank with those of the leading cities. Businesses in Milwaukee are trying to grow. One of their biggest problems is finding qualified employees. I am not a sociologist, so I won't try and tell you how to solve social problems, but I have been a banker and businessman here for over fifty years, and I can tell you that the path to success and a good middle-class life starts with education—high school, college, and vocational.

So where do the Board of Regents and the University of Wisconsin System come in? The University of Wisconsin-Milwaukee is the largest institution in this part of the state. As a public university, it is a force that can make the largest impact on the future of this area, along with MPS. Through its educational programs and development efforts, it is the logical venue for the citizens of the Milwaukee area to acquire advanced education.

We must recognize that a high percentage of our central city people are poor and come from distressed backgrounds. This is a fact. I know UW-Milwaukee is working hard to carry out its educational mandate for these citizens. What it needs is more of the resources from the UW System. With that support, UW-Milwaukee can be a real engine for bringing the economy of the city and in turn the state back to prosperity. Without these resources, the future is very gray.

In simplest terms, I am saying that more money, more faculty, and more programs, all of which will lead to more engineers, more teachers, more business school graduates, and more productive and creative citizens, is what is required. The UW System, through its judicious allocation of funding, can be the difference. As I said, Milwaukee's problems are also the state's, and Milwaukee's success will be the State of Wisconsin's as well.

As Regents, you were appointed by a Democratic governor (my friend Jim Doyle), and he in turn is working with a Democratic legislature. I am asking you to take ownership in this situation and carry this message to them and to your president and my friend, Kevin Reilly.

The Object of Life
University School of Milwaukee Graduation
May 20, 2012

Good afternoon and sincere congratulations to all of you graduates who have worked so diligently to get to this unforgettable moment. Let me also congratulate the faculty and staff of the University School and, of course, the graduates' loyal supporters: parents, families, and friends of the graduates. You have all done your jobs well or they wouldn't be here today. And with your permission an additional congratulation from me to my grandson, Patrick Lubar. Good job, Patrick. We're proud of you and your classmates.

At the outset, I promise you that I will adhere to the advice of President Franklin Roosevelt on speech-making: "Be sincere, be brief, be seated." You have my word on this.

As you might have guessed, if only by looking at me, I have been around a long time. I have traveled the world, climbed mountains, and been involved in many businesses, the government, and philanthropy. I have worked with important as well as not important people, and have generally accomplished what I set out to do. But above all I have had a very happy life, thanks to my wife of sixty years, Marianne, our four children (two of whom graduated from the University School), and eleven grandchildren (eight of whom attended or graduated from the University School). In addition to my family, I have loved my work.

I intend to make two points in my remarks to you, two thoughts that I hope you will remember and use to your advantage as you travel your own particular pathway through life. First, what is the object of life? Second, how can you achieve this objective?

What is the object of life? What constitutes a "good life"? Simply put, I believe happiness is the ultimate object of life. But what is happiness? The best definition I know of happiness is a sense of lasting and justified satisfaction with one's own life as a whole. Satisfaction with your own actions and behavior. The pleasure you enjoy because of what has happened as a result of your efforts. Being a good student brings happiness. Later in life, being a good parent qualifies. Providing a good life for your family qualifies. Achieving goals you have set for yourself qualifies. Contributing to your community and country qualifies, but in the end you yourself are the best judge of what qualifies as a happy life.

I recently read a part of one of the Federalist Papers, Number 62, which was probably authored by James Madison, but, as you know, the authors are anonymous. Permit me to quote from that paper: "The object of government is the happiness of the people." A simple but true statement. There is no reference in this paper to prosperity, security, or even equality—only happiness. This thought was repeated in the preamble to the Declaration of Independence, in which the Founders wrote that "all men (and women) are created equal, that they are endowed by their creator with certain unalienable rights, that among these are Life, Liberty and the Pursuit of Happiness."

Being proud of yourself and what you do, being decent and civil, will make you a happy person.

The other message I have for you today is live in the present. Make each day a gift and be grateful for it. Plan ahead, but don't be worried about the future. My approach was to pursue life in short, attainable segments. Have short-term objectives that are goals along your lifetime path. I have found that there are perhaps only a half-dozen decisions one will make in a lifetime that are truly life-changing. One of these decisions should be your commitment to continuing lifetime education after your college days are over. Whom you marry and what kind of home you both seek are also life-changers.

Your choice of careers is another key decision, and it may not start with your first job. Although that job may turn out to be your lifetime career, it may also only be experience in preparation for your lifetime career. Or you might follow my path and have many careers. Also, don't be afraid to experiment. Don't be afraid to fail. None of us wants to fail, but it is a price one must be ready to pay for experimenting and trying new ways. Should you fail, learn from that experience, then get up and start again. It is the sum of all of your experiences along the way, and your willingness to try new things, that will result in the satisfactions I spoke of earlier, and that I believe will bring you a happy life. It did for me.

There is not a doubt in my mind that I am speaking to a graduating class that will produce the intellectual, business, and social leaders our country needs so badly today. I don't think any of you realize how much you are needed and how much of a difference you can each make. Without hesitation, I predict you all have the ability to live happy and productive lives and that you will make yourselves and your families proud. Henry David Thoreau said, "The world is but a canvas to our imagination." To that I add, "Trust your imagination and follow your dreams."

I end with wishes for good luck, calm seas ahead, and thanks for having me today. God bless each and everyone here, and God bless our country.

Chapter 3

The U.S. Economy

How to Encourage Saving

Statement to the U.S. Senate Finance Committee

Apr. 21, 1980

As a commissioner of the White House Commission on Small Business, my particular responsibility during the past fifteen months has been to examine the issues of capital formation and retention. This, along with twenty-seven years of experience in banking, investments, and venture capital, are my qualifications for making this statement. I regret that I was not able to appear in person, but if called upon in the future, I will make myself available.

Simply stated, capital is formed through the savings of individuals and businesses. That is all there is to it, nothing more. If a citizen's personal expenditures and tax liabilities are less than his total income, the difference is savings, and capital is created. If a business makes a profit after taxes, what is left after dividends to stockholders is retained earnings, and again capital is created. All business activity and employment is dependent on the flow and creation of capital.

The problem existing in our country today results from more than forty years of encouraging consumption and borrowing on the part of our citizens and penalizing savings and investment by means of tax policy. If you question this, then consider that the fruits of typical savings and investments come in the form of interest and dividends. Assume you are a married taxpayer and together with your wife have a total income of $55,000. You could save. However, your 50-percent earned income bracket means that the interest from your savings is taxed at rates between 50 and 70 percent. Since most saving and investment comes from persons in this or higher income brackets—not families with, say, $20,000 of annual income who are barely making it—it is understandable why the savings rate in the United States has sunk to just over 3 percent of disposable income—the lowest of any developed country. Our declining competitive position with countries such as Germany and Japan, whose citizens save at a 14-percent rate, also becomes understandable.

Without oversimplifying, the solution to this problem could be found in three changes to our tax laws:

1. Eliminate any differentiation between the tax treatment of "earned" vs. "unearned" income. Initially this would mean a top personal tax bracket of 50 percent.
2. Reduce corporate taxes, especially those of small business, the sector that represents the most dynamic portion of our economy. Allow these companies to keep more of their "seed" or retained earnings so that they can build and grow.
3. Allow for more rapid depreciation of business assets. Our tax laws provide one of the slowest rates of capital recovery in the world. In some countries, business assets can be written off in one year. If we are to improve productivity and compete in a worldwide economy, faster capital recovery is a financial necessity.

Since high levels of inflation and a rapidly escalating cost of living index bear on the feasibility of fiscal measures such as I have proposed, let me briefly comment on these issues. In recent years, the cost of living index has been used by many as the measure of inflation, which has confused the issue and the policies necessary to deal with inflation. Inflation results from an increase in the volume of money and credit beyond the real growth of the economy. A balanced budget at the lowest possible level of expenditure will ultimately bring inflation to a halt.

Cost of living is an index of a market basket of consumer needs, and hence is a measure of buying power. Therefore, inputs such as higher interest rates feed into this index, along with every OPEC increase in oil prices, wage increases of each worker with a cost of living escalator, etc. The cost of living index will stabilize when the budget is balanced at a reasonable level of expenditure, the free market price of energy has worked its way through the economy, and the confidence of our people in this country's ability to sensibly grow is restored. Use of this index to escalate wages, government pensions, Social Security payments, and so on is distortive, and it unfairly transfers money from taxpaying citizens to specially designated recipients.

In summary, sound economic policies take five or ten years to be effective. Change is not instantaneous. What is needed today are the tax measures referred to earlier, the discipline of a budget balanced with a restraint on spending, and the patience to allow these measures to become effective.

Business in Milwaukee 2000: The Road Back
UW-Milwaukee
Graduate School of Business
Oct. 29, 1982

Of course, anyone who would dare stand up before an educated and informed audience such as yourselves on October 29, 1982, and forecast or predict where the Milwaukee business economy will be in the year 2000 is either a fool or a dreamer. Since I don't consider myself either, my comments today are aimed at reviewing very briefly where we have been, determining what course we are on nationally, and then suggesting that we in Milwaukee have to steer our own boat if we want to get our share of America's dynamic future. To put it another way, I don 't believe much in luck. I think we largely make our own luck. Where we will be in the year 2000 is dependent only on our resourcefulness, our intelligence, and the intensity of our commitment.

First of all, where we have been. We can best understand the context in which we are operating and living by reviewing a few important facts:

1. The economic base of Milwaukee and Wisconsin has been, and is, manufacturing. However, its importance is declining because of a changing economy and the depression in durable goods.

Manufacturing as a % of Total Employment

	1959	1969	1975	1979
Milwaukee	50.2	44.3	39.1	36.4
Wisconsin	48.3	42.6	37.9	35.8
U.S.A.	38.7	35.8	30.3	28.8

2. In the last ten years, the population of the Milwaukee metro area has declined 0.4 percent while state population has increased 7 percent and U.S. population has increased 11 percent. This indicates that we are a low- or no-growth area.

3. In the nation as a whole, the service sector of the economy has shown the fastest growth, and almost 50 percent of all jobs are now service-based, an increase of 30 percent since 1970. This reflects an increase in activities such as hotels, restaurants, tourism, financial services, etc. Perhaps equally significant is the increase in government social services resulting from the growing elderly segment of the population.

4. For almost fifteen years, our government has been embarked on ever-worsening inflationary policies, both fiscal (spending and taxes) and monetary (money creation). Consider these statistics if you are interested in a growth industry :

National Health Expenditures

YEAR	GNP	TOTAL	PER CAPITA	% GNP	% PRIVATE	% PUBLIC
1940	$100B	$4.0B	$29.62	4	79.7	20.3
1960	506	26.9	146.30	5.3	75.3	24.7
1970	982.4	74.9	359.41	7.6	62.9	37.1
1981	2864	278.5	1216	9.7	56.6	43.3
1990	7587	821	3309	10.8	53.6	46.4

In 1981 the public cost of health expenditures was $120.8 billion and represented a major element of total public spending. Though health expenditures are an important component of government spending and inflation, I don't mean to hold them out as the sole cause. It is an important one of many. Transfer payment programs, largely consisting of Social Security, resulted in 1981 expenditures of $279.7 billion. That number is growing, and it has a significant impact on inflation. Remember, I am not judging these programs, only considering their impact on our financial markets and business affairs. The excessive government spending and deficits that I am alluding to have resulted in inflation, and equally important inflationary expectations.

Now consider these levels of past inflation and the prevailing public expectations. Try to think back on how people were conducting their financial affairs:

1960 1.5% (expected to stay level)
1970 5%   (expected to drop with decline in Vietnam War and Great Society)
1980 13% (expected to increase)

What I am getting at in the briefest possible way is that what has happened to Milwaukee over the past ten years, and certainly the past three years, is directly related to the national inflation we have endured. Remember, more than the rest of the country, we are a manufacturing-based economy, not an area whose prosperity is based on population expansion, government services, or a financial or commercial center. We are a place where durable and capital goods are developed and produced. No manufacturing business system can function when inflationary expectations soar to the moon.

Let me move on to where we are headed. Since only the federal government can cause inflation—by incurring deficits that are settled by printing money—only the government can stop it. And it is being stopped, or at least substantially reduced. The medicine we are now enduring is bitter and has resulted in high unemployment and low or no profits. Business failures are increasing, and even the financial system is showing some cracks. For Milwaukee and Wisconsin, whose industries do well when people are buying cars and houses, and businesses buy new machinery, the impact of reducing inflation through monetary policy has been bone-crunching.

If President Carter's inflation rates had not been brought under control in an orderly way in President Reagan's first term, the inflation cycle would probably have ended in a crash—a truly frightening possibility. With even 13-percent annual inflation, any dollar you lend is worth only 30 cents when the borrower repays it in ten years, so by the late 1970s Americans had figured the game out, that they should always a borrower and never a lender be. It really is not a coincidence that ever since President Johnson's program of "guns and butter" started the great inflation in 1968, the common stockholder has been an uncommon fool. Only in the last sixty days has the market returned to its early 1973 level. Constructive investing in the past ten years made less sense than acquiring gold, art, antique furniture, or race horses. Personal savings were down to 3 or 4 percent of GNP, and buying a vacation home was considered smart investing. All of this is being corrected—granted, with real pain for many. Although it may not be apparent from where we probably are at the bottom of the trough, we are now on a very slow upswing from a depression or recession. If we hold to the steady course we are on, as a nation, we are probably headed to:

- Annual inflation of 5 percent and hopefully less.
- Lower interest rates, although not the 6-percent prime rate of the past.
- Higher savings rates, perhaps 8 to 9 percent.

What it all indicates is that there are dynamic possibilities ahead. At the outset I referred to getting our share of America's dynamic future. So let me go on the record as one who believes that the possibilities ahead of us dwarf what has been achieved to date.

In terms of the scientific and technological changes we can look for in the years ahead, you can be assured that they will be numerous. I won't take your time by star-gazing or indulging in likely scientific possibilities, but I can highlight some of the very exciting technologies already known to us:

- The communication transformation, including video phones and conferencing, video newspapers, cable TV, entertainment, and data transmission.
- Computerization of the household and financial industry, with major impacts on banking and shopping.
- Age of information, with widespread access to computer knowledge banks.
- The factory of the future, which will incorporate robotics.
- Genetic engineering.
- Organ transplants.
- Space platforms and exploration.
- Deep-sea engineering and farming.

As exciting as these industries will be, let us not forget the business activity that will result from meeting such well-known and basic needs as new housing, rehabilitating the existing housing stock, replacing the aging and to some extent energy-inefficient auto stock, rebuilding our highways and road system, rebuilding sewer systems, continuing development of domestic energy, development of fossil-fuel substitutes, and I could go on. The possibilities are exciting beyond anything ever considered.

Let me summarize what I have been trying to say:

- The base of Milwaukee and Wisconsin is still manufacturing.
- This base has been severely and negatively impacted by inflation and resulting high interest levels.
- We know we have a fine pool of skilled labor. Although competitive wages in our area are above levels elsewhere on the Great Lakes, or in the Sunbelt and the U.S. generally, the free labor marketplace will sort this out in the near future. Our labor force is one of our major assets, not a liability.
- President Reagan's policies, although painful, have reduced inflation and interest rates, and more improvement lies ahead if we hold our course.
- The technological base of ideas and knowledge exists today for a period of dynamic growth ahead.

Bottom line, this means that barring the horrible and unexpected, e.g., nuclear war, calamity in the Mideast, a banking collapse, or some other catastrophe, the years ahead to 2000 should indeed be very good ones.

So how do we position Milwaukee and Wisconsin for their fair share? If it is the desire of the people of this city and state to share in this prosperous period in the years to 2000, then we are going to have to act. Passiveness is not how you make your own luck. To make the future what we, the people of Milwaukee and Wisconsin, want, we need focused and pragmatic action on both the public and private fronts. On the public side, let me tell you what I believe is needed:

1. Recognize that no family, business, or government can regularly spend more than it takes in. If we do, the result is inflation or bankruptcy. Hence, since we are all human, to effect the necessary fiscal discipline, Congress needs to pass a "balanced budget amendment." This means spending priorities will be established and inflation controlled.
2. Tell your congresspeople that it isn't fair or possible to continue to fully index Social Security payments. Even more important, it will be the elderly, those largely dependent

on Social Security, who will be really devastated if the system stops working because workers believe it is unfair.

3. Since further drops in inflation are crucial, don't vote for people who block imports of cheap European steel or Japanese cars or Taiwanese textiles. For balanced trade, fight for equality and not protective tariffs.

4. The key to improving our business climate is intelligent leadership from the governor and legislature. Wisconsin must be a competitive place to live, work, and ultimately die. Don't vote for people who want to do good deeds with more government programs and more of your tax dollars. The history books are full of their failures. We must keep ourselves competitive with the rest of the country in terms of taxes and government cost.

5. Finally, administrative agencies in the state must stop acting as though our citizens are helpless and stupid. This means a shift from regulation of everything to a disclosure approach, from antagonism to cooperation. I am particularly thinking of our securities laws, but I also seek an end to the hassle government gives most businessmen in Wisconsin.

So much for the government. On the private side, there is at least an equal amount to do. We in business must become innovators. Attracting and creating high-technology companies is a high priority and one that deserves a maximum effort and perhaps even another speech by me.

But a more important and significant challenge for us is how to manage a slow-growing company in a mature industry. Because so much of our business here might fit this description, the challenge is more major than it might be if we were in the Sunbelt. It has been my experience that some of our best-performing companies have been those in mature industries that focused their efforts on a few major businesses and continued to "grow" them by identifying new opportunities within these mature areas.

All of you joggers out there, consider that staid old industry, athletic footwear or, in the vernacular, "sneakers." Nike went from nothing a few years back to almost $700 million of profitable volume. It met the unsatisfied market demand for better-engineered and better-styled athletic footwear. The potential demand existed before this company satisfied it. Previous industry participants had ignored these market needs, and their failure to innovate resulted in an industry that was, at least temporarily, slow-growing and mature. A strategist who had not thoroughly analyzed the industry would have looked at the statistics, labeled it mature, and concluded it offered little investment opportunity.

This same explosion of growth occurs regularly in segments of one of our oldest industries: clothing. Designer blue jeans, active sportswear, panty hose, and western clothing have shown us that innovation in a mature industry can cause dramatic growth for the innovator. In addition, volume increases can be on a much larger scale than is possible in an embryonic, high-technology industry where the market is still relatively small and undeveloped.

I speak with conviction about the potential and profitability of innovation in mature companies, because I have built a career and a business on doing just that. Over the past twenty years, I and my firm, Lubar & Co., have engineered and been involved in at least a dozen acquisitions of companies in various businesses that had only one thing in common: they were in mature industries. I can't tell you that every one of these companies turned into a high-growth success story, but I can say most of them did.

What I can tell you is that five years after acquisition, the successful companies didn't look anything like the companies we had acquired. The results were more and better jobs for the employees and excellent investment for the owners.

What I am pointing to is that for alert management in a mature industry, which is what we have much of in the U.S. and especially in Milwaukee and Wisconsin, the growth opportunities compare favorably with those in less-developed embryonic or growth markets. The important reasons are :

1. Mature industries provide a much larger hunting ground to explore for opportunities. The number of mature industries is sizable compared to the small number of growth industries.
2. If success is gained, the markets are much larger, and much greater sales and profit increases are possible.
3. The financing of new opportunities is considerably easier in a mature industry, as the industry is usually well-serviced by financial institutions that understand the business.
4. There is less competition to find opportunities. Mature industries are unglamorous places to be, according to today's wisdom. For those who enjoy holding contrary opinion, it suggests that this is the best place to make money.
5. The vulnerability of competitors in mature industries is often substantial. If the competitors are part of a large corporation, they are often entangled in bureaucracy and are less reactive. Usually they are milking their mature businesses and ignoring the opportunities that exist.

As businesspeople attempting to build a high-growth business environment in Milwaukee and Wisconsin, the challenge must be to create this growth through innovation and the renewal of our existing and seemingly mature companies. Indeed, here in Milwaukee we have no other choice. These are the only places large enough to provide a meaningful impact. This is what I am doing as we move to the year 2000, and this is what I urge all of you to consider.

Let me sign off with an excerpt from *Alice In Wonderland*. Said Alice to the Cheshire Cat, "Would you tell me, please, which way I ought to walk from here?"

"That depends a good deal on where you want to get to," replied the cat.

"I don't much care where," said Alice.

"Then it doesn't matter which way you walk," said the cat.

"So long as I get somewhere," Alice added.

"Oh, you're sure to do that," said the cat, "if you only walk long enough."

Capitalism and the Prophetic Ethic
Congregation Sinai, Fox Point, WI
Jan. 12, 1985

The two ancient enemies of the human race are poverty and tyranny. In a civilized world both must be eliminated. Life with either is unacceptable and unfulfilled. Most of us would stipulate to this. The issue for this evening is what economic system will best see to their elimination.

I hold that today's American system of capitalism, among all workable societies past and present, serves best to uplift the poor, provide freedom and dignity for the human person, makes possible the growth and development of all its citizens of every sort, and establishes a more voluntary and open form of life than any other society of the past, present, or foreseeable future. In other words, it alone best achieves the highest of what the prophets sought.

That the vanquishing of poverty and injustice is not yet complete does not mean that our system is not the best. It means that the system has not yet achieved perfection. Our challenge is to proceed toward this goal and develop workable solutions to the problem.

In support of my position, I would like to discuss capitalism, profit, and poverty. R. H. Tawney, the socialist historian, selected acquisitiveness as the fundamental motive of capitalist economic activity. I fear acquisitiveness confuses two quite different motivations. Truly, the miser is acquisitive; he hoards, holds, wants to possess. The miser's behavior is quite different from that of the investor, the entrepreneur, and the inventor. Two key words in a capitalist civilization are "new" and "improved." Business reaches out to create new things and often fails. Technological invention in one place also means obsolescence in another. It is not having and grasping that characterize the capitalist spirit, but letting go and venturing, creating and rendering obsolete. Max Weber was far more penetrating than Tawney:

The impulse to acquisition, pursuit of gain, of money, of the greatest possible amount of money, has in itself nothing to do with capitalism. This impulse exists and has existed among waiters, physicians, coachmen, artists, prostitutes, dishonest officials, soldiers, nobles, crusaders, gamblers, and beggars. One may say that it has been common to all sorts and conditions of men at all times and in all countries of the earth, wherever the objective possibility of it is or has been given. It should be taught in the kindergarten of cultural history that this naive idea of capitalism must be given up once and for all. Unlimited greed for gain is not in the least identical with capitalism and is still less its spirit.

What does define a capitalist order is, rather, the habit of abstaining from consumption and from miserly hoarding in order to invest in creative ventures. Capitalism is saving and investing. The aim is to produce new wealth in a sustained way, generating more new wealth that is invested in its turn.

Why should one do this? Individuals each have their own purposes, but clearly the economic development of the planet demands it, so long as poverty exists. The aim of the capitalist is not to live sumptuously or even comfortably, as was the spirit of pre-capitalist persons of wealth, but to create ever-new wealth in a sustained and systematic way. "Acquisitiveness" and "possessiveness" are not the objectives of the capitalists; building, creating, and developing are.

The semantic confusion is just as great with the word "profit." Most persons confuse profit with mark-up. They further intuitively confuse profit with cash taken out of the business by owners or managers. They think that the capitalist spirit is to "buy cheap, sell dear," and that profits "go into the pocket" of those who make them.

There is a need to understand that profit is another word for development. Not to earn profit is to be economically stagnant or going backwards. Businesses that don't earn profits eventually cease to exist. In our day, perhaps as many as half of all Americans whose family income is more than $30,000 a year are engaged in activities of government, teaching, research, and other activities that earn no profit.

No wonder many have an inadequate conception of profit; they have no experience of earning it in a sustained, creative, venturesome way.

If they did understand, they would see that most profit is a cost of doing productive work. Some of it goes to retire the loans used to start up a business. Some of it is invested in improving the product or in finding new markets for it. By far the largest proportion of profit is reinvested. Typically, only a small proportion of profit is used in paying dividends to the original investors and in raising salaries. One may say that dividends and salaries go "into someone's pockets," but often enough that money, too, is reinvested. Savings from earnings and profits is what creates capital to invest.

Some may retort that this is how "the rich get richer." Yet, as John Stuart Mill pointed out in *The Principles of Political Economy*, there is a keen difference between wealth and capital. Wealth merely hoarded or used for consumption is unproductive. Capital is that portion of wealth which is reinvested in productive activities. It creates jobs and incomes, which in turn eliminate poverty. Wealth may or may not be socially useful, but it provides many benefits in the form of new employment, goods, services, invention, and new wealth for all citizens. It provides the funds which are paid both into nonprofit activities and into taxes. Profit is also the source of funds for the research and development on which future prosperity depends.

Those who are in favor of doing away with profits are necessarily in favor of halting the production of new wealth. If they retort that their wish is rather to socialize profit, by yielding all profit to the state, they disregard human motivations and the natural order of humans. Such disregard does not serve the common good. It is a fact that our system and the taxes it has produced have provided many times the money that is needed to totally eliminate poverty. No other system has even remotely approached ours.

Next I'd like to discuss poverty. The figures on poverty in the U. S. produced annually by the Census Bureau are based upon a strictly monetary calculation. The poverty level for 1982 was defined as an annual income below about $10,000 for a non-farm family of four. Any person or family falling below that line is considered poor no matter where or in what circumstances they live. Although this income in a small town in Wisconsin has a different meaning from what it may be in New York City, the Census Bureau treats all alike.

A further problem of this calculation is that many Americans have experienced this income without feeling poor. My point is that the Census Bureau figures exaggerate the magnitude of poverty in the U.S. In any case, the total number of persons included is 34,398,000. Of these, 23,517,000 are white, 9,697,000 black, and 4,301,000 Hispanic. In terms of age, 11,587,000 are under 15, and 6,606,000 are young singles (15 to 24). Only 19,000,000 were between the ages of 15 and 64—the working ages. Of these 19,000,000, 4,300,000 were keeping house, and 3,000,000 were ill or disabled. Thus only 12,000,000 of the poor are potentially able to work, and of these, 9,000,000 worked for pay at least part of the time in 1982.

The vast majority of the poor are truly dependent. The reasons for their poverty are multiple, including health, education, and the environment. Through no fault of their own, they are not able to be self-reliant. Other studies show that individuals typically move into and out of the poverty ranks with considerable volatility. A study by the University of Michigan showed that only 17 percent of the poor surveyed over a ten-year period had been in poverty for as long as two years consecutively. Poverty for most, the researchers concluded, tends not to be a permanent condition. Individuals in great numbers fall into it temporarily and rise again. This is important in countering the myth of a permanent underclass.

As a group, the poor in 1982 earned enough as a class to come within $45 billion of lifting the entire group completely out of poverty. Now, consider that federal expenditures (which have increased by twenty-one times since 1960) targeted solely for the poor exceed the $45 billion "poverty shortfall" by a considerable margin—in fact, by two to one. This does not count state or private assistance. The American people have been generous and civilized. It is clearly their will that a "safety net" or "floor" be placed under every American citizen, and Congress has voted more than enough federal funds to have achieved this years ago.

We must conclude that the problem of poverty does not consist of a lack of funding. Clearly the problem is not one of money alone. More money is being spent than would be necessary to eliminate poverty, as measured by the monetary standards of the Census Bureau, by simply giving the money directly to the poor. Hence, I conclude the problem does not lie in the economic system. Indeed, as I have shown, the economic system has produced the necessary wealth to solve the problem. The problem lies in the ability of all of us to use the fruits of the system to solve the problem of poverty.

A full discussion of the problem would lead one to believe that the missing ingredient in the solution is the family unit. We have failed to preserve the family unit. This is despite the fact that twenty years ago welfare programs were designed to stress the integrity and preservation of the family unit. Why has exactly the reverse occurred?

If you are interested, I could give you reams of statistics about poor families without fathers, of illegitimate children, and of the declining age of mothers of illegitimate children. We are seeing the feminization of poverty. Yet as poverty grows in this area, substantial progress has been made in other areas. In 1959, 35 percent of the elderly were poor, and by 1982 this figure had declined to 15 percent. Based on my experience in Washington, I can tell you that prior to 1940, most of the elderly lived in substandard housing. When I left Washington in 1975, only 2 percent were in substandard units, and 98% were in safe, sanitary housing. I regret to say that the family has been neglected as we have moved forward in other areas.

In conclusion, two centuries ago poverty was virtually a universal condition. The very idea that sufficient wealth could be created to make the dream of eliminating poverty possible was unbelievable even after Adam Smith first articulated it. Today, seeing the incredible vitality of free economies—the U. S. doubled its GNP in real terms between 1960 and 1983—we can truly see that the elimination of poverty is within reach. What is needed is a new approach, not a new economic system.

The Corporate Board in Crisis
UW- Milwaukee Executive MBA Program
Harvard Seminar
Nov. 2, 2002

The integrity and decency of corporate America is being questioned today as it has not been since the Great Crash of 1929 and the catastrophic depression that followed. From those events came years of congressional hearings, investigations, and regulation that included the creation of the Securities and Exchange Commission, the Public Utilities Act, the Investment Company Act, and also the conviction and jailing of the head of the New York Stock Exchange, Richard Whitney.

Along with the scandals of Enron, WorldCom, Qwest, and a host of others, investors have lost huge amounts of their capital—$7 trillion by some estimates. When the public loses on such an enormous scale, they will want satisfaction and answers to why and who is responsible and what can be done to fix the system. They are clamoring for blood, scalps, heads, and perhaps more. Our elected officials cannot afford to disappoint them. I suggest the show is only beginning.

Adding to the public's lust for vengeance has been the disclosure that while the public was being fleeced of their shirts, socks, and capital, certain CEO's, executives, and stockbrokers had made hundreds of millions of dollars selling stock. I might add that certain venture capital firms, particularly in Silicon Valley, got in, sold out, and banked the loot. As if this wasn't enough, we are now hearing about the unconscionable compensation packages of former corporate icons like Jack Welch.

So what will be done about all of this? Corporations are governed by boards of directors who are elected by shareholders to represent their interests. At the end of the day, it is the board of directors that bears the responsibility. It is the board of directors that must demand and initiate common sense and common decency through their corporate governance. Until recently, corporate governance was not a commonly discussed subject. Today knowledgeable investors and money managers are focusing on corporate governance as never before.

To support this view, I would like to quote from a recent "Heard on the Street" article published in the *Wall Street Journal:*

> A year ago, many investors couldn't have cared less if a corporate board's outside directors were named Larry, Moe and Curly. Now, everyone is a corporate-governance expert, opining on conflicts of interest, stock options and financial disclosure. The problem, however, is that figuring out the details of a company's governance can be time-consuming and frustrating.
>
> That is changing as a handful of new and established players in the corporate-governance field vie to sell their research to both investors and the companies themselves. The end product will be a simple rating system that will give investors a quick overview of where companies rank on governance issues. Ranging from Standard & Poor's, which will release corporate governance scores on all of the companies that make up its big-company S&P 500 stock index, to Governance Metrics International, a start-up that hopes to sell access to a database with all kinds of detailed information, the providers are trying to tap into the growing interest in the area.

The quality of corporate governance will also continue to be reflected in a company's market valuation. A well-governed company is worth more in the market. A McKinsey study conducted in 1999 surveyed 200 institutional investors who manage a total of $3.25 trillion in assets. Three-fourths of the survey respondents gave as much weight to board practices as to financial performance when evaluating a company. When choosing between two companies with equal financial performances, institutional investors indicated the quality of governance is a factor. More than 80 percent of the respondents said they would pay more for a well-governed company than for one with poor governance. On average, these investors would pay 18 percent more.

If the quality of governance makes a company worth more, acting in the best interests of shareholders takes on a new dimension. Directors will have to continue to improve governance to fulfill their roles as fiduciaries.

The Subprime Crisis
Milwaukee Country Club
May 21, 2008

Raise your hand if you don't really understand the current financial situation.... Everybody? I thought so. Let me tell you what I see. What is most visible is that, in the last nine months, the public has become aware that thousands of people bought homes they couldn't afford, often encouraged by banks and mortgage banks. Their credit wasn't verified, even the value of the house wasn't verified, and virtually all of the loans were packaged into mortgage-backed bonds and sold to institutions all over the world.

The buyer's expectation was that real estate values would continue to rise, every buyer would make money, the loans would be repaid, and everyone would live happily ever after. The one thing we know for certain is that real estate values started to weaken in 2007 and continue to do so. As values declined and the over-stretched borrowers realized they couldn't meet the monthly payments, and as the amount of the mortgage exceeded the market value of the house, delinquencies started to rise. The subprime crisis had started and was about to spread.

First of all, what is "subprime"? It's the term applied to the lowest of three main quality categories—prime, Alt-A, and subprime—that are used to classify home loans in the U.S. mortgage market. The classifications are based on the size of a mortgage borrower's initial payment, or "down payment," and his or her credit quality.

- Prime mortgages are for amounts that are relatively small compared to the value of the property; they are granted to a borrower who has a clean credit history and sufficient current income to meet payments.
- Alt-A lies between prime and subprime in terms of loan quality. Basically, three types of borrowers fall into this category: those who have no credit history, good or bad, but who may otherwise be considered prime; those who

borrow for a house they will not occupy themselves; and those who, for whatever reason, do not disclose necessary data like their current income.

- Subprime borrowers have a credit quality that is too low for prime mortgages. The reasons can include a flawed credit history or low income levels relative to the necessary mortgage payments.

Why did banks lend to subprime borrowers? To start with, subprime mortgages offered access to credit to borrowers with weak credit records, enabling them to purchase homes, finance other forms of spending, or pay down high-interest-rate consumer debt. As real estate prices continued to rise, subprime borrowers were able to roll over their mortgages after a specified number of years by repaying the outstanding loan with funds from a new mortgage loan based on the higher valuation of the property. Thus borrowers realized the gain on the property. But the frequent rollovers prevented the build-up of valuation reserves in outstanding mortgage contracts, leaving no cushion for a decline in property values.

Even with soaring house prices, banks probably would not have issued so much mortgage debt to low-quality borrowers without the one big innovation that emerged in recent years: "securitization." Previously, mortgages appeared directly on a bank's balance sheet and had to be backed with a certain amount of the bank's equity capital, and the amount of required equity increased as the credit quality of borrowers declined. Securitization has allowed banks to bundle many loans into a single tradable security. This simple-sounding innovation enabled banks to sell part of their loan risks to other banks and investors. Once they could transfer risk off their books, banks were able to issue more mortgage loans per given amount of their equity. They were leveraging their earning power. A typical securitization of a residential mortgage-backed security (RMBS) would consist of four tranches, and the mathematics were based on expected delinquencies and loan losses. Many assumed a one-percent loss.

- Tranche 1, the AAA-rated tranche, has a senior claim on all interest and principal payments of the mortgage pool. No other tranche may receive any cash flows as long as all payments on the AAA tranche are unmet. Its size equals 80 percent of the overall volume of the mortgage pool, or 0.8 times, for example, $300 million.
- Tranche 2, the A-rated tranche, is subordinated to the AAA tranche, but senior to all remaining tranches. It has 12 percent of the overall volume, or 0.12 times $300 million.
- Tranche 3, the BB-rated or High Yield tranche represents another 5 percent of the overall volume and is subordinated to both higher-rated tranches.
- The lowest tranche is called the Equity tranche. It equals 3 percent of the pool volume and receives anything that is left over after all other tranches are fully serviced. Toxic waste, in other words.

The shares of the tranches and their coupons are merely indicative, but they give an idea of how this structure was set up. If the losses remain within the expected one percent of loans, the Equity tranche takes all losses, while all other tranches receive the full amount of interest and principal payments. Even with a cyclical rise in default rates, the AAA tranche would be well-protected from losses, as the overall loss rate could rise to 20 percent without endangering the cash flows for AAA investors.

As delinquencies rose from the expected levels of say 4 or 5 percent to 25 percent or even higher, accounting rules forced the banks to establish market values for the securities they backed with mortgages that they held. This is where the big write-down of the banks, investment banks, and other financial institutions have come from. You might ask if these write-downs are really losses. The answer is "Yes." Total losses are estimated to be from $400 billion to $1 trillion worldwide.

So how has our financial system changed to get to where it is today? Has it migrated into a system of fewer, bigger players who are protected against collapse by the Federal Reserve Bank?

Things started to change for Wall Street with the end of fixed commissions about twenty years ago. The financial sector's earnings dropped substantially, and its leaders looked for other sources of income. Investment banks started having IPOs to raise capital, but going public meant pressure to show earnings per share. The banks saw what private firms were doing with LBOs, then proprietary trading, and they finally realized that, with high borrowing, or leverage, they would make more money from their balance sheets. (Bear Stearns was leveraged 44 to 1 when it collapsed.)

While all this was going on, the Fed lobbied Congress to allow banks to get into the securities business, and before anyone realized it, both the commercial banks and the investment banks had gotten into each other's business and turned the financial system into a giant gambling den. Then came the growth of hedge funds, which soon had $2 to $3 trillion in assets; derivatives (another $61 trillion); innovative new securities, including subprime mortgages; endowments; and other institutional investors looking for high returns. They all fed huge amounts of money into the system, and pretty soon our financial system morphed into this enormous speculative casino.

What lies ahead of us? The conventional view is that we are, or soon will be, in a recession. Treasury Secretary Paulsen says the crisis is more "fear-based" than fundamental. Whatever you call it, things are slowing in the U.S. and to a lesser extent around the world.

I am not as pessimistic as most. The biggest problem is here in the U.S. There are many things we could do to clean up our act:

- Stop the level of spending in Iraq.
- Use the savings to rebuild our infrastructure here at home.
- Establish a sensible energy policy that focuses on incentives to use small, gas-saving cars; develop other energy alternatives; drill off-shore and in Alaska; and adopt disincentives for excessive consumption.
- Institute sensible re-regulation of our financial markets.

If we could accomplish all of that, we would restore the world's respect for the U.S. and the prosperity of our people.

Chapter 4

Milwaukee and Wisconsin Issues

Betting on Wisconsin
Alpha Kappa Psi
Annual Business Banquet
Oct. 30, 1985

The full title of my remarks this evening is: If you have a college degree, good health, a willingness to work, and a desire to achieve, should you bet your future on Wisconsin? In my judgment the answer to that question is an emphatic YES! That concludes the formal portion of my presentation. Are there any questions from the floor?

If there are none at this point, let me expand on my answer a bit. You should know that I also believe the time to buy straw hats is in fall, and that you should get your skis in spring. Sell on good news and buy when things look the worst. Am I a contrarian? Not really, but neither do I follow the crowd. As a matter of fact, if I am certain of anything in this uncertain world, it's that ultimately the crowd is always wrong.

Right now the crowd is saying that Wisconsin is one of the rustiest states in the entire "Rust Belt." They point out that, compared to the "Sun Belt," unemployment, taxes, and living costs are high, while economic growth and opportunity are low. Worse yet, there are growing numbers in the crowd who say that the leadership and legislature of this state are largely made up of a bunch of lunkheads who have as much business making the strategic policy choices this state requires as I have to pilot the next space vehicle to the moon.

Is all of this true? Could it be that the crowd is right this time? Let's take a few minutes and examine the indictment against Wisconsin before arriving at our verdict. Almost two years ago, I spoke to the International Institute of Management Consultants and discussed the strengths and weaknesses of Wisconsin. If we can do a quick review of these factors, I believe you will see where I am coming from. First the strengths:

1. Availability of skilled labor.
2. Excellent academic institutions, both secondary and university. This is exceedingly important, since education is perhaps any area's principal resource.
3. A diverse economy, strong in manufacturing, agriculture, tourism, and growing in services.
4. The cost of living (e.g., taxes) is competitive. Real estate is inexpensive. There's plenty of land.
5. A good transportation system.
6. Cultural amenities, including a high quality of living and good recreational opportunities.
7. A location close to markets.
8. A good infrastructure, including roads, sewers, police, and a reputation for honest government.

Next our weaknesses:

1. Comparatively high labor costs.
2. Few natural resources, such as energy, which, combined with our climate, make this a high-cost energy state.
3. Most significant, in my view, is that we lack an entrepreneurial environment. Specifically, this refers to our tax levels, which result from the high spending level at which the state operates, and regulation, particularly, from my perspective, securities regulation.

There has been real progress. They're starting to recognize the problems over there in Madison, and that's half the battle. Just a few hard decisions, that may initially be unpopular in the eyes of some, and the legislation necessary to implement them, and Wisconsin could be one of the economically dynamic places in the nation. Remember, for the first half of this century, that's what it was.

So you can see we have the basic ingredients of a dynamic economy working for us here. Most important, the attitudes are changing. The attitude of the people is changing; they realize that economic development must be helped, not hindered. And the attitude of the legislature is changing. If you get to know these people, you will see that the majority of them are not lunkheads, and they are trying to get things changed. If you don't agree with that last statement, you can get involved and start changing the cast of characters in Madison. (As a matter of fact, a change of not too many faces in the legislature would give the Republicans control and lead to a new direction.)

I have one final argument to prove my case that Wisconsin is now the place to bet your future. As I said earlier, the crowd always lags; they fail to recognize the signals of change. As the great Friedrich Schiller said: "Anyone taken as an individual is tolerably sensible and reasonable. As a member of a crowd, he at once becomes a blockhead." If you don't believe that, why have there been lynch mobs, or Crusades, or runs on banks, or fires where people would have escaped with their lives if they hadn't panicked?

I have read the book *Extraordinary Popular Delusions and the Madness of Crowds*. If you haven't, you should. In his foreword to the October, 1932, edition, Bernard Baruch wrote that reading the book saved him millions of dollars. The month he wrote the foreword marked the absolute bottom of the stock market crash that had begun three years earlier. The Dow Jones Average had plunged to 41. Greed and speculation had turned to fear. In the midst of all this, Baruch wrote: "I have always thought that if, even in the presence of dizzily spiraling stock prices, we had all continuously repeated, 'Two plus two still make four,' much of this evil might have been averted."

Therefore, as you might imagine, I was encouraged when I attended the 1986 Economic and Financial Outlook program sponsored by the First Wisconsin Bank. In response to the question, "How much progress is Wisconsin making toward improving its business climate?," 0 percent of the people said "Great," 44 percent said "Some," and 56 percent said "None."

If the crowd is always wrong, ladies and gentlemen, I rest my case for Wisconsin.

Growing an Entrepreneurial State
Governor's Summit on Capital
Mar. 20, 2002

My charge today was to present twenty minutes of stimulating, wise, and witty remarks to three or four hundred successful business people and venture capitalists and, as a throw-in, come up with some solid ideas for attracting more equity and venture money into our great state. Since I have never faded from challenges, I accepted the invitation without hesitation. Although talking in front of this group could be intimidating, I remembered what Woody Allen said, "Two-thirds of life is just showing up!" So here I am.

My firm, Lubar & Co., is in the private investment and venture capital business. We act for our own account acquiring companies, often in mature industries. Our objective is to make these companies into better and faster-growing businesses through innovation and renewal. In these situations, we encourage management to introduce new products, reduce costs through modern equipment and technology, seek better marketing and the efficiencies of advanced information systems. We are also in the venture capital business, investing in growth and start-up companies. I consider what we do to be entrepreneurship. We are professional owners or entrepreneurs working with professional managers.

The proposition I will put to you today is that there is no real shortage of venture capital or, for that matter, any tangible capital. Rather the shortage that exists is of entrepreneurs. I will try to point out that:

- Education leads to a knowledgeable, skilled work pool.
- From such a work pool of engineers, scientists, business graduates, and skilled tradespersons come entrepreneurs.
- It is the entrepreneurs who create opportunities.
- And finally, capital flows to opportunity if there is an environment of lawfulness and stability and if the regulatory and tax climate is competitive.

I would like first to talk about entrepreneurship, which I believe is the force that attracts capital. Peter Drucker, the internationally known consultant and author on management, asks the question: "What do the few truly successful businesses do which the others do not?" The answer is not that they are in the "right business," because that is not an accident, nor is it that the people are more able, because most of us are pretty much made of the same stuff. The difference, he says, lies in entrepreneurship.

Let me illustrate what I think entrepreneurship is. The special concern of entrepreneurship is effectiveness—doing the right things. To put matters in their proper perspective, I should add that the concern of management is efficiency—doing things the right way, for example by lowering costs, training people, etc. Efficiency is not unimportant; a business can die of inefficiency. But no business can grow, let alone survive, just because it is efficient. The classic example of this is the much-maligned buggy-whip business. If 100 years ago you were in the business of making buggy whips, no amount of efficiency would have allowed you to survive in that activity alone. The subject of entrepreneurship is therefore what things to do; it is not how to do them.

There is a basic principle to entrepreneurship. It is that whatever is already being done is by definition obsolete. In other words, recognize that the world is dynamic and that change is constant.

Entrepreneurship is essentially the acceptance of change as an opportunity. The acceptance of the leadership in change is the unique task of the entrepreneur. It was the success of ocean liners and railroads that prepared the way for airplanes. Propeller airplanes opened the way for jet airplanes. The development of the automobile created the motel, road-building, and drive-ins. The story is the same in communications and every other industry I can think of. At this time, when change is occurring faster than ever before, it means that opportunity for the entrepreneur is greater than ever. Entrepreneurship in effect means finding and utilizing opportunity. It is opportunity-focused and not problem-focused. Management deals with problems. Entrepreneurship deals with opportunity.

Actually, the specific task for the entrepreneur is to create and then to exploit risk. Without risk there can be no genuine profit, nor can there be any justification for profit. No-risk activities are paid for with wages. Profits belong to risk-takers. The entrepreneur is the systematic risk-maker and risk-taker. He discharges this function by looking for and finding opportunity.

Managing a business for growth involves risks. Starting new businesses involves even greater risks. Entrepreneurs take on these risks in return for the opportunity to make and keep money. This is what creates a dynamic economy. Without this process of constant renewal and creation, you have a downward cycle as businesses mature and decline in their normal course.

As I said earlier, the stated focus of this summit conference is on increasing equity capital for Wisconsin-based businesses. The reality is that tangible capital is fungible. Capital is like sand particles on the beach, or kernels of grain in a bin, and it flows to where the return is highest in relation to the perceived risks. Entrepreneurs create opportunities that attract capital. In theory, no place in the United States is without capital because it flows to where it finds the best opportunity. However, we know that some states are more hospitable or attractive to entrepreneurs and that capital flows more constantly in their direction. Certainly states like

Texas, Florida, and Arizona, without income taxes, have an advantage over states with income taxes. States with lower income-tax structures have advantages over states with higher tax structures. States with well-regarded educational infrastructures have advantages over those that don't. States noted for fair judicial systems and honest government have advantages over those who are not perceived to be as fair and honest. So clearly a state can improve its economic situation if it makes itself more hospitable to investors than its competitor states.

In the short time I have left with you today, I would like to address certain specific issues for attracting capital, what kind of capital we are seeking to attract, where I believe we stand here in Wisconsin on these issues, and what we might consider doing to improve our situation.

First, let's define what we mean by capital. My definition will be in the context of recognizing that the overall objective is to combine capital with labor to maximize economic development, create more high-paying jobs, and also lift those at the bottom of the income scale up. Although there are other forms of capital, I am talking about, first, human capital and, secondly, tangible capital. By human capital, I mean the level of skill, education, and talent that exists in the labor force. Indeed, it's the level of learning that is retained, because knowledge represents any community's greatest resource. If you don't believe this, look at the Middle East, whose countries are rich in resources but low in education, and hence the bulk of the population lives poorly.

How are we doing here in Wisconsin in the education department? When it comes to post-secondary education, we are doing exceptionally well. We have many fine private colleges and universities and, in my judgment, the premier state university system in the USA. The UW System, with thirteen degree-granting universities and thirteen two-year campuses, is tops. In fact, our flagship university in Madison last year attracted close to $600 million in research funds and is second only to Johns Hopkins in this regard. It is the world's leader in stem cell research and other areas of the life sciences. Regrettably, the Board of Regents and the legislature are currently unhappy with each other, but since they both know the extraordinary value of our university system to the state and the nation, I expect they will come to a satisfactory resolution soon.

But what about those critical early years of education— K through 12? We don't look very good here, and it is vital to our future to change this broken, non-performing system. As a Milwaukeean, I am most familiar with the Milwaukee Public Schools, but my comments apply to public schools in general. We have an enrollment in the city of Milwaukee of about 100,000 students, mostly minority kids. The annual budget of the MPS System is about $1 billion, or $10,000 per student. According to a recent *Milwaukee Journal Sentinel* article, truancy averages 50 percent daily. Here alone we are wasting one-half of our budget dollars. Even worse, the dropout rate before graduation is more than 50 percent, and those graduating may often be uneducated to the point of being unprepared for college or even illiterate. You all must know that without a high school diploma, and probably a college degree, a young person's future is dismal. They are left to compete with the workers of Third World countries for whatever low-paying jobs are available. This situation is a disgrace. I am ashamed and share guilt with the rest of our community for allowing this to go on. We cannot leave behind more than half of our minority young people and expect to have a talented workforce, a quality community, and a dynamic economy.

So what can we do? Our leadership—mayor, county exec, governor, legislators, city and county officials—can recognize what is happening. They can recognize that there is no accountability. Ten years ago, we had 100,000 welfare cases. Today we have none. We must do the same with those public school systems that are not performing and not accountable. This means radically changing the system and the people that are causing the system to fail.

Turning to tangible capital. What we mean here is money, investable funds, and tangible assets: inventories, buildings, and machines.

The higher the quality of our human capital, the more we can expect to attract tangible capital. This is the controlling principle of how free markets work today.

In the years I have been in this business, Wisconsin has done some good things to make itself more attractive to capital. Income-tax rates were reduced. However, we are still a high-tax state. Capital gains are taxed at a lesser rate than they were fifteen years ago, and the inheritance tax has been largely abolished. However, there are still an enormous number of improvements that the state must make if it is to become competitive with the high-growth states. Generally speaking, Wisconsin's economic performance has been average to a bit below average. According to a recently published report by the La Follette School of Public Affairs, Wisconsin's population grew more or less steadily over the past thirty years, from about 4.4 million in 1969 to about 5.3 million today. This growth rate is a little over half the national average over the period. Wisconsin's employment also grew more or less steadily over the past thirty years, from about 1.9 million to about 3.3 million jobs. This growth is just slightly below the national level over this period. In 1969, Wisconsin's income per capita was about $14,400, compared with $14,800 for the United States as a whole (in today's dollars). Over the past thirty years, Wisconsin's real per-capita income grew at about 2.2 percent per annum, to about $27,300, while the United States as a whole grew at a rate of 2.3 percent, to about $29,600. Wisconsin should not be a sub-average state.

Although Joe Hildebrandt has written a white paper enumerating forty-four proposals for enhancing capital investments, I would offer the following specific suggestions to create an environment attractive to entrepreneurs:

1. Boldly address and reverse the deterioration and non-performance of our public school systems.
2. Lower income tax and capital gain tax rates, ideally across the board, but if that isn't doable, at least reduce them on start-up productive companies.

3. Direct the State Investment Board to invest in Wisconsin venture capital. (I don't mean New York buy-out funds.) An allocation of at least $5 billion spread out over ten years would put the issue of a venture capital shortage to rest.
4. Continue to work on our securities laws so that public markets for small company shares become more possible.
5. Create incentives for graduates with engineering, scientific, and business degrees to remain in Wisconsin, possibly including some level of student loan forgiveness.

Having told our government what they can do to help, let me leave you with this final thought: "Free enterprise creates wealth. Entrepreneurs create wealth, not government." I didn't originate this thought. Lady Margaret Thatcher did, and she transformed her country from decadent socialism to prospering free enterprise.

A County in Crisis
Greater Milwaukee Committee
Sept. 11, 2006

I am here to summarize the GMC's report on reforming Milwaukee County's current fiscal situation and getting the county back on track with a balanced budget and providing the necessary services expected by its citizens. Let me start by stating that with sensible decisions and the required political will, these problems are solvable. Needless to say, as in solving all difficulties, there will be some pain, and part of the solution is distributing this pain fairly.

I want to emphasize that the purpose of our report is not to fix blame for the current situation. Rather, we view the GMC's role as a catalyst and facilitator for the solution. Our message is simple and basic: County expenses need to be lowered and controlled. Tax increases should be a last resort. This means that county officials, the county executive, and the Board of Supervisors must step up and do the job for which they are responsible. If not, the alternative is for the governor and the legislature to create a Fiscal Control Board that is empowered to do the job.

Our committee has spent much time this year meeting with labor leaders, County Executive Walker, county supervisors, Mayor Barrett, state and county officials, budget and legal experts, and others to acquire a deeper understanding of the issues driving this fiscal crisis. The persons we talked with were informed and decent, and most recognized the seriousness of the problems we saw.

We discovered three key areas responsible for the current situation:

1. Communication between the county executive and the Board of Supervisors is poor. County governance is further complicated and made more difficult by the numerous spending and taxing authorities that exist outside of county control and oversight. These authorities include: Milwaukee Metropolitan Sewerage district, Milwaukee Area Technical College, Wisconsin Center District, and the Miller Park Stadium District. To these you can add Milwaukee Public Schools, which does have an elected board. The actions of these authorities impact the tax bills of county residents, and accountability to the county does not exist.
2. There have been huge cost increases relating to county employee health care and pensions.
3. There is a lack of coordination and duplication of services between local governments, resulting in unnecessarily high costs of operations and services.

We also came up with what we believe to be effective, realistic solutions to the county's budget crisis:

1. Lowering active employee and retiree health care costs, for a potential annual savings of $28 million.
2. Contracting with the state for criminal justice services. Milwaukee County could pursue, for 2007 and beyond, the option of paying the State of Wisconsin to take over pieces of the criminal justice system.

3. Contracting with the state to take over the Milwaukee County prosecutorial system and cover the management and financing of that system, with the exception of the district attorney's compensation.
4. Changing the way the county finances its pension obligation by replacing its current pension liabilities with pension obligation bonds.
5. Developing a coherent, defensible, and widely supported policy for disposing of unneeded and under/unused non-parkland assets.
6. Coordinating services through intergovernmental agreements. If the county could contract for "overhead" and public safety costs with other governments at 90 percent of its current costs, the resulting 10-percent savings would equal at least $9 million per year, much of which would result in property tax savings.

We believe the short-term solution to the County budget issues rests with the county executive and the Board of Supervisors, whom we urge to consider these recommendations for the 2007 budget:

1. Revise both the county retiree and active health care plans as outlined in the report appendix.
2. Have the Milwaukee County Transit System follow the revised county health care plan as part of the provision of additional resources to the system, and cease the practice of offering lifetime health insurance benefits.
3. Dedicate a portion of the savings identified in this report to restoring transit services, rebuilding our parks, and restoring funding to the cultural and arts institutions currently supported by the county.
4. Bid out Milwaukee County's "overhead services" to other governments in the area.

As I said earlier, reviewing our governance system is also a key recommendation for solving the county's budget crisis. Toward this objective we propose:

1. An elected oversight board which would approve all expenditures and all property and sales tax levies for the autonomous taxing authorities in Milwaukee County, including Milwaukee Metropolitan Sewerage District, Milwaukee Area Technical College, Wisconsin Center District, and Southeastern Wisconsin Regional Ballpark District;
2. Studying the creation of a board or committee of multi-governmental entities to oversee coordination of less costly, more efficient, countywide service delivery through intergovernmental agreements.
3. Reviewing our current safety and emergency services within the county to eliminate areas of duplication and overlap.

Finally, we recommend the following to the state task force studying the Milwaukee County budget crisis:

1. Change state law to allow Milwaukee County as well as other local governments to incur 30-year or longer-term debt for the sole purpose of reducing unfunded pension liabilities.
2. Identify and recommend removal of any statutory impediments to the county's ability to purchase state criminal justice and prosecutorial services.
3. Urge state agencies to contract criminal justice and health and social services to Milwaukee County.
4. Have the county set clear benchmarks for achieving fiscal soundness and quality of service, to be reviewed by the state for compliance.

Both the State of Wisconsin and the City of Milwaukee successfully dealt with unfunded liabilities for pension and health care cost in a responsible and timely manner. The mounting budget dilemma caused by rising health care and pension costs for Milwaukee County is solvable as well.

We take the strong position that our county leadership must step up to the challenge, set aside the past squabbles and attacks, and focus instead on the difficult decisions needed to turn around the county's very vulnerable fiscal position. Our citizens expect and deserve quality and effective services. These services need to continue without interruption, whether provided under the county's current governance structure or under a Fiscal Control Board.

The Outlook for our City and State
Milwaukee Press Club
Gridiron Headliner Award
Apr. 28, 2007

I am truly honored to accept this award. I follow in the footsteps of men and women who were the leaders of Milwaukee when I arrived on the business scene in October, 1953. They are all people I respected. One Headliner I will never forget is Eliot Fitch, president of the Marine National Exchange Bank, who hired me fresh out of law school in 1953. It was the beginning of my career.

When Roger Stafford and I met this past winter to talk about this award, he asked me if I had ever been in the Milwaukee Press Club. I told him that from 1967 to 1973 I was the president of Mortgage Associates. My office was on the fifth floor of 125 E. Wells Street, and the Press Club was on the second or third floor. Not only that, but the Press Club was a regular place for lunch. More important, I told Roger that I had concluded that newspaper reporters made very good investment analysts, and I was in the investment business. The reason, I explained, was that the typical young analyst visits a company, sits down with his pad and pencil, interviews the president, writes down all the responses, and then comes back to the office to write his report, reflecting all he heard in the interview, whereas an experienced reporter assumes that everyone is a liar and proceeds to challenge everything said and eventually does get the real story. I told Roger that I had shared this view with a close friend and former *Sun-Times* reporter from Chicago a few years ago, and he asked if I had ever been in the Chicago Press Club. I said, "No, just Milwaukee's." "Well," he said, "over the doors it says, 'If your mother says she loves you, check it out.'" See what I mean?

While I have this stage and this very influential audience, please allow me to focus for a few minutes on a most serious topic: the outlook for our city, county, and state. This past year I spent a good amount of my time as the co-chair of the State

Task Force on Milwaukee County Finances as well as co-chair of a Greater Milwaukee Committee dealing with the same subject. I would expect you are all familiar with what we found: generous and underfunded pensions, generous and underfunded health care, outdated management systems, elected officials who barely communicate with one another, duplication of services, and, perhaps most serious, multiple non-elected boards and commissions with taxing authority. Specifically, that includes Milwaukee Area Technical College, the Metropolitan Sewerage Commission, the Wisconsin Center, and, though the school boards are elected, I would add them to this broad number of spenders who have little or no oversight.

If that isn't enough, consider that Wisconsin has always had a high proportion of its work force in agriculture and manufacturing —two sectors in decline due to global competition. Meanwhile, as the more prosperous states in our country are transitioning into the knowledge industries, since 1991 our state government has been drawing back on its funding for the University of Wisconsin System. That's where fully one out of three state high school graduates receive their college education, and it is our best vehicle for preparing for a knowledge-based economy. Nor have the public school systems in cities like Milwaukee been able to educate our young people at an acceptable level. Yet we all know that education is everyone's ticket to a good future.

Oh, yes, one more thing. Despite being a high-tax state, neither the city nor the county nor the state can satisfactorily balance its budget. We have some very big-time systemic problems that must be addressed. Sadly, I can tell you that the well-intentioned elected officials I worked with are as frustrated as you and I, but feel powerless to change the system.

So what to do? We need leadership from the mayor, the county executive, the chairman of the Board of Supervisors, and the governor to collect a group of the best people at our universities, in the government, and in business and have them develop a governance plan that addresses:

- The ideal organization and governance system for our public schools.
- A streamlined governance system for city, county, and possibly metropolitan governments.
- A full review of our state tax system and the development of a more realistic and competitive system.
- Finally, a means and a plan to implement these needed changes.

We must act if we want to enter a new and better era. It will take leadership and sacrifice on the political side, and an open mind on the part of all citizens, but it can be done.

Again, thank you from the bottom of my heart for this wonderful recognition, and thank you for letting me get all of what I said off my chest.

The Devolution of Milwaukee County Government
Rotary Club of Milwaukee
Apr. 29, 2008

Most of you know that my career has been in business management and finance. I don't claim to be an authority on municipal finance or Milwaukee metropolitan politics but, then again, many elected officials lack a background in business management and don't seem to have a record of understanding finance, so we'll call it even. I also believe my record will show that I am a common-sense person with the ability to recognize changing circumstances and change with them.

During the past two years, I co-chaired the Greater Milwaukee Committee's Task Force on Milwaukee County Finances. I also co-chaired Governor Doyle's Task Force on Milwaukee County's Finances. In the time we have together here, I will share with you what I learned, the problems I perceived, why they occurred, and, most importantly, what I believe the solutions are.

First, I want to acknowledge that all of the county officials and employees I encountered were decent and intelligent people. Many want to do the right thing, but they're mired in a bureaucracy that won't let them. County governance has grown into a dysfunctional system that wouldn't work if Jesus was the county executive and Moses chaired the Board of Supervisors.

Let me start by giving you some background. During the last sixteen years, despite closing County Hospital and shifting services for both welfare (W-2) and child welfare to the state, Milwaukee County's budget has grown by 50 percent. In 1990, the county spent $857 million; by 2006 that budget ballooned to $1.25 billion. The property tax levy has also grown by more than 50 percent, from $147 million in 1990 to $233 million in 2006. During that same period, the county's residential population has decreased by about 44,000 people.

But as Milwaukee County's budget and levy have risen, the portion of the county budget and levy dedicated to services that the average person cares about most—namely parks, transit, the zoo, the arts and cultural centers—has declined. Of the total budget, only about 13.5 percent was spent on these services. Almost half the budget consists of health and human service spending.

Let's examine some of the County's problems and their causes in more detail:

1. Pensions. As recently as January, 2001, the county's pension system was more than fully funded. In fact, it was 108.6-percent funded. So what was done? A series of irresponsible benefit increases were implemented. The former surplus soon became a liability of almost $500 million. You know you have a pension problem on your hands when an area reporter writes about our pension problems and how we got there and wins a Pulitzer Prize for it—as we just saw happen with Dave Umhoefer of the *Journal Sentinel*. By the way, congratulations, Dave. But Dave, like the rest of us, is now stuck paying to cover these pension obligations.

The situation was recently addressed by the legislature and Governor Doyle, when they authorized Milwaukee county to issue thirty-year Pension Obligation Bonds. This was a key recommendation of both the GMC's and State Task Force's reports. While that does indeed help, this is still a liability that shouldn't have happened.

2. Rising health care costs and early retirement of county employees. Unlike the pension problem, this is an issue for every American, whether you're in Milwaukee County or not. But faced with a fiscal crisis, a rapid spike of younger retirees, and a commitment of lifetime health insurance for all employees hired before 1994, the county is in a tougher position than most when it comes to funding health care responsibilities. Again, some poor decisions of the past that we are paying for today.

3. State mandates that impose costs without full revenue-sharing to pay for them. In the past, the county has been burdened with costs mandated by the State of Wisconsin— mandates that require the county to provide a service or fulfill a duty without providing the funds needed to do it. In the case of Milwaukee County, the financial situation simply doesn't allow the room for unfunded mandates. This is an example of how many in the county who want to do the right thing are put in a position of funding the priorities of others.

4. Costs imposed by independent authorities, many non-elected. Look at your property tax bill. There are not only assessments from Milwaukee County and your local municipality. You pay MMSD for water treatment, MATC for technical schools in the area, local school districts, and so on, and so on. There are multiple, independent authorities, many of whom do not face voters but have the power to add to the tax bill, and in too many cases with little or no oversight over what they do. Do you think these independent taxing authorities pay close attention to the overall tax burden, or do they just focus on what their needs are?

5. Duplication of services. Fire, police, maintenance crews—in too many cases, multiple agencies are responding to a single need. A sensible way to lower the tax burden and increase efficiency would be to eliminate duplication of services. Consolidation of some services, as was done with the creation of the North Shore Fire Department in the early 1990s, is an example of a good way to go. The mentality of government should be to find these efficiencies and make cross-agreements to implement them.

6. Communication between the County Executive and the County Board. It's no secret that the relationship between County Executive Scott Walker and many members of the County Board has been quite adversarial. Infighting and political maneuvers are certainly not productive, and they don't help the county and the taxpayer to get things done. I understand the county executive is trying for better relationships, but the system is not built to create collaboration.

The result of all of this lack of expenditure control, high employee costs, duplication of services, and past poor judgments is that we have one of the highest property tax rates in the country. And despite these high tax burdens, Milwaukee County is not adequately supporting key assets and fundamental services to its residents, its businesses, or its visitors. I am talking about building maintenance and infrastructure needs in general.

Meanwhile, we're top-heavy with governance. The 2007 tax levy cost for the Milwaukee County Board of Supervisors Department was about $5.6 million. In a fully incorporated county, where there are governing municipalities covering every inch of ground, do we really need a nineteen-member Board of Supervisors who each get paid over $50,000 per year with full benefits in what is essentially a part-time job?

Some may argue that other Wisconsin counties have more board members, and that's true, but they don't get paid this much, and they have non-incorporated areas for which they are responsible. Let's look at Milwaukee County compared to other major urban counties in the United States. We have nineteen supervisors and a population of about 900,000. Meanwhile, Hennepin County, Minnesota, which contains Minneapolis and a large number of suburbs totaling just over one million people, has seven on its county board. Alameda County in California, which contains Oakland and parts of the East Bay with 1.4 million residents, has just five. Fast-growing Tarrant County, Texas, which includes Fort Worth, has 1.6 million people and will soon hold the headquarters of the United States Bowling Congress, but needs just five supervisors to oversee rapid growth and an increasing quality of life. Why do we need nineteen supervisors?

We haven't asked much from them, but even something reasonable like an ethics code—something much needed—meets with resistance. As the *Journal Sentinel* Editorial Board noted on April 13, just over two weeks ago, "The Milwaukee County Board's trashing of a proposed and very much needed revamp of the county's ethics code was way over the top." We could save time with this ethics issue by not having a County Board in the first place.

Meanwhile, Milwaukee is challenged economically, struggling to move ahead in a world where the speeds required to keep up continue to accelerate. How can we keep up when we're bogged down with glaring redundancies and inefficiencies in a government that works with the speed of a horse and buggy in the age of the satellite? For Milwaukee, both the city and the county, as well as the seven-county region we are part of, to have a prosperous future, we must break free of our outdated past and recognize the need to change and deliver.

Studies show time and time again that larger legislatures are positively correlated with higher government spending. One study found a close link between larger county boards and significant increases in county social and criminal justice spending. Perhaps that's not news to many of you, but this is just to prove that, upon true examination, the evidence is there that wherever you go, larger government bodies equal larger government spending, which means they need more tax money. Eventually, government grows to the detriment of the area it's supposed to serve.

The time has come for county government to retire itself in an orderly fashion, reduce the burden on area taxpayers, and reshape the way taxes are collected, services are delivered, and thereby create a better economy and quality of life in Milwaukee.

As promised, I come not only to point out the problems, but to offer solutions. First, we can change the system by means of a process of devolution, and then develop a strong, accountable Fiscal Oversight Board to manage budgets for the area. We can devolve and eliminate county government by passing down the various services that the county is responsible for to a combination of state, existing municipal, and certain independent authorities. The county is a child of the state and exists at the pleasure of the state. The state, through the actions of the legislature and the governor, can devolve what the state has imposed but is no longer relevant or needed.

Nineteen municipalities in the county maintain all the key services locally, such as police, fire and, through cooperative arrangements, services like animal control. We could return the parks to local municipalities with the county's former share of property tax to maintain them or, if municipalities desire, create a Parks Authority whose budget and taxing limits would be subject to the Fiscal Oversight Board. The state is able to assume administration over remaining social services that are now handled by the county. The state can also run the public safety (sheriff, etc.) and corrections functions, along with social services such as income maintenance and food stamps. The governor's recent budget even included provisions for funding of the General Assistance Medical Program. The judicial system is currently split between the state and county, but the state could do it all.

With respect to cultural assets, Milwaukee County could cede to the various governing boards responsibility for their physical facilities and collections, along with funds and/or endowments to repair and maintain them. Better yet, other communities have created cultural districts governed by authorities comprised of board representatives of their various cultural institutions. The legislation exists within current state law to create a Cultural District within Milwaukee.

Independent authorities, requiring far less administration and expense, can take over transit, airports, and perhaps the parks to bring a more comprehensive, regional focus that benefits not only city and county of Milwaukee residents, but those residing in other counties in the region. Coordinated planning and a larger view would be very beneficial.

For example, a Regional Transit Authority could run the buses with a regional view, or at least develop a memorandum of understanding with other adjoining communities, resulting in a system that works better for everyone and has a wider source of funding with lower administrative costs. Larger transportation visions, such as commuter rail and interconnecting modes of transport systems, including consideration of roads and highways, are also much better planned and executed on a regional scale.

Airports can be part of this also. A Regional Airport Authority, perhaps as part of the Regional Transit Authority, could handle not only Mitchell International Airport and Timmerman Field, but take in and coordinate nearby airports such as Crites Field in Waukesha, John Batten Airport in Racine, and Kenosha Regional.

These proposed solutions are based on three key assumptions:

1. It is possible, and beneficial, to create an overarching mechanism to review and approve the budgets and tax levies for those services provided by the county and the various authorities;
2. There is a need to create a system that governs based on citizens' needs today—not on the distance that can be covered in a day's horseback ride by a circuit court judge, which was the criterion for drawing county lines 150 years ago.
3. The appropriate services must be provided by a simplified, cost-effective system. We must unpeel the onion of multiple, redundant layers of government.

This may sound radical to some, but only because it is a new and different structure. It would be designed to meet today's needs.

It's been done around the country, however, in one form or another, in a number of cities and counties. Over the past two years, Wyandotte County and its county seat, Kansas City, Kansas, have merged services and passed much of the savings back to taxpayers, who are repaying the area with increased investment, business activity, and economic growth. Jefferson County, Kentucky, merged with Louisville in 2003 and provides a wealth of good examples of how to consolidate its transit authority, park system, and school systems. Indianapolis and Nashville are also good examples of devolution, and of how consolidation of city and county government can work. If you haven't noticed, all the cities and metro areas I just mentioned are doing quite well right now and have moved up the list of the top fifty high-growth municipalities. In May, 1997, the county executive of Essex County, New Jersey, proposed abolishing his job along with the entire county government.

We're struggling to keep up. In 1970, the city of Milwaukee ranked twelfth-largest in the U.S., with 717,000 people. Today the city has fallen to twenty-second, after losing over 110,000 of those residents. Even more illustrative of our situation, the Milwaukee metro area was seventeenth in the U.S. in population in 1970; today it has fallen to thirty-seventh. Our economic and political muscle has shrunk proportionately.

The cities and metros I just mentioned that have consolidated or devolved duplicative governments are doing well by comparison: Kansas City is seeing 6-percent population growth, while Louisville's metro has increased 4 percent. Meanwhile, Nashville is hot on our heels as a metro, ranking thirty-ninth, and will soon surpass us with its 8.4-percent growth rate. Austin, Texas, will also, since it's thirty-eighth, with 14.3-percent growth. We currently have 0.8-percent growth—stagnant at best.

But one of the reasons I'm talking with you today is because we want to change that. It's quite evident that Milwaukee County can learn from examples like these and realize that it can be done. In 2006, as a result of in-depth, inclusive research, the GMC published *Reforming Milwaukee County—A Response to the Fiscal Crisis,* the final report of a task force that I co-chaired. This report outlined causes and included specific recommendations to save taxpayers millions of dollars in 2007 and even more in future years. The ideas I have shared with you today represent a continuation of this GMC work. The GMC remains committed to moving this issue forward, and an action plan will be developed in the next few months.

So, what's next? The involvement of the legislature, the governor, the local communities, and all citizens is critical. This can't be done easily, but it can be done. A lot of entities and individuals must come together, agree in principle on what I have generally put forth today, and take the steps to make this happen. It would take the action of the State of Wisconsin, Milwaukee County, the City of Milwaukee, and the municipalities in the county. It has been done before, and it can be done now. The time to make it happen is now.

This is our opportunity. We can change the future of Milwaukee County for the better. We've done it before. County government's last major structural overhaul came in 1960, when John Doyne was elected the first county executive. This is simply part of changing with the times, of becoming more responsible with taxpayer money, more growth-oriented, and adding opportunities to everyone's future and ensuring that Milwaukee's next great era lies ahead. The most courageous among us will make it happen. Will you join us?

Remaking Milwaukee County
Milwaukee Journal Sentinel
Sept. 30, 2008

Let me start with a short quotation from *The Lessons of History*, by Will and Ariel Durant: "On one point all are agreed: civilizations begin, flourish, decline, and disappear—or linger on as stagnant pools left by once life-giving streams. What are the causes of development, and what are the causes of decay?"

Kiril Sokoloff recently wrote of the fragility of complex civilizations. Drawing from books like Thomas Homer-Dixon's *The Upside of Down* and Joseph Tainter's *The Collapse of Complex Societies*, he set forth a simple thesis: As societies evolve, they become more complex. For example, a simple agrarian society develops an irrigation system after its crops fail because of insufficient rainfall. As the population grows, so do the number of irrigation canals. In order to maintain and repair the canals, a management bureaucracy is put in place, and the people are taxed to pay for it. To counter the people's complaints, a tax collector is invented, and so on and so on.

Sokoloff maintains that every extra layer of organization imposes a cost. As complexity increases, returns diminish. As you have to feed more canal-builders and tax collectors, your extra crop yields disappear. Also, once a society develops beyond a certain level of complexity, it becomes increasingly fragile. A relatively minor disturbance can bring everything crashing down. We saw this at Milwaukee County with the pension scandal a few years ago. We are seeing it today with the current financial crisis that has endangered the entire world financial system.

Is there an alternative to collapse? There's only one that I know of: change. Milwaukee County and ultimately the city and MPS must change. At the Greater Milwaukee Committee, we are working on a plan to simplify and change the county's governance system to make it more effective and less costly—and to reduce property taxes. We have informed the chairman of the Board of Supervisors, the county executive, the governor of Wisconsin, and the mayor of Milwaukee of what we are working on, and we have asked for their collaboration in developing a proposal for change. The willingness of these leaders to consider our ideas and combine them with theirs makes me hopeful that together we can produce a better system for all our citizens and taxpayers.

Here are the key elements of our proposal:

1. Negotiate a fifty-year lease of the airport and use the funds to retire unfunded pension and health care liability, along with other debt. If any surplus remains, place it in a rainy-day fund.
2. Outsource most county services to state or local municipalities.
3. Create a Parks and Cultural Assets Authority and fund it with a sales tax.
4. Eliminate the county executive and his staff.
5. Replace the Board of Supervisors with a Fiscal Oversight Board that would approve all expenditures supported by property taxes, with the size of the body and its appointees by the governor to be determined.
6 Create a Regional Transit Authority.

Fixing Milwaukee
Rotary Club of Milwaukee
Dec. 1, 2009

I want to speak to you today about three principal subjects that we as Milwaukee citizens we must address if we are to prevent our city and county from crashing. They are:

1. County governance and county fiscal management.
2. The Milwaukee Public School system, its importance, and its failure to date.
3. The economic future of Milwaukee and the role of the University of Wisconsin-Milwaukee as a research university in leading a new era of economic growth.

On April 29, 2008, I spoke to your Rotary Club describing what I had learned about Milwaukee County's fiscal crisis. What we learned in our studies is that the county governance system consisting of a county executive and a large county board that do not work together had resulted in gridlock. In short, there are ongoing, critical problems, and no action is taken to solve them.

Since then, the problems have worsened, according to a recent study by the Public Policy Forum. Last week Rob Henken of PPF reported this to you in detail. The county has now seen its unfunded employee pension and health care benefits grow to $2.4 billion, and it is struggling with a structural annual deficit that is projected to grow from $78 million in 2010 to $153 million in 2014. To put this in perspective, the total budget today is about $1.4 billion. County employee salaries and wages are projected to increase from about $280 million in 2010 to almost $350 million in 2015, employee health care benefits from just under $150 million to $230 million in 2015, and pension contributions from $70-plus million to over $100 million in 2015, if no changes are made.

Needless to say, the government would implode before this would occur, but is this level of recklessness something a citizen should even have to contemplate? Must we not start by recognizing we live under a dysfunctional governmental system? A system that favors the elected officials, who seek re-election, and government employees, and particular voting groups that they favor?

Unlike cities and villages, counties do not have broad "home rule" authority; they may only undertake functions expressly authorized by the state. In fact, they are children of the state, often called "administrative arms" of the higher level of government. Certain county offices are specified in the Wisconsin constitution— sheriff, register of deeds, district attorney, county clerk, and county treasurer—but everything else about county government exists at the will of the legislature and governor.

The main reasons for eliminating county government are these:

1. To end the growth of legacy costs, meaning pensions and health care.
2. To properly manage county expenditures.
3. To stop the county government from diminishing county services such as parks, recreation, and transit.

4. To potentially use existing county assets as part of a liability reduction program.

There are other reasons, but the four I have listed are reason enough.

Eliminating a government with a $1.4 billion budget, 5,700 full-time employees, several critical state-mandated functions, and unfunded retirement and health care liabilities of $2.4 billion is far easier said than done. But it is very possible and has been done in other jurisdictions. This issue is what the GMC task force that I chair is working on, along with the Public Policy Forum. We have to date released some of the analyses I have just referred to, and our final report will be released in late January, 2010, along with our recommendations for change.

It was inevitable, as county government's fiscal problems worsened during the past three years, and as its elected leadership failed to agree even on the nature and scope of the problems, that some of us would begin asking whether county government was needed at all. I know I did, but I was not the first. As early as 1969, Supervisor Richard Nowakowski introduced legislation to the County Board to create a commission to determine which county services should be abolished or curtailed. I don't think it got off the ground, but time has proved it was needed. Just consider the current round of agonizing and bitter budget deliberations between the county executive and the Board of Supervisors. I was encouraged when the county executive joined the chorus of those advocating the elimination of the county and the transfer of its assets, authority, and duties to the state and other municipalities in the county. Stay tuned for the GMC recommendations on this critical issue, and most important, make your views known.

Finally on this subject, be certain that next fall, when you vote for governor, you are well aware of where each candidate stands on this subject. Ask yourself, "Where do I want to see the county in five or ten years? Who has a plan that will take us there? Is it an achievable plan that makes sense? Who is best able to lead this effort?"

And yet the county isn't the worst of our problems. The future of our city depends on a public educational system that prepares our young people for suitable employment and a pathway to a middle-class life. In addition to the 3Rs, we should be able to expect a well-functioning school system to teach our students civil behavior, discipline, and the importance of a supportive family. On all counts, MPS has failed. I realize there are many persons and groups responsible for the failure of the public school system, but we must start by changing the MPS system itself. The current changes being sought by Governor Doyle and Mayor Barrett must be embraced as a first step. It is a modest beginning, but it is a first step.

Recently President Obama was in the state, and in his remarks he said what all of us already knew: "Nothing will determine our future more than education." Mayor Barrett added, "The future of Milwaukee is inextricably intertwined with MPS, and we can no longer embrace the status quo. We need real change." Who can disagree with those statements? How can any even half-informed person question the need to change MPS?

Regardless of the reasons, the MPS system is a failure. There are approximately 86,000 students in the MPS system, which has a budget of $1.24 billion, or about $14,400 per student. By comparison, Chicago schools spend about $11,000 per student, and the national average is around $10,000, so it certainly isn't lack of funding. The high school graduation rate at MPS is less than 50 percent. In the case of male African-American students, only about 32 percent graduate in Milwaukee schools. Is there any wonder that in the city of Milwaukee the unemployment rate for African-American men is about 50 percent? Compare that with some suburban schools that graduate 98 percent of all students and have a go-to-college rate of more than 90 percent. I am talking about schools that have 10 to 20 percent of their students in the 220 Program, which means they are bussed in. I recognize that there are racial differences, family differences, and union differences. But above all there are organizational differences and system differences that have led to failure at MPS and not at the other schools in the county. As Condoleezza

Rice said here in Milwaukee a few weeks ago, "We must get past the situation where simply a student's ZIP code will tell us whether they are getting a good education."

The first step in change is for the legislature and governor to allow the mayor to appoint the MPS superintendent. The next step is to change the way the system is organized and governed. The price of not implementing change and not acting now is to sentence another generation of central-city children to a dark, bleak future. This is not acceptable in a civilized country. It is not an affordable option for the taxpayers of Wisconsin.

Lastly, let's talk about the economic future of Milwaukee and the role of a public state university like the University of Wisconsin-Milwaukee. First, I want to tell you a story. This is a true story, and it is one of the most amazing stories I know concerning economic development, wealth creation, and the ultimate monetary value of education. This is the story of how a backwater area of California grew into what is now called "Silicon Valley." It is the story of Stanford University, located in Palo Alto, California, and Professor Frederick Terman, who became dean of the Stanford Engineering School. Besides being an outstanding educator, he was an entrepreneur and a manager. Perhaps most important is to recognize that the product he developed through his efforts at Stanford was people—people who study, think, and act, the characteristics of all effective leaders.

The principle Professor Terman developed was what he called "Steeples of Excellence." The theory he proved was that the quality of a university is determined largely by these "steeples of excellence," in which each steeple is formed by a group of capable faculty members having closely related interests and collaborating—working together. He said an illustration of how this steeple concept works is that an electrical engineering department will achieve much more national recognition if it has five good men, all of whom specialize in one of the important areas within electrical engineering, such as solid-state electronics or control systems, as compared with an electrical engineering department that has five equally good men distributed one in each of five fashionable areas of electrical engineering acting by themselves.

This latter arrangement, where individuals work without close colleagues, is much less effective and adds up to very little of significance. The former can lead to national distinction. It takes a critical mass of talent concentrated in an individual specialty to make an impact. Think of UWM's effort to be a leader in the science of water.

Terman acknowledged that excellence costs money. But he felt that in many cases it would be less expensive than generally expected. He felt an increment of no more than $5,000 or $10,000 for each of five positions could make the difference. (In fairness to today, I must tell you that in Terman's final faculty year at Stanford—1964-65—he was provost, dean of engineering, and vice-president of Stanford at a salary of $37,500, so I grant you we are at different levels today.)

Terman summed up his strategy for achieving excellence by quoting from a speech Governor Fritz Hollings of South Carolina made to his legislature in early 1963, upon the occasion of his retirement from the governorship. In this speech, Hollings spoke of the South in general and South Carolina in particular as being "always too late with too little." He spoke of the state having "one last shot" and then continued:

> But what is this one shot we in South Carolina are to use? A college professor. You say we have lots of those, and we do have many good ones. But we don't have one with a National Aeronautics Space Administration grant, or one who is a member of the National Academy of Sciences. We don't have one internationally famous who will attract leading scholars and professors. You say that's Harvard thinking. South Carolina can't afford it. Any money available should go to the teachers, and not to these "ivory tower" professors. But I disagree. We can't afford not to do it.
>
> Suppose we had a faculty budget of $60,000 for five professors. The ordinary way, the South Carolina way, is to hire five good professors at $12,000 each. But the space-age approach is to retain an outstanding one at $20,000 and hire the other four at $10,000 apiece. The $10,000 ones are just as good, perhaps better than the original $12,000 professors, for this type will sacrifice to associate with the outstanding. And you haven't

spent any more money in total. In fact, you've made money as a result of the grants and contracts and students that the outstanding professor and his associates attract.

This one shot—the outstanding professor—has a snowballing effect. First, you have the professor, then his associates, then talented students, then contracts and grants, then quality education, then leadership. Multiply this by five or ten professors and it's easy to see the effect.

The outstanding professor also gives us the quality we've been looking for. Raising the pay of the incompetent teacher won't make him competent. But raising the level of higher education elevates all levels of education. The professor will be more talented, his associates brighter, the students more challenged, the new graduating teachers will be better trained and more inspired. And your children and mine when they graduate from high school can get into college and compete in society.

Our one shot may be the UW-Milwaukee Freshwater Research Institute School, or it may be some other research endeavor at the Business School or the Engineering School. But whatever it is, let's be sure it is a "Steeple of Excellence."

What I am able to tell you today is that directly flowing from Fred Terman's leadership were the people who formed Hewlett-Packard, Google, Intel, and hundreds more of the high-tech companies that now make up Silicon Valley. Nor is California the only state where this is going on. It is happening at the University of Texas in Austin, in the Research Triangle of North Carolina, certainly around the many universities in Boston, and close to home at the University of Wisconsin-Madison. It can happen in Milwaukee also, but we need a push to get our fair share of the UW budget.

Well, that's it for now. I thank you all for your attention. My hope is that you will think about what I have said, and that your consideration will lead you to join our efforts to:

1. Change the system of governance of Milwaukee County.

2. Recognize the need to drastically change the governance of MPS by transferring the authority to make the necessary changes to the mayor of Milwaukee.

3. And finally, understand that the real engines of economic development in the world are not generous giveaways by the state, or clever advertising, but the development of outstanding research institutions that persons like Chancellor Carlos Santiago are struggling to accomplish here in Milwaukee.

Restoring Civility
BizTimes Bravo! Entrepreneur
Lifetime Achievement Award
May 7, 2012

Thank you to the *Biz Times* for this recognition, and thank you to my family, friends, and everyone here for being with me today. I appreciate all of you more than I can say. At the outset, I assure you that I will hold to my time limit of twelve minutes. I won't be talking about my career or all of the good things my family and I have worked on in the past. My remarks today are more important than that and deal with the future—in truth, all of our futures.

I want to talk to you about the polarization and bitterness that has descended on our great state of Wisconsin this past year. I have spoken to no one who isn't unhappy and worried about the state of affairs that we are all experiencing in Wisconsin. So whether Scott Walker is your courageous hero or Tom Barrett is your savior sent from heaven, each of us will make that decision, and I implore all of my fellow citizens to vote your own conscience on June 5. But after that let's get on with it; let's roll up our sleeves and go to work together.

We must respect each other and understand that none of us are always right or always wrong. We must recognize that as citizens we are all going downhill unless we make the needed changes to our schools and government and work together toward the common goals that will solve our problems.

I consider both of the candidates in this election friends of mine, and I respect them both. A few years ago, I chaired several studies of the causes and potential cures of Milwaukee County's fiscal crisis. As you recall, this situation had been brought to light by the pension scandal, which led to the resignation of County Executive Tom Ament and the recalls of several county supervisors. Scott Walker was elected to replace Ament, and by all measures he did an excellent job. I know he worked with our group and helped us in every way he could. In the case of Tom Barrett, I first met him while he was serving in the State Senate. I had been nominated to the Board of Regents of the University of Wisconsin System by Governor Tommy Thompson, and he sent me around to meet every senator in advance of my confirmation hearings. Tom stood out. He is a man of honesty and high intelligence. I have always supported his actions as mayor of Milwaukee,.

As you can see, I admire both of these gentlemen, although I can only vote for one—one a Republican and one a Democrat. So where am I going with this? In the past, and I mean while I was in college, I considered myself a Republican. Over the years, I have received appointments from both Republican and Democratic presidents and Republican and Democratic governors. In considering this issue, I have concluded that these party labels have lost their meaning to me. My politics are for what is right, what makes common sense, what is decent, what will create prosperity and a good life. I am for civility.

So what is civility? Webster defines "civil," "civility," and "civilization" as follows:

- A community of citizens. A rational and fair government.
- Being polite and courteous.
- Civil law is derived from Roman law and is a basis of our common law.
- Civility is a high stage of cultural, social, and intellectual development.
- Civility is positive and sincere consideration of others.
- Also consider that "chivalrous" is derived from "civil" and means gallant, noble, protector of the weak.

I believe that the founders of our great country sought to create a nation of civility. They sought to create a nation that elected leaders who could recognize both sides of all issues and through honest and informed debate could and would resolve differences fairly and then move ahead. Remember that the early part of our Declaration of Independence states: "We hold these truths to be self-evident, that all men are created equal, that they are endowed by their Creator with certain unalienable Rights, that among these are Life, Liberty and the pursuit of Happiness." Happiness is a state of civility.

We need people like you and me to stand up and declare we have had enough. We must ask for civility whatever the outcome of the recall election. No, we must insist on civility, and insist that these two leaders of their respective parties collaborate and recognize the problems facing Wisconsin and compromise to achieve effective solutions. We cannot heal or move ahead unless these two leaders commit to returning civility to Wisconsin. I hope you agree with me. Thank you. I appreciate this award, and ON WISCONSIN!

Chapter 5

Housing in the 1970s

Housing at the Crossroads
Wisconsin Builders Association
Sept. 29, 1973

It is a great pleasure to come home to Milwaukee, and the pleasure is doubly enhanced by this opportunity to meet with the Wisconsin Builders Association. I say "doubly" because, first, you represent one of our country's most basic and vital industries—home-building—here in the best state of the Union. Second, you have invited me here at a time of crisis for all of the home-building and home-financing industry in America. I don't think there can be any doubt in your mind—there certainly is none in mine —that we now stand at the crossroads.

One of the two roads we can choose to follow is essentially a loop back to the past. It means that we can simply continue down the path we have taken in the past. And what have we found along that road up to this point? On the bright side, we have seen a quantitative record in housing production over the past five years; new starts over the past few years have been at or above 2 million units annually. In 1972 we had an all-time record. The number of housing starts was more than double the average for the previous two decades, and we expect this year to be another good one.

The same applies to what you, the builders, and we in the government have been able to do for low- and moderate-income families. In these past five years, you have built and the federal government has subsidized nearly 1.6 million units of new housing and over 400,000 units of existing and rehabilitated housing.

For perspective, that is more subsidized housing than was produced in the entire preceding thirty-four years of our national housing program. In short, more has been done in the way of housing for low-income families—and for everyone else—than during any other presidential administration in our two centuries as a nation.

If the pictures were all that encouraging, I guess we wouldn't have to be meeting here today. But where else has this old road led us? Two of the most prominent warning signs were the credit crunches of 1966 and 1969, with their debilitating stop-and-go, on-again/off-again results. The cost of that kind of dislocation—to the builder and the buyer of housing—is impossible to calculate, but it has to be enormous. And here we are again in 1973, only perhaps even more so. There is a dearth of money in our thrift institutions, and record-high mortgage interest rates.

Another landmark along the road of the past is a Federal Housing Administration reeling from the costly failures of our subsidized housing programs. Let's look at the record. With what we've subsidized so far—and I mean if we never put another penny of public money into housing subsidies—we have already committed American taxpayers to something between 65 and 85 billion dollars over the next thirty to forty years.

Well, okay, our children and their children will have to shoulder that huge burden, but the tragedy is that, with all that enormous commitment, we have not achieved our national goal of a decent home and a suitable living environment for all Americans. On the contrary, of every fifteen persons eligible for housing assistance in this country, one—only one—is actually getting help out of current programs. That's a very unsatisfactory 6 percent getting the benefit of that 65 to 85 billion dollars.

Even worse, we have had to take back, so far, more than 200,000 properties and assigned mortgages under default, with the default rate being the worst in the subsidized units. We have an FHA suffering from inner-city mortgage-financing efforts that have resulted in mass foreclosures, scandals, huge losses to the taxpayers, and a host of disillusioned homebuyers.

And, finally, we have an FHA steeped in so much red tape, front-end processing requirements, and lack of confidence stemming from the failures of old programs, that positive action is only a dim and fond remembrance from the past.

That is what we have so far bought for the very huge expenditures to which we have committed the nation. We could, as I say, continue down that same dreary and hazardous road, never planning any further than the next crisis, fighting deep-rooted ills with the well-known Band-Aid. Or we can do what reason and common sense demand, which is what I think all of you would do if you had to make the decision. And that is exactly what President Nixon did last January 5, when he ordered a suspension of new subsidized housing commitments, to be followed by a deep and comprehensive study of the entire U.S. housing picture, out of which new housing policy recommendations would emerge.

The study, involving more than six months of intensive work, began at HUD shortly thereafter. It was a full-scale review of the federal government's role in housing production and finance, including all the housing programs not only of our own department, but of the Department of Agriculture and the Veterans Administration as well. In addition, the study explored the housing role of private and government lending institutions and the regulatory agencies.

Because of this broad scope, our Housing Policy Review Team relied heavily on participants from other departments and agencies, including HEW, Agriculture, the Office of Management and Budget, the Federal Reserve Board, and the Census Bureau. In all, we detailed 135 temporary and career employees to the study, and hired 17 full-time consultants from outside the department. Beyond that, we contracted for 99 consulting studies and considered 508 public responses to our request for comments, ideas, and suggestions. These more than 500 responses, adding up to over 8,000 pages, came from knowledgeable individuals and from such interest groups as realtors, builders, mortgage bankers, urban organizations, and civil rights groups.

This broad-based, in-depth analysis reinforced what the hand-writing on the wall had been pointing to for sometime: our old subsidized housing programs have not benefited the poor people for whom they were designed in any degree commensurate with the vast commitment of public resources.

I've already detailed the 65-to-85-billion-dollar commitment, the 6 percent of eligible households receiving help, and the unsatisfactory—to say the least—default and foreclosure record. The study further unearthed these kinds of findings:

- Forty percent of the people in the United States are technically eligible for the subsidies as the laws now stand, as against the 12 percent who are actually below the poverty level.
- Taking public housing and the subsidy programs of the 1968 Act together, 6 million people have been helped to acquire housing, as against the 24.5 million Americans living in poverty.
- The average income of a family of four owning its own home under the Section 235 program is $6,500. Under the Section 236 apartment rental program, the average is $5,500. Both figures are well above the poverty level.
- Some families benefiting from subsidy assistance have incomes of more than $12,000 a year.
- We found that overall it costs between 15 and 40 percent more for the government to provide housing than for people to acquire that same housing themselves on the private market.
- And we determined that assisting all eligible households under the former new-construction-oriented approach would cost about 34 billion dollars a year.

Findings such as those dramatically underscore what the president said in his Community Development message of last March:

... all too frequently the needy have not been the primary beneficiaries of these programs; ... the programs have been riddled with inequities; and ... the cost for each unit of subsidized housing produced under those programs has been too high.

This study, together with one by the Hunt Commission on US Financial Institutions—embodied in the presidential recommendations on August 3—represents an excellent map of the other road we can take from the crossroads. That new road is a studied, well-thought-out approach to achieving our national goal of "a decent home and a suitable living environment for every American Family" in the fairest, most direct, and most economical way.

I would therefore like to take the rest of my time to describe to you some of the more important elements of this combination of recommendations. But first, for a fuller perspective, let me quote what President Nixon wrote to the Congress in announcing his recommendations ten days ago:

> The state of America's housing will continue to depend on the state of America's economy more than on any other factor. Specific policies aimed at housing can help. But, as our housing study concludes, the forces which will do the most to shape the future of housing in America will be the forces of the marketplace: families with sufficient real income and sufficient confidence to create an effective demand for better housing on the one hand, and builders and credit institutions able to respond to that demand on the other.

To those ends, the president's legislative and administrative proposals cover a number of tightly related areas. Let's concentrate specifically on these three:

1. Easing the current tight mortgage credit situation
2. Making it easier for all homeowners, urban and rural, to obtain decent housing; or, in other words, assuring the flow of mortgage credit over the longer pull
3. Assisting low-income families to obtain decent housing.

Easing the Current Situation

When we talk about the current crunch, we have to realize that the fight against inflation is our foremost domestic problem and priority. Since measures to control inflation—including the necessity to hold down federal spending—are essential to holding down the price of both housing and money, there is necessarily a limit to what can be prudently done to stimulate housing credit in the short run.

And yet, on the other hand, no one wants the burden of fighting inflation to fall unfairly and disproportionately on those who want to buy or sell a home. For that reason, a number of remedial actions have already been taken. The Committee on Interest and Dividends, for example, has instituted voluntary guidelines to encourage banks to keep up their levels of mortgage lending. The Federal Reserve Board has made similar moves. FNMA has stepped up its mortgage commitment and purchasing operations to free up funds for further lending. And the Federal Home Loan Bank Board has lowered the reserve requirements for lending operations of its member institutions, and has stepped up its advancement of funds to them.

The president has further proposed to ease mortgage credit in these three ways:

First, the Federal Home Loan Bank Board will authorize a new program of "forward commitments" to savings and loan associations, promising to loan them money at a future date if they need it to cover commitments they are now making. This authority will cover up to 2.5 billion dollars in loan commitments.

Second, HUD will reinstate the "Tandem Plan" under the Government National Mortgage Association. GNMA will provide money for FHA-insured residential mortgages at an interest rate somewhat below current market rates. In order to encourage new construction, only mortgages on new starts will qualify—and up to 3 billion dollars in mortgages will be assisted under this arrangement. Incidentally, we are also considering an increase of the mortgage amount limitation for Tandem Plan purchase beyond the present

$22,000 limit. The intent here, of course, is to enable the plan to reach a broader spectrum of potential American homebuyers.

And third, we're asking the Congress to authorize—immediately if not sooner—increases in the permissible mortgage amounts of FHA-insured loans for both single and multi-family units. At the same time, we are requesting appropriate adjustment of the loan-to-equity restriction. The present limits had some basis in reality when they were set in 1968, but the ceiling and downpayment terms are totally unrealistic in today's market. This authorization to adjust to current realities would bring the advantages of FHA insurance to many homebuyers who cannot obtain conventional loans in the current mortgage market.

Assuring Credit Flow over the Long Haul

All that is for right now. To make it easier for urban and rural homebuyers to obtain mortgages not only in today's tight squeeze, but over the long term as well, we have made four legislative proposals:

1. To permit homebuyers to pay market-level interest rates and still be eligible for federal mortgage insurance. This procedure would eliminate the necessity for discount "points," which too often raise the price of the home, the size of the down payment, the cost of insuring the property, and the magnitude of the property taxes and mortgage payments. It would also eliminate the inequity that arises when a home is resold before the mortgage term as run its course, which is the usual case. Since, as you know, the points were paid to compensate the lender for what he would lose in interest over the full term of the mortgage, the lender can reap an unfair profit when the mortgage is paid off early.
2. To authorize more flexible repayment plans under federally insured mortgages. What we're after here is the authority to innovate on a carefully experimental basis. One possibility we'd like to explore, for example, is gearing the level of repayments to expected changes in family income.

273

A young family just starting out would make smaller payments in the earlier years—when they are harder pressed—and larger payments as their income grows with the years. Not only would they be able to purchase a home earlier in life, but they would be able to arrive at their more-or-less ultimate—or at least intermediate—home at an earlier stage. We would also like to experiment with negative payment clauses, which would obviate foreclosures when default is caused by a temporary interruption of income due to illness or loss of job.

3. To establish a mortgage interest tax credit to ensure a steady supply of housing credit. A tax credit on interest on earnings—of up to 3.5 percent—would be given to financial institutions that invest a certain percentage of their portfolios in residential mortgages. The higher the proportion invested in such mortgages, the greater the tax credit on interest earned by the mortgages in the portfolio. This credit would rise to the full 3.5 percent when at least 70 percent of a portfolio was invested in residential mortgages. Thus investment in housing loans would be made more attractive in two ways. First, it would be more attractive to those institutions that have traditionally provided mortgage money. And second, it would provide incentive to institutions not heavily involved in mortgage lending to do so.

4. To further the development and institutional acceptance of private mortgage insurance companies. Such private companies—performing a function like those of FHA, VA, and FMHA, but at lower premium rates—have become a significant factor in the housing market in recent years. We should certainly do everything possible to encourage their continued development. Our legislative proposal is therefore aimed at allowing these companies to purchase inexpensive federal reinsurance in much the same way as FDIC insures bank depositors. This would have the two-fold effect of providing added protection to the owner of a mortgage, and accelerating

the acceptance of private mortgage insurance, especially in the secondary markets. The desired end result, of course, would be additional sources of low-down-payment, long-term home financing for prospective homebuyers.

Both the immediate and longer-term improvements in credit flow and availability, of course, should bring back to the housing market many Americans who are currently unable to enter that market because of high down-payment requirements and the relative unavailability of mortgage commitments.

Assisting Low-Income Families

But what of those who, no matter how easily credit may be flowing or how generous the terms, cannot provide themselves with decent, safe, and sanitary housing out of their own resources? It is, after all, in helping the families of low and moderate income that our housing programs have shown the least return for the amount of treasure expended.

The underlying assumption of the present construction-oriented programs has been that the basic problem of the poor is a lack of housing. Our studies have shown, however, that what the poor really suffer from—and this should come as no surprise to anyone—is a lack of income. They have too little money to pay for food, to pay for clothes, to buy light bulbs, health care—practically everything—and certainly housing.

But instead of treating the root cause of the problem—the inability to pay for housing—we've been attacking the symptom with our federal programs. We've been helping the poor only indirectly—and only a chosen few of them, and with no real efficiency—rather than providing assistance directly to low-income families. I've already spelled out quite a few of the negative results of all that, in both social and economic terms.

You know there has to be a better way to help the three million American households that still live in substandard housing. Our determination is to make decent housing available for all low-income families—without the housing-project stigma, the lack of freedom of choice, and the excessively high costs of current programs.

All right, so how do we go about it? First, the president has identified direct cash assistance as the most promising principal approach to helping such families obtain decent housing. By this means we would make maximum use of existing decent housing, afford them the freedom and dignity of choice, and reduce the cost per family as compared with the present approach of concentrating on new housing construction.

Second, we have to take steps to complete the development and evaluation of an operational program based on direct cash housing assistance. This would be scaled to make up the difference between what a family could afford for housing on its own and the actual cost of decent housing in their area. What we're talking about here is an estimated 8 to 11 billion dollars a year, so this kind of program would have to be phased in over a number of years. The first phase, quite probably, would cover the elderly poor. Incidentally, even though 8 to 11 billion a year is a substantial amount, it's only about a third or less of the 34 billion I mentioned earlier as the cost of extending present construction programs to everyone who is eligible under the law.

Third, we will continue to undertake limited programs for subsidized housing, since obviously there are areas where existing housing is in tight supply. Here we would be making use of some existing programs, but revised to eliminate past abuses. This part of the program could result in the additional approval, this fiscal year, of 200,000 subsidized units, 150,000 of which would be new construction. I would expect about half of these to be constructed under the 236 program to honor assurances to urban renewal agencies and community developers, and as part of rehabilitation compacts and agreements with local governments.

We would administer one of the existing programs—Section 23, construction-for-leasing—to make maximum use of the freedom-of-choice principle inherent in the concept of direct cash assistance. Eventually, with congressional authorization of our proposed new construction program, we would expand the development and ownership of projects under Section 23 to private builders.

Fourth and finally, we need to improve the operation of existing public housing projects by:

- providing realistic and workable incentives for effective management
- taking a more realistic approach to rents
- appropriately allocating the responsibilities of local authorities and the federal government
- adjusting the current level of federal operating subsidy if necessary for the continued sound operation and maintenance of the projects

There you have, in essence, our new policy recommendations, the administrative steps we are taking to implement part of them, and the new laws that will be required for the rest. As you evaluate these proposals, I ask that you keep in mind that we are addressing two related but quite different goals. One goal certainly is to make sure that those poorer Americans who are still in substandard housing shall get decent housing. We are committed to that goal, but decent housing certainly does not, in most cases, mean new housing. A quite separate goal is a healthy housing industry capable of meeting the continued very high level of demand for housing middle America that we anticipate to continue for many years.

To confuse the one goal with the other is what leads some to believe that the needs of our lower-income families have to be met primarily by new construction. Please believe me, however well placed the sentiment, such thinking does a real disservice to those who need help. Because to focus on new construction as the primary way of helping low-income people get decent housing, is to do three things: 1) it deprives them of freedom of choice; 2) it is unacceptably expensive and wasteful; and 3) because of the huge amount it would cost, new construction alone practically guarantees that we will never achieve the goal of decent housing for all.

Confusion of the two goals is also contrary to your own best interests, because the health of the housing industry cannot and should not depend on the "crutch" of building new for the poor.

The long-range, overall health of your vital industry is built upon the demand of the growing numbers of Americans who have the jobs and the money to afford better housing—and upon the availability of credit to make that demand meaningful in the market place.

So ask yourselves what you really want. I think the answer will be a healthy, growing economy with stable increases in real income and with inflation firmly under control. And superimposed upon that attractive picture, the kinds of fine tuning we need to get rid of the feast-or-famine credit situation that has plagued us all—and you most of all—in recent years.

I would conclude by saying to you that the picture I have just painted describes precisely what President Nixon and all of us are certain we can achieve under his new housing policy

---

Fixing the FHA
National Housing Conference
March 4, 1974

My job is managing the subsidized and unsubsidized federal housing programs and making appropriate policy recommendations. Briefly, let me summarize some of the broad and critical problems we are faced with in this area:

1. Increasing cost of homes, which eliminates purchasers with less than $15,000 to $20,000 of annual income.
2. Uneven and volatile flow of mortgage money, causing the home-building industry to be the most cyclical, boom-or-bust business in the country, resulting in inefficiencies and cost escalation.
3. High defaults and losses in central-city areas and in the subsidized programs. Also associated with such failures are scandals and exploitation of the consumer by some builders, lenders, and certain FHA employees.

4. Slow processing, caused largely by the imposition of various social objectives on the use of FHA mortgage insurance, outdated maximum loan limits (currently $33,000), and obsolete down payment requirements. These have all but eliminated the use of FHA insurance in new construction.
5. Implementation of effective and improved public housing.

I have been in my job eight months. I am not satisfied with the progress that has been made, but let me tell you what we have been and are doing to find solutions to the problems I have outlined.

First, to assure an even flow of mortgage funds into the market and assure an ample, steady number of housing starts, we need a well-functioning FRA and an active secondary mortgage market for FHA-VA and conventional loans.

To improve the secondary market for conventional loans, we have proposed legislation for the re-insurance of private mortgage insurance companies. The object would be to expand the acceptability of private mortgage insurance to investors other than savings and loans.

Still another way to attract greater and steadier flows of credit into home mortgages is by means of a mortgage interest investment tax credit. We feel that this proposal, which is part of the general restructuring of our financial institutions, would not only help to stabilize the thrift industry, but would also provide incentives for others, such as commercial banks and private groups of investors, to contribute to the supply of home mortgage credit.

To make the FHA perform again, we must redesign our approach so as to cut through the tangle of mortgage-processing requirements that have built up over the years. As one method of achieving that goal, we propose to make use of co-insurance programs, which would be offered in addition to existing full-coverage FHA programs. By co-insurance, I mean risk-sharing. Obviously, when risk is shared, those who share in it are motivated to recognize their responsibilities—and to carry them out. Let's call it enlightened self-interest. If the originator of a mortgage assumes a small portion of the risk, we would expect improved underwriting quality and more constructive servicing. In return, the originator would be delegated all loan processing, and probably a share of the mortgage insurance premium, for the extra risk he is assuming.

We know that co-insurance works. In 1954, our Title I property improvement and mobile home loan programs were a disgrace. But since adopting co-insurance for these programs, we have had excellent results. The loss ratio on these programs, which cover almost 13 million loans of more than 14.5 billion dollars, has been less than nine-tenths of one percent, while on some of our unsubsidized home mortgage programs without co-insurance, the loss ratio has been as high as 20 percent.

Certainly another co-insurance success story is the record of the VA system of home loan guarantees. Furthermore, co-insured loans can be the underlying security for GNMA mortgage-backed securities, as they are in our Title I mobile home loan program. Also, I can envision active co-insurance programs with state finance corporations.

To achieve a better basis of dealing with central-city problems, we are administratively working with the FHLBB, the Federal Reserve Board, and other agencies concerned with home mortgage lending to coordinate our activities and get greater involvement of local savings and loans and banks in their own central cities. In addition, we will seek in each city participation from local city government, business persons, and civic leaders.

Other changes we are seeking include:

1. Increased loan amounts on FHA-insured mortgages, to meet the realities of today's market, together with higher loan-to-equity ratios.
2. Experimental financing, which would allow flexible terms to accommodate changing levels of income and life styles.
3. Free or market rates for federally backed mortgages, along with the elimination of discount points.
4. Administratively, we seek to serve the consumer by such measures as updated minimum property standards aimed at thermal conservation, Truth-in-Housing, Full Disclosure

to buyers, and encouragement of measures such as the National Association of Home Builders home construction warranty program.

Finally, for those low-income persons that are not reached by any of these measures, we have identified a system of direct cash assistance as the most promising approach. As an interim program until direct cash assistance is thoroughly tested, we are moving ahead with a new Section 23 leased public housing program as a means of making the best use of decent existing housing, as well as providing new construction where the supply of existing units is inadequate.

The emphasis in Section 23 is upon private developers and owners, privately financed, making a portion of their units available for lower-income residents. The federal government would then pay the developer the difference between the fair market rental on such units and what the low-income families can afford to pay. The local housing authority would be involved in certifying tenants for eligibility, inspection of units, and, in certain instances, managing units.

In summary, if we can carry through on these proposals, we believe we will be on the way to providing a sound basis for housing and upgrading all of our citizens.

The Future of FHA
Texas Mortgage Bankers Association
May 2, 1974

The president of the United States is vitally concerned with the housing and housing finance industry. Furthermore, the president, Secretary Lynn, and I are committed to a strong, viable FHA—an FHA that will change and develop to meet the needs of the 1970s, not the 1930s.

Let me tell you what we're trying to do at HUD in Washington. As an ex-member of your profession, I feel particularly able to tell it like it is. The basic philosophy of this administration is "New Federalism." The individual is responsible for himself in all matters that are within his power to control. Those things for which he cannot exercise individual responsibility, or which private business cannot fulfill, should be undertaken by that level of government closest to the people—local, state, and only what is left by federal.

The administration's basic philosophy on subsidized housing is to subsidize the individual, not the unit. That approach allows free choice of location, encourages dignity and responsibility, and puts management in the hands of the owners.

What has changed in the past forty years? In the 1930s, the market's confidence was based on primary lenders originating loans for their own portfolios. In the 1970s, secondary-market investors play the dominant role. We have also added social objectives to our housing policies, including equal opportunity in buying and renting units, affirmative marketing, and payment of prevailing local wages on federally funded projects. Environmental concerns have become another priority, including noise abatement and mitigating lead-based paint exposure. On top of all this, the federal housing programs have undergone a sweeping reorganization.

This brings us up to today. We are again facing a period of high interest rates and credit stringency. Home-building and finance are once again threatened. In the past six months, we have offered at least three separate legislative proposals to improve this serious situation. To date, no action has been produced. What happens will be largely up to you and the other housing industry groups.

There is much to do. We must create two principal funds: an actuarially sound program under the general fund that would include coinsurance, and a special fund for high-risk and subsidized cases whose reserves would be replenished by appropriations. We must restore soundness to all our programs. We must further develop the secondary market, especially the secondary market for conventional loans. We must simplify and delegate loan-processing. We must develop new programs for condominiums and mobile homes, and new forms of financing to meet today's changing lifestyles.

Will you spend your time longing for the old days, or will you face the future and take a part in developing it? This is your FHA, and its future is up to you.

New Directions in Indian Housing
Indian Housing Conference
June 6, 1974

It is widely recognized that the quality of Indian housing is below that of any other minority in this country. In the 28 states which had Indian populations of 5,000 or more at the time of the 1970 Census, there were 166,000 Indian households reported. The adequacy of their housing, if one uses plumbing facilities and overcrowding as measures, shows that approximately 73,000, or 45 percent, of all the housing units for Indian families in these 28 states was inadequate. The Department of Housing and Urban Development is deeply concerned with the development of a comprehensive housing program that will establish priority objectives to improve housing conditions for native Americans.

Perhaps the most meaningful effort to improve the housing conditions of Indian families has been taken by HUD under the public housing program. This effort began in 1961, when the legal determination was made that Indian tribes have sufficient sovereignty to establish local housing authorities and participate in the public housing program.

In May, 1968, representatives of HUD, HEW, and Interior signed an agreement that provided for cooperative efforts of the three departments to produce housing on Indian reservations. Through June of this year, funds will have been provided to produce all but 4,900 of the 30,000 units agreed to in that proposal.

During the next fiscal year, beginning July 1, HUD will continue to provide new construction subsidies to Indians at a level at least comparable to those of previous years. We anticipate that up to 7,500 units of housing for Indian families would be obligated for FY 1975. This assistance will be made available through HUD's revised leasing program when possible, and through the Mutual Self-help or Turnkey III homeownership program in other instances. For the longer term, the administration is studying what is the most appropriate production program that would be needed to complement a national direct cash assistance approach for housing on Indian reservations.

In addition, funding for new units is also available through several Farmers Home programs and to a lesser extent through the BIA's Housing Improvement Program.

We all recognize that circumstances unique to the Indian reservation system, or to particular federally recognized Indian communities, may render a housing program designed for broad national needs ineffective in particular localities. Therefore, the Office of Management and Budget has asked the Bureau of Indian Affairs to review the reservation housing situation and identify steps to tailor a housing program to unique Indian needs. We at HUD will cooperate fully and support the effort to consolidate and make more efficient Indian housing programs as administered by all federal agencies.

In addition to providing funding and technical assistance to Indian housing authorities for the production of needed housing for Indian families, we will continue to develop a more viable program of homeownership education to be used especially in Indian territories. We are also currently working with the Department of Labor on a joint venture to implement a special building trades apprenticeship training program to ensure that Indians will participate in employment opportunities associated with HUD-assisted housing on Indian lands.

As you can see, we have made some progress but we recognize there is a long road to travel, and we will continue to support the goals and objectives to provide a decent living environment on Indian lands.

The Federal Role in Housing:
Has HUD Taken New Directions?
National Association of Home Builders
June 11, 1974

The two broadest and most critical problems facing the areas of housing and housing finance in America are these:
1. Sharply increasing or inflating cost of homes, which deprives many citizens of the option of homeownership
2. Uneven and volatile supply of mortgage money, which has made the home-building industry the most cyclical and boom-or-bust industry in the country, resulting in inefficiencies and cost escalation.

At the heart of these problems is inflation—inflation of costs and inflation leading to an absence of mortgage money. The chain of events is becoming all too familiar:
1. High rate of inflation
2. Federal Reserve monetary restraint
3. High short-term interest rates
4. Disintermediation of thrift institutions, the major suppliers of mortgage funds
5. Lack of mortgage money
6. Depressed housing market

In addition to these broad problems, some of the other critical problems the federal government is faced with are:
1. Implementation of the most effective and equitable manner to provide safe and decent housing for those citizens with insufficient incomes to do it themselves
2. A viable program for central city lending, which is typically higher-risk and often involves first-time, low-income buyers and declining real estate values.
3. Gradual elimination of the use of FHA mortgage insurance in new construction. Since FHA-VA loans are virtually the

only mortgages with ready access to secondary mortgage markets, this has been a damaging event to home-building.

The causes of this decline in mortgage insurance are numerous: outdated loan ceilings (currently $33,000, a figure set in 1968); outdated down payment requirements; slow, laborious processing, resulting from the imposition of various social objectives on the use of FHA insurance, past reorganizations of the department, and reluctance of employees to act decisively because of scandals and investigations; expiration of FHA insuring authority caused by Congress, which was in effect from June 30, 1973, to October 1, 1973, and really damaged a long-lead business; and past excessive discounts caused by large variances between the "fixed" rate and "market" rates.

What are we doing to face these problems?

1. Regarding inflation, we must have greater fiscal restraint. We can't do it with monetary policy alone, especially during times like this, when there is a shortage of the industrial plant and expansion needed to meet demand. Furthermore, we can't expect housing to assume the disproportionate burden of restraint it has in the past.

2. Regarding low-income persons, the results of the National Housing Study show us that the most equitable and efficient way to provide decent housing for those whose incomes won't support it is through direct cash assistance, because it gets the poorest first, allows freedom of choice, and gets the government out of ownership and management. Section 23 can be used as an interim solution. In 1974 we have 118,000 Section 23 units; in 1975, there will be 300,000 units.

3. We must make FHA programs and access to secondary markets available to a broader sector of the population. That means increased loan amounts (to $45,000), increased loan-to-value ratios, a free rate, experimental

authority, and coinsurance. Coinsurance will delegate processing to private originators on a sensible basis and handle expected large volumes of the future, return programs to an actuarially sound basis, and lessen possibilities of scandals and bribery.

4. We must develop secondary mortgage markets for conventional loans, including a PMI guarantee program and mortgage-backed securities.

Better Times Ahead
Institutional Investors Real Estate Conference
June 19, 1974

We meet today to discuss real estate and housing at a time when interest rates are at previously unthinkably high levels, home prices are escalating to levels out of the reach of more and more of our people, new home starts are declining, and the conventional suppliers of mortgage money—the thrift institutions—are once again experiencing disintermediation and are unable to furnish an adequate supply of mortgage funds for the construction, purchase, and sale of houses.

The principal problem we must face in this depressed market is inflation. This inflation is the inevitable result of years of lack of fiscal discipline and, most recently, sharply rising energy costs, which pervade virtually the entire cost side of an industrialized society.

The effects on housing have been enormous:

- The sharply increasing or inflating cost of homes has deprived many citizens of the option of home ownership.
- The uneven and volatile supply of mortgage money has made the home-building industry the most cyclical and boom-or-bust industry in the country, resulting in inefficiencies and cost escalation.

- Finally, since monetary policy is aimed principally at the users of credit, and no activity in our economy is more capital-intensive than housing, the impact there has been disproportional. I have heard some economists say that housing absorbs two-thirds of the total cutback in durables, while it comprises only 10 to 15 percent of the total.

No significant progress can be made in providing more and better housing for our people until inflation is brought under control and our money markets are restored to order. And to do this we must face the hard choices involved in ordering national priorities and recognizing the limits of our resources at any one time.

Along with these broad economic and fiscal problems, there are also numerous and specific programmatic problems relating to previous and existing federal programs. All of this leads to the basic questions: What is federal policy relating to housing, and what is being done to achieve it?

The national objective of "a decent home and suitable living environment for every American family" is still intact, but the method of getting there has changed. First, as regards persons whose income won't support decent housing, the results of the National Housing Policy Review, completed in September, 1973, convinced this administration that the most efficient and equitable way to help lower income persons was through direct cash assistance—a method of subsidizing the individual, not the housing unit. This approach reaches the poorest first, allows freedom of choice, and gets the government out of ownership and management.

Currently, HUD is experimenting with direct cash assistance in twelve cities, and Congress is considering legislation for going forward with a nationwide program. In the meantime, the department is proceeding on an interim basis through the use of Section 23 Leased Public Housing to provide low-income housing on a basis as close to direct cash assistance as possible. There are 416,000 units provided for the rest of this year and fiscal 1975, and we anticipate that they will be apportioned to provide 290,000 new units and 126,000 existing.

Since the lifeblood of housing is credit or mortgage money, we cannot consider the area of unsubsidized housing without first recognizing that the financial markets have changed dramatically over the past ten years, and that our financial institutions must change with them if they are to be viable. Anyone who questions that change is necessary need only recall the credit crunch of 1966, the monetary and gold crisis of 1968, the severe squeeze of 1969-70, and the interest rate crunch of 1973 to show that our system does not adjust well to short-term changes in economic and financial conditions. The administration is addressing this situation in the proposed Financial Institution Act presently before Congress.

Briefly, the act seeks to improve the efficiency and independence of all institutions within our financial structure through greater reliance on market determination of the cost and availability of credit, safeguarded by existing regulatory agencies. The entire thrust of this legislation is to create greater flexibility on both the asset and the liability sides of all institutions. The housing sector would, of course, benefit generally by stronger institutions and specifically by the incentive of a mortgage interest tax credit which we believe would attract more participants in the home mortgage market.

To make the FHA effective and to provide access to secondary mortgage markets for a broader base of home-buyers, we have proposed legislation to achieve the following:

1. Increased loan amounts, to $45,000.
2. Increased loan-to-value ratio.
3. Free rate.
4. Experimental authority, including variable payment mortgages.
5. Co-insurance authority, the objectives of which are to delegate processing to private originators on a sensible basis and handle expected large volumes of the future, to return programs to an actuarially sound basis, and to lessen possibilities of scandals and bribery.

Although we intend to continue to develop secondary mortgage market sources for FHA-VA loans, we believe that there is great potential for a secondary market for conventional insured loans. The first attempt at creating the necessary investor confidence is our PMI Guaranty Bill which was sent to the Hill for discussion. The object is to create an FDIC for private mortgage insurance companies which would do for mortgage investors what the FDIC does for bank depositors.

Given these changes, most of which I believe Congress will act upon very shortly, and with the mental toughness to restrain spending and force down inflation, we would find ourselves in the midst of the greatest era housing has known.

We know that the demand is there. The Harvard-MIT study estimates that the demand for unsubsidized new homes over the next decade is 23 million units. Add to this subsidized needs and you get some idea of the backlog of demand that is building up. So stay strong. Better times are ahead.

Index